New 9th

NEW JERSEY DAY TRIPS

A GUIDE TO OUTINGS IN NEW JERSEY, NEW YORK, PENNSYLVANIA & DELAWARE

Revised and Updated

BARBARA HUDGINS

Woodmont Press
P.O. Box 108
Green Village, NJ 07935
www.woodmontpress.com

If a copy of this book is not available at your local bookstore, you may order one by sending $14.00 plus $2.50 shipping to:

The Woodmont Press
P.O. Box 108
Green Village, NJ 07935

Visit us at http://www.woodmontpress.com

ISBN 0-9607762-8-1
Printed in the United States of America

DEDICATION

To all the friends and family
who trudged through countless
amusement parks
and reconstructed villages
to help me with my book.

ACKNOWLEDGEMENTS

Much gratitude and thanks to:

All the driving companions who searched out New Jersey's nooks and crannies with me. In particular: Carol Arnold, Sue Donecker, Ada Dougherty, Mary Duffy, Pat Hammes, Nancy Boucher, Sue Meehan, Pam Morse, Gail Poblicki, Carol Potter, Kathy Slack, Laszlo Vasko, Lynn Wyatt and the Wemple family.

Those who helped with the book production beyond the call of duty, particularly: Pam Morse for copyreading and organization, Jack Krug and Irene Rich for editorial help and Linda Kimler for pictures and general support.

And to Lani and Robert for their help and comments.

Some of these entries have appeared in somewhat different form in *The Bernardsville News* and other Recorder newspapers.

Book design and composition by Dorothy Shubert of Triart Graphics.

FOREWORD

There are several ways to put together a guidebook. One can do it regionally (e.g., all attractions in Sussex County are listed together), chronologically (everything open in winter is listed in one section) or by subject (all zoos are listed together, and all museums are listed together). There is no perfect way.

My book is set up primarily by subject. However, there are chapters that differ from this approach. The first chapter, "Unique Towns, Places to Browse" covers such towns as Atlantic City, New Hope, Princeton and various walking tours. Here I write about the town as a whole and include all the sites available. In the chapter "Museums of All Kinds," the listings proved to be so huge that I subdivided the sections geographically (N.Y., NJ. and PA.) and then subdivided New Jersey museums.

You will find some of my listings to be purely arbitrary. When a particular place could belong to more than one category, I simply chose the one where I felt it fit in best. Pennsbury Manor, for instance, the reconstructed estate of William Penn, could fit in either the chapter titled "Homes of the Rich and Famous" or the one on restored villages.

The advantage of listing attractions by subject is that someone interested in a particular sport or hobby can easily find what is available at a glance. A newcomer wants to know what ski areas are near - a garden club president wants to know where to take her group on a trip - a parent asks a history teacher what Revolutionary War sites are around - and so forth.

However, because many people want to know what is available in their immediate geographical area, I have included a regional index in the back of the book, which appears after the main alphabetical index. Here the listings for New Jersey are under each county, and those for out-of-state are under a specific area (e.g.: The Poconos, Hudson Valley or New York City). One caution however — always check the main listings before you set out. There are many attractions that are open on a limited basis. Other places change guise with the season, so that summer action parks become winter ski areas, and August racetracks become September flea markets.

I wish you many hours of pleasurable day-tripping in and around New Jersey.

Ten Tips for Day Trippers

1. Always telephone first. Places may be closed unexpectedly for any number of reasons. Or they may change their public hours at any moment.

2. Check websites when they are available— (we have added some for this edition.) However, we noticed that when it comes to hours and prices, they may not be as up-to-date as the telephone message. Websites are fine for "seeing the place" first and for traveling directions.

3. Take along a full-size map, drinks, snacks, flashlight, an extra jacket, etc.

4. Do not show up at the last half-hour. Places that require guided tours often refuse admittance one hour before closing.

5. Use coupons and "two-fers". Most amusement parks have marketing arrangements with companies for two-for-one admission with the requisite can or coupon. Also check for discount coupons in brochures, flyers and newspapers.

6. Go on free days. The Philadelphia Museum is free Sunday mornings. New Jersey state parks are free off-season.

7. Buy season tickets. This makes sense if you live within close range. Or become a member of a local museum, garden, or zoo (which will also get you discounts for the gift shop and trips).

8. Use your corporate or organizational clout. When corporations support institutions, their employees may get a free "corporate" day, or a discount. Members of AAA and AARP often get discounts. Check with your town's Recreation Department—they may have discount tickets for attractions & events.

9. "Suggested donation" means just that. If you are visiting for a short period of time or have a large family with you, you do not have to pay the full "suggested donation", although you must pay something.

10. Watch out for "extras", like parking fees and sales tax. Always take along more money than you think you will need.

CONTENTS

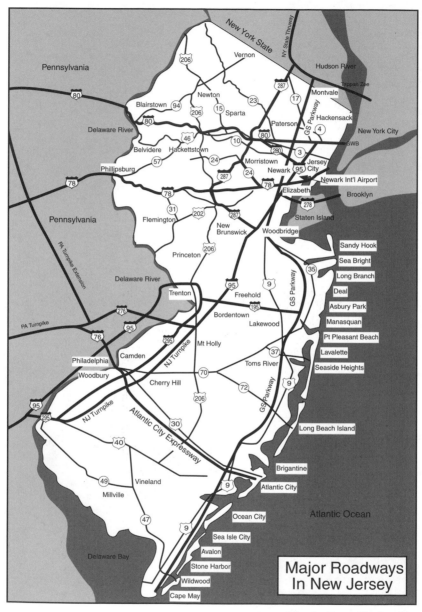

Map by Set A Bit Graphics

For general reference only. Use in conjunction with a road map.

UNIQUE TOWNS,
PLACES TO BROWSE,
GUIDED WALKING TOURS

Photo: Cape May County Division of Tourism

In This Chapter You Will Find:

Atlantic City, NJ
Princeton, NJ
New Hope, PA
Lahaska, PA
Cape May, NJ
Chinatown, NY
Other NY Tours

Walking Tours for:
  Paterson, NJ
  Bordentown, NJ
  Burlington, NJ
  Mount Holly, NJ
  Other NJ Tours
  Philadelphia, PA

ATLANTIC CITY

Atlantic City keeps trying to redo itself with new looks, new styles, new owners, in a constant balancing act between an old-fashioned New Jersey shore resort and a Las Vegas imitation. A new Convention Hall and a Lighthouse replica now create a dramatic entrance into the city. Construction cranes are always working—whether on a tunnel to the marina side or new condos or apartments.

On the boardwalk, newly refurbished casino-hotels are taking over more space from small shops and tacky stands. But it is still a pastiche of monolithic hotels, amusement areas, parking garages, concession stands and elegant stores. Crowds of people, rolling chairs, and sometimes teenage rollerbladers pass by. The beach is bumpy with sand dunes. Over at the marina, there are lots of boats and the Harrah's and Trump hotels. A third hotel is slated to join them.

Here's what you will find:

Parking: Valet parking is available at the hotels if you are staying over or using the casino. Most offer free parking for a 3 or 6 hour stay. However, getting into town on a busy summer weekend can be full of traffic delays.

Transportation: Once you have parked your car, the best way to get around town is to take the small jitneys that operate along Pacific Avenue. They come frequently and cost $1.50. On the boardwalk you can walk on a nice day or take the push-along rolling chairs that cost about $5 for every six blocks. Cabs are plentiful (at the hotel entrances) if you want to get away from the boardwalk area. And NJ Transit buses serve the length of the island 24 hours a day. They run along Atlantic Ave.

Bus Tours: Still the favorite way for most people to make a one day visit — fares vary from point of embarkation. It costs around $19 from north Jersey, but the casinos give you a voucher for money and other freebies when you arrive. You must stay 6 hours if you take a bus tour. These casino-subsidized buses travel to Atlantic City from all points. Groups often charter their own buses. Regular NJ Transit buses and trains also service the town.

The Hotels: Casino-hotels change their names more often than Hollywood stars change husbands. On the boardwalk they stretch from *The Hilton* (formerly Bally's Grand) to the *Showboat* at the north end. In between, a number of modestly priced chain hotels have popped up. Many large hotels now feature a dramatic theme. At Bally's *Wild,Wild West* you get a domed ceiling that simulates a real sky with sunsets and thunderstorms. *Showboat* has mechanical cats that play jazz (and live musicians as well). *Caesar's Palace* is now fitted out with marble atriums, fountains and statues worthy of Augustus.

The Casinos: If your idea of a casino is garnered from the movies and you expect evening dresses and tuxedos, leisurely gaming tables and James Bond types floating around, forget it! This is supermarket gambling, where little old ladies with shopping bags hover over slot machines. Roulette, blackjack and craps tables are placed side by side, but the noise comes from the ringing of the slot machines. The big spenders get special rooms for Baccarat and other exotic games. Minimum bets are posted at each table—and they keep going up as the afternoon wears on.

Casinos now offer lots of variety—Pai Kow, fancy looking Wheels of Fortune and an ever-expanding variety of slot machines. You can put dollars straight into the slot machines now, so you don't have to bother with getting change from the cashier. But to transform a bucketful of coins into dollars, you still must hike over to the Coin Banks, usually located way across the room.

The casinos try mightily to keep their customers loyal. The gimmick of choice is a card (something like a credit card) which you get by joining a particular casino's "club". This card gives you back points every time you use the slot machines or tables, so that eventually, if you spend enough money, you get enough "comps" to eat in the fancy restaurants, buy in the gift shops or sleep in the hotel rooms.

Food: There are plenty of first class restaurants, both in the casinos and the streets beyond. And every casino has a buffet. They are not as elegant as they were years ago, but they're cheaper. But since they're often crowded, reserve your time as soon as you arrive. Then there are the theme restaurants: *Planet Hollywood* at Caesars, the *Hard Rock Cafe* and the *All-Star Cafe* at the Taj Mahal are popular with families. Coffee shops and delis are also plentiful. Big Spenders go to the super-deluxe restaurants— often open only five nights a week.

Entertainment: First class shows, chorus girls and big name stars appear at the hotels, but the big names are usually weekend events. Besides the big shows, there are piano lounges, boxing matches and all sorts of tournaments. As for teenagers, they will find video game rooms in the hotels and some on the boardwalk also.

On the boardwalk, during summer, **The Steel Pier** (across from the Taj Mahal) offers amusement rides which include roller coasters, whirlwind rides and interactive thrills. The usual hot dog stands and games of chance bring back the flavor of the "old" Atlantic City. The biggest indoor attraction is **Ripley's Believe It Or Not Museum** at New York Ave. It features a tipsy building leaning over the boardwalk. Inside, there are displays of the world's tallest man, the double-eyed man from China and a model of the Sydney Harbor Bridge made out of matchsticks. Try walking the swaying bridge in the mining tunnel.(About $10 admission.) Tel.: 609-347-2001. At **Ocean One Mall** (which looks like a cruise ship berthed across from Caesars) there are three floors of stores and a profusion of restaurants and fast food joints.

For nostalgia buffs, there's a museum devoted to Atlantic City history, plus an art museum at **The Garden Pier,** which is on the boardwalk north of the Showboat hotel. The historical museum contains a vast amount of facts, and displays everything from Miss America's tiara to a video of historical trends in seaside resorts. It's free and could use some customers. (Tel. 609-347-5839). And Absecon Lighthouse, the tallest of such structures in New Jersey, has reopened. It stands on a square of sand at Vermont and Pacific Ave. Call 609-449-1360 for hours.

On the inlet side, besides the large Farley Marina, there is *Historic Gardeners Basin*. A new aquarium called **Ocean Life Center** (q.v.) has helped stir up some interest. The nautical theme is reiterated in the restaurant *The Flying Cloud*, plus a café that sells good clam chowder and a seashore-souvenir shack. You can also catch boat rides here— dolphin watching excursions, and deep-sea fishing charters for example. The Basin hosts an annual Seafood Festival in June.

For those who want to venture beyond Atlantic City, there are a few attractions. One is **Lucy, The Margate Elephant** a 65-foot high, tin-plated Victorian architectural "folly". During the season, you can walk through its wooden interior (which is actually a museum) with a guided tour for a reasonable fee. You can even step outside onto the Howdah on top and view the surroundings. Lucy is located at Decatur and Atlantic Avenues, in Margate, a few miles south of Atlantic City. Call 609-822-6519.

Other standard side trips from Atlantic City are: the tour at Renault Winery, the Historic Towne of Smithville and Wheaton Village, all of which are mentioned elsewhere in this book. And of course, there is always the Atlantic City beach, which has lots of sand dunes in some places, but unlike most New Jersey beaches, it is free.

DIRECTIONS: Garden State Parkway to Exit 40 and 38S, or NJ Tpke. to Atlantic City Expressway.

TELEPHONE: 800-BOARDWK ext 797. www.atlanticcitynj.com

PRINCETON

Shades of F. Scott Fitzgerald! Golden lads and lasses walk the well-clipped paths between venerable University halls while russet leaves flutter overhead from rows of sturdy trees. Time, scholarships, and the inclusion of girls have changed the atmosphere at this Ivy League bastion somewhat. But still, for a trip to a true University town that combines history, culture and typical collegiate Gothic architecture, nothing beats a visit to Princeton.

The best way to see the campus sights is to take the free tours offered by the *Orange Key Guide Service* –just go to MacLean House on campus during college season. Tours leave at 10 AM, 11 AM, 1:30 PM, and 3:30 PM weekdays and Saturdays. Sunday tours are 1:30 and 3:30 PM. The telephone number is 609-258-3603 but it is not necessary for individuals to reserve in advance. Here are some campus sights included in the tour:

Nassau Hall: Built in 1756, this Georgian stone structure has survived pillage and fire (by the British, not the students) over the years. It served as a barracks and hospital for troops of both sides during the Revolutionary War. In 1783 Congress met here and drafted the Constitution while Princeton was still the capital. It now serves as an administrative office for the University. A painting of Washington at the Battle of Trenton by Charles Willson Peale is to be found here.

Firestone Library: A beautiful two-million volume library built in 1948, it is the embodiment of the Collegiate Gothic style. Major collections include the papers of F. Scott Fitzgerald, Adlai E. Stevenson, John Foster Dulles, Woodrow Wilson and other famous graduates. A changing exhibit of rare books is also on display.

Woodrow Wilson School of Public and International Affairs: Guides will show you the outside of this striking building, one of the few modern structures on campus. Designed by Minoru Yamasaki, it includes a reflecting pool and the Fountain of Freedom by James Fitzgerald.

The University Chapel: Built in a Gothic design by Ralph Adams Cram in 1928, it is the third largest university chapel in the country, seating 1800. A 16th Century carved oak pulpit and some of the finest stained glass to be seen this side of the Atlantic Ocean makes the Chapel an outstanding part of the Princeton trip.

The Putnam Sculptures: These are a series of massive metal and stone sculptures scattered around the campus as if a giant had decided to distribute his toys among the college buildings. Sir Henry Moore, Jacques Lipchitz, Louise Nevelson and Pablo Picasso are among the sculptors represented here.

6

The Prospect: A Tuscan villa built in 1949, it is now used as a Faculty Club and not open to the public. However, the formally designed garden to the rear is open for browsing and is very pleasant

Not included in the tour, but an important stop, is **The Princeton Art Museum.** This is a first-rate museum and wonder of wonders—its free! Paintings include a generous sampling of Americana, Italian Renaissance and French Baroque. You'll find a good collection of Chinese bronzes as well as artifacts from Central and South America. A top collection of prints, a statue of Diana, and a separate medieval room that includes part of the stained-glass window from the Cathedral at Chartes are also "must sees." Special changing exhibits are of a high order. Call 609-258-3788 for more information. And don't forget Guyot Hall with its Museum of Natural History and dinosaur bones. Call 609-258-5807 for hours.

Besides the university, Princeton has pleasant shopping along Nassau Street and Palmer Square, and many good restaurants (among them *Lahiere's, The Nassau Inn* and the *Alchemist and Barrister*). You might also want to look at the **Princeton Cemetery** at Wiggins and Witherspoon, which holds the remains of Aaron Burr and Grover Cleveland among its many notables. The Princeton Battle Monument, a fifty-foot structure, stands imposingly at Nassau and Mercer Streets, while a walking tour of the area will take you past many lovely old houses. Albert Einstein's former home, at 112 Mercer St., is not open to the public. However, many people take a photograph of it as they pass by. A short drive away is **Princeton Battlefield Park**, which has lots of greenery and a colonial house that is open sporadically.

Morven, at 55 Stockton Street is open to public tours on Wednesdays from 11-3. This lovely Georgian Mansion has lost most of the beautiful furnishings it had as a governor's mansion. **Drumthwacket**, the present governor's residence, and the **Bainbridge House** have separate listings in this book. Self-guided tour maps can be picked up at the Bainbridge House (158 Nassau St.). And anyone can join their walking tours on Sundays at 2 PM.

The McCarter Theater on University Ave. runs a full program of professional plays, movies, ballet and concerts. Call 609-258-ARTS for particulars. There are also a good number of fairs and community doings going on.

DIRECTIONS: Route 206 or 27 to Princeton. The University is on
                 Nassau Street

7

NEW HOPE, PENNSYLVANIA

There are a number of small towns in the United States that seem to survive simply by being picturesque. A combination of natural beauty, historical significance and the establishment of an art colony (followed inevitably by a writer's colony and a rustic theater) creates that certain atmosphere that brings the tourists out in droves. Whether the original tourist impetus was the antiques in the historical part of town or the artworks in the art colony, the more people arrive, the more craft shops, antique stores, boites, boutiques and charm-laden restaurants open.

New Hope, Pennsylvania has long been the cultural and picturesque capital of Bucks County. On any fall weekend the narrow sidewalks of this sophisticated oasis set in Pennsylvania farm country are simply jammed.

In the 1920's landscape painters settled here, bringing with them the excitement of the creative world. By the Thirties, Bucks County had become well known as a quiet weekend haven for novelists, poets and playwrights. And in 1939 a gristmill in the center of town was transformed into the **Bucks County Playhouse.** It has been a stalwart of the summer circuit ever since. The season now begins in the late spring and extends well into the fall. Since the theater offers family musicals and matinee performances it is one of New Hope's biggest draws. (Telephone: 215-862-0220).

Another warm weather attraction is the **New Hope Mule Drawn Barge Ride** which offers an one-hour ride down the old canal works. It is a slow and easy way to see the town. It departs from the barge landing at New Street, and usually several rides are offered during the afternoon. Call 215-862-0758 for details.

A popular pontoon ride is **Coryell's Ferry** which offers scenic rides on the Delaware. It loads behind Gerensees Exotic Ice Cream Store, 22 S. Main St. (Telephone: 215-862-2050). And railroad enthusiasts will enjoy the **New Hope and Ivyland Steam Railway** which operates between May and October. It leaves from a picturesque station at Stockton and W. Bridge St. and steams through the Bucks County countryside. Call 215-862-2332 for information.

Historic house lovers will enjoy the **Parry Mansion** at South Main and Parry Streets. Guided tours of ten rooms that run the gamut from Colonial to early 20th century are available. The rooms were furnished by a professional interior decorator and each reflects a different period— Federal, Victorian— in the history of the house. It's quite well done. The house is open seasonally. Call 215-862-5652 for additional information.

8

But even without these extras there is plenty to see in New Hope. Stroll along the leaf-strewn streets and visit the shops. There are plenty of shops featuring memorabilia in town, and if you collect old sheet music, military hats or miniature dolls, you'll find much to pick from. If you're tired, there are horse-drawn carriage rides that leave from The Logan Inn.

Art galleries can be found on Main Street, Mechanic Street and Route 202. Phillips Mill, just two miles outside New Hope, hosts an art festival and has galleries too. Besides the standard landscape of Pennsylvania red barn country you can find modernistic sculpture and paintings also. The kids will be more interested in the toyshops, the knickknack and the candy shops.

One of the charms of visiting a quaint riverside town is eating in a quaint interesting restaurant and there are plenty of them in New Hope, most of them along the main drag. Whether you opt for the casual *Mother's,* the glossy *Hacienda,* or the cutesy *Picnic Basket* you will be satisfied. The better places fill up on weekends, though, so you'd better make reservations as soon as you hit town. There are a variety of nightspots that gives the place a jazzier tone after 7 PM. Check the Information Center at 1 W. Mechanic Street, or call 215-862-5880.

Lambertville, on the Jersey side of the river, now rivals New Hope in the number of good restaurants, antique shops and ambience. Read more about Lambertville in the chapter on Flea Markets.

DIRECTIONS: Route 202 across Delaware River, then US or take Rte. 179 to 29 to Lambertville and cross bridge.

LAHASKA, PENNSYLVANIA

Having gone as far as New Hope, you might as well go the extra four miles on Route 202 to Lahaska and the Peddlers Village area. The road still has some antique shops (which brought this area to prominence in the first place) but housing developments are filling up the landscape fast. **Peddler's Village** is one of those reconstructed outdoor shopping malls that combine the brick walls and lamps on the 18th Century plus very pretty landscaping with astute 20th Century commercialism. This one has a great big waterwheel and lovely floral beds to give it the proper atmosphere. It even has its own Bed and Breakfast inn, one of the many in Bucks County.

Many people who visit New Hope like to go on to Lahaska to eat, since Peddler's Village features free parking and several different eating spots. The Village also includes many shops that sell china, leather, children's clothes, and handicrafts in specialized boutiques. There are also special events on weekends - everything from a Strawberry Festival to a Teddy Bear Picnic.

Across Route 202, **Penn's Purchase Outlet Mall** has a constellation of discount and outlet stores designed to attract the bargain-minded crowd. You'll find Hanes, Bass, etc. and a fast food shop here.

LOCATION: Routes 202 & 263, Lahaska, PA.
HOURS: 10-5:30 daily for shops. Fridays until 9. Sun.: 1-5:30. Restaurants are open later.
TELEPHONE: 215-794-4000

CAPE MAY

When the Bed and Breakfast boom started in the 1970s, New Jersey was hardly mentioned in all those B&B books. But now, architectural buffs have discovered the Victorian summer homes of Cape May and have converted them into inns. Gone are the dull, old-fashioned guesthouses whose porches always seemed to show peeling white paint. In their stead there is a whole array of Victorian homes, sporting the sprightly colors of pink, blue and maroon. Gothic cottages, Italian villas, Mansard and Stick style buildings have metamorphosed into charming, whimsical Bed and Breakfast homes, restaurants, antique stores and art galleries. And the interest in this Victorian revitalization has led the town of Cape May to extend its season beyond the ten weeks of summer.

You can now take walking tours, house tours, trolley tours, and tulip tours on weekends from May through October. A special Victorian Week, held in October, features ten days of antiques, crafts, fashion shows and tours. Another special event is the Christmas candlelight tours. The group that runs many of these festivities is the *Mid-Atlantic Center for the Arts*, which operates out of the **Emlen Physick Estate.** The Physick house itself is the scene of a popular tour. This sprawling 1881 Stick Style home is typical of the late Victorian era, both in its exterior and its somewhat fussy furnishings. There's even a tearoom and a gift shop (open during season) on the estate grounds. A trolley car tour that leaves from here travels to the more colorful beachfront area, where houses trimmed in carpenter's lace and fancy restaurants await the visitor. Another interesting mode of travel is the Cape May Seashore Lines train from the city to stops in the county like the zoo and Historic Cold Spring Village. Call 609-884-5300 for this one.

Cape May has long been a part of the summer scene (see the chapter on the Jersey Shore) and the beachfront has a few modern motels and video game arcades along with the older hostelries. But the major ambience of the town is the restoration of its Victorian past. *The Washington Street Mall* is a focal point for shoppers and you can find any number of boutiques and outdoor cafes in this pleasant outdoor mall. You can also catch both trolley and horse-drawn carriage rides at the mall entrance. For more information on the various tours and inns, contact *The Mid-Atlantic Center for the Arts*, P.O. Box 340, Cape May, NJ. 08204, or telephone 800-275-4278. For other information call the Chamber of Commerce at 609-884-5508.

DIRECTIONS: Garden State Parkway to Exit 0. Follow signs to historic area.

CHINATOWN, NEW YORK

There are many unique neighborhoods in nearby New York, but the one that stands out as the last of the true ethnic neighborhoods is Chinatown. In fact Chinatown keeps spreading so that it now includes much of what was formerly called *Little Italy* and the *Lower East Side*. It is packed with six-story tenements and a huge variety of shops and restaurants. Pagoda-shaped telephone booths, a Chinese movie, and Buddhist temples add touches of the Orient. But it is the smell of spices in the streets, the gnarled looking vegetables in the grocery shops and the tinkling brass bells in the curio shops that gives Chinatown its special flavor.

Most of all it is the restaurants that pull the crowds to Chinatown. You can find hot and spicy Northern cooking, the traditional Cantonese cuisine, and the small tea shops that serve dim sum lunches. Sunday is the big day for tourists, so it gets terribly crowded. Try Saturday, or get there early on Sunday if you want to find a parking space. This is the closest you'll get to a foreign country without leaving the United States.

DIRECTIONS: Use Holland Tunnel. Keep straight on Canal Street to Pell St or Mott streets in lower Manhattan.

NEW YORK TOURS

Since New York is a center for art and theater and New Yorkers are traditionally preoccupied with being "In," it is only natural that some of the most popular tours here are of the behind-the-scenes variety.

Lincoln Center, for instance, runs escorted tours through the whole complex. That means you get a peek at the Vivian Beaumont Theater, the opera and the State Theater all on the one ticket. You may buy tickets at the Tour Desk in the downstairs concourse—they run four tours daily. Call 212-875-5350 for information and reservations. For the one and one-half hour backstage tour of the **Metropolitan Opera** (which runs at 3:45 PM on weekdays and 10 AM on Saturday) you don't have to be a phantom, but you do have to make reservations. Highly supervised, but you get to see everything from scenery and costume rooms to a view of the Met stage from the wings. Call 212-769-7020.

NBC Television Tours: These are extremely popular although only a few programs still originate from this building. However, you get a lot of history and inside information on the way TV really works. The tours run every thirty minutes from 9:30 to 4:30 and leave from the main floor of 30 Rockefeller Plaza. Children under 6 are not permitted. It is best to get your tickets as early as possible, since the tours do fill up. Tickets go on sale at 9 AM. If you're early enough you might get to see the Today show through the window at 10 Rockefeller Plaza beforehand. For information call 212-664-3700.

Sports lovers and kids will enjoy the behind the scenes tour of **Madison Square Garden** which are run frequently at the 7th Ave. & 33rd Street site. The arenas, locker room and suites are covered in this one-hour tour. Tickets are available at the box office, but call first to make sure. Telephone: 212-465-5800.

For those interested in the backstage machinations of the capitalist world, the **New York Stock Exchange,** 20 Broad St, in the Wall Street area, has been allowing visitors for years. You get a quick glimpse of the Exchange floor from a high window. Otherwise, there's plenty of information and hands-on computer stuff to play with. It's free, but access is limited. Call 212-656-5167 for further information.

WALKING TOURS

There are two kinds of walking tours. One is the self-guided type where you begin with a map and a brochure (usually provided by the local historical society) and hoof it yourself. The other is the pre-arranged group tour wherein you reach your destination by bus or car and then proceed *en masse* down the street following a highly knowledgeable leader who tells you what you are seeing. Group tours often include one or two private houses where you enter by special permission.

Here is a sampling of some of the many guided and self-guided tours available.

PATERSON TOURS

Do-it-yourself tours, guided group tours, visits to the variegated ethnic churches or simply a walking tour of the public statues of Gaetano Federici—these are some of the many tour possibilities you find in the city of Paterson. This industrial city is proud of its history as one of the earliest manufacturing sites in the United States. Its tours emphasize the historic district of *The Society for Useful Manufactures,* a section of the city that was planned for commerce by Alexander Hamilton back in 1791.

The Great Falls of Paterson: A spectacular waterfall completely surrounded by concrete and urban landscape is the focal point of the S.U.M. Tours. The Society for Useful Manufacture's Historic District covers the area of mills and plants that were once the heart and breath of the city. Paterson's Golden Age began early in the 19th Century when power from the falls created an industrial bonanza. **The Rogers Locomotive Works** building (which now contains the Paterson Museum and a host of interesting exhibits), and the silk mills that made Paterson the center of that industry are included in the tour. Some of these brick and stone edifices contain artist's studios.

The **Great Falls Development Corporation** runs tours that take you to the scenes of Paterson's industrial past, but they also will custom-tailor tours to the interests of the group. Popular stops on all the tours are the Farmer's Market which offers vegetables, cheeses and other fresh items; or the great stone churches with their stained glass windows.

CONTACT- Great Falls Visitor Center, 65 McBride Ave., Paterson, NJ. 07501. Telephone: 973-279-9587.

BORDENTOWN TOUR

One of the oldest historic towns in New Jersey, Bordentown is no longer the Quaker enclave it once was. Nor is it the large metropolis (the major boat and coach stop on the route to Philadelphia) of yore. Several famous citizens once made their abodes here - among them Clara Barton, Thomas Paine, Francis Hopkinson (another Revolutionary notable) and Joseph Bonaparte, brother of Napoleon. There are many Quaker buildings still standing and the homes of the famous are here but are private for the most part. And even though the town is primarily working class, there is still an aura of quaintness and history here.

Self-guided walking tours begin with a brochure from the Historical Society which is located in the **Old City Hall.** The hall itself has many interesting rooms - among them an one-room courthouse upstairs and a four-cell jail downstairs. The jail demonstrates how economically space was used in the old days - a criminal was sentenced upstairs and jailed within the same building, right away. The City Hall is open to the public Tues.- Thurs., 9:30-11 & 12:30- Fri.: 9:30-11; Sat.: 10-3. For those individuals who take the brochure and proceed from City Hall, it is mostly a matter of looking at the outside of the historic buildings. However, if you book a group tour (ten or more) you may get a peek inside. The group tour I took had as our first stop the **Gilder House.** As we entered the front hall, we noticed an elaborate rendition of a family tree. But it is the furniture from Joseph Bonaparte's estate that creates the most interest here. An elaborate buffet, a blue couch with eagles, and a gold-trimmed tea set in the Empire style are some of the remnants the rich and proud French family left in this small New Jersey town. The guide also pointed out a painting of sheep by artist Susan Waters. She is another Bordentown native whose fame is growing with the stronger appreciation of American itinerant painters.

Next, we saw the **Clara Barton Schoolhouse,** a prime historical site in town. Actually Miss Barton taught here for a very short time but she made quite an impact on the town. Until then, middle class children went to private school while public schools were considered to be for paupers. Miss Barton had to persuade local schoolchildren to attend. There was no fee, but each child was required to bring a stick of wood to keep the woodstove going. The small red brick building has benches and a raised platform where the teacher sat (in the back of the room, not the front).

Other houses included on the self-guided tour are: The Friends Meeting House, Shippen House, Francis Hopkinson House, Thomas Paine House and the Joseph Borden House. While most of these are private they are often opened up for Bordentown's *"Open House Tour"* which takes place in mid-October. The Gilder House is open certain Saturdays in summer.

CONTACT- Bordentown Historical Society P.O. Box 182, 302 Farnsworth Ave., Bordentown, NJ. 08505. Telephone: 609-298-1740 (12-3 PM except Mondays).

BURLINGTON

Another town that saw its heyday years ago at a time when it was the capital of West Jersey and a stronghold of Quakerism is Burlington. Among the many buildings that still stand are the **Friends Meeting House, the Revell House,** and the **Ulysses S. Grant House,** plus several prominent churches.

A very active Historical Society operates a museum here comprised of five houses. One is the house once rented by the family of America's first novelist and is named, appropriately, the **James Fenimore Cooper House,** although the writer only spent the first thirteen months of his life here. The **Captain James Lawrence House** is right next door and is dedicated to pictures and memorabilia of the War of 1812 hero who is best known for his words, "Don't Give Up The Ship!" (You find out, during the tour here, that they did give up the ship, and the British won the battle, but what the heck, a good phrase is hard to find.) Although small, this is a well furnished and very interesting place.

These side-by-side houses are located at 457 and 459 High Street. **The Pearson How House** (453 High St) the **Delia Pugh Library and the Alice Wolcott Museum make** up the rest of the complex. For hours of visitation or special arrangements call 609-386-4773. Usually, they are Mon. - Thurs., 14; Sun., 2-4.

Aside from its historical district, Burlington also offers the Burlington Coat Factory on Route 130, which is home base for a well-known outlet chain. There is also a small mall of outlet shops called The Burlington Mart. And down by the riverfront you can find an old-fashioned walk with a nice view.

A brochure for a self-guided walking tour of the historical district is available from City Hall. You can also make arrangements for guided group tours from there.

CONTACT: City Hall, Burlington, NJ. 08016. Telephone: 609-386-3993.

MOUNT HOLLY

The county seat of Burlington was a center of Quakerism in New Jersey. This quiet little town has several buildings of note on its walking tour. You may obtain a pamphlet for the self-guided tour from: Township Hall, 23 Washington St, Mt. Holly, NJ. 08060. Telephone: 609-267-0170.

Among the noteworthy buildings are: The **Burlington County Prison-Museum,** designed by Robert Mills, architect of the Washington Monument, the **Mill Street Hotel, The John Woolman Memorial** and a restored 1759 schoolhouse where Woolman, the famous Quaker abolitionist, once taught. Most of these are heavy old stone buildings that really set you back in time. A few miles outside of Mt. Holly there stands the historic mansion of **Smithville** (not to be confused with the historic town of Smithville in Atlantic County). This large columned house includes a museum of bicycles and is open for tours from May through October. Telephone 609-261-3780 for further information.

OTHER NEW JERSEY TOURS

SALEM TOUR: Salem was an early Quaker settlement in West Jersey in the county of the same name. The town boasts a large number of authentic 18th Century houses. The headquarters of the Salem Historical Society is the **Alexander Grant House** at 79-83 Market Street. It is maintained as a museum and offers nineteen rooms of early American furniture and decorative arts. Living rooms, bedrooms, featherbeds, rooms full of dolls and much more are on view here. Open Tues.-Fri. from 12-4 p.m., plus the 2nd Sat. of the month. There is a nominal fee for the museum. This is where you pick up the map for a walking tour of the local historic area. Among the important sights are the Old Court House and the ancient Salem Oak. And once a year, Salem hosts an open house of its historic buildings. It's on the first Saturday in May. *Telephone:* 856-935-5004.

GLOUCESTER COUNTY: For those who wish to see the many historical buildings in the small towns that dot the county of Gloucester, the County Historical Society has prepared a map which lists forty-eight of them and gives a short history of each. Many are privately owned, but **The Hunter-Lawrence House,** 58 North Broad St., Woodbury, is now a historical museum filled with artifacts and furniture. It is open to the public Mon., Wed. & Fri., from 1-4 p.m. The library at 17 Hunter St. is the headquarters of the Historical Society and you may stop there for the map before you set out *Telephone*. 856-845-4771.

BRIDGETON: Yet another southwestern Jersey town trying for a Renaissance of its heyday. The town includes New Jersey's largest historic district with over 2000 homes and buildings from the Colonial, Federal and Victorian eras all in various stages of repair. The strongest ambience here is Victorian, with many large homes on hand. The Cohansey River runs through town and a pleasant riverfront plaza has been built to host concerts, fairs and walking tours. A large park, which includes the Nail Museum and the good-sized Cohansic zoo is on the other side of the river. A few boutique shops have opened in the riverfront area, but the town has a long way to go to rival Cape May in interest. Maps, a slide film and arrangements for guided bus and walking tours are available at the Bridgeton-Cumberland Tourist Association at Routes 49 & 77, Bridgeton. Telephone: 856-451-4802.

CRANBURY: A charming little town below New Brunswick that has at various times been called Cranberry and Cranberrytown. Many of the houses standing on the tree-lined streets were built between 1820 and 1880. Washington dined here during the battle of Monmouth (although not at the Cranbury Inn, which has a Dickensian ambience). The Historical Society runs a museum at 4 Park Place (open Sat & Sun. from 1-4) with early Victorian furnishings. They also supply a walking map of the sites in the historic district. Write Cranbury Historical Society, 4 Park Place, Cranbury, 08512.

NEWARK: You can reserve walking tours through the Ironbound and visit the bakery and produce shops in this heavily Portuguese and Spanish district. And for bus groups, a very knowledgeable guide will board the bus and give a tour of Newark that includes downtown, the Newark "subway", the parks, the slums, the grand old houses and the magnificent **Sacred Heart Cathedral, which** you may enter. This huge Gothic cathedral rivals its European counterparts in beauty, if not in age. You also get to see the edge of Branch Brook Park which is especially lovely in cherry-blossom season. For the tours: Telephone: 973-621-8900, ask for Liz Del Tufo.

SEASONAL TOURS: Many towns now concentrate their efforts on a once a year "Open House" sort of thing. Among these is **Plainfield,** which boasts many beautifully restored Victorian homes. Its hospital tour, usually in May, includes some old-style wrap-around porch houses of the late Victorian era that makes this town so distinctive.

Hoboken celebrates its railroad station in the fall (varies from September to October) with festivities, tours of the Byzantine station, jazz concerts and walks through some of the restored brownstones. Of course one can visit the many bars, jazz spots, clubs and restaurants in this one-mile square city at any time. It's a favorite of the twenty and thirty-something age crowd.

November is the season for **Sergeantsville's** "Thanksgiving In The Country" tour wherein the whole town makes soup for the church luncheon and runs buses back and forth to the various open houses.

PHILADELPHIA TOURS

Probably the best known self-guided tour is that of Independence National Historical Park (Independence Mall) which is treated in the chapter entitled "Classics". Other popular tours in Philadelphia are:

UNITED STATES MINT: Within the downtown historic area (it's located at Arch & 5th Sts) is the building where the coins we use are produced. No, they don't give free samples, but you can buy special sets and commemorative coins from the sales counter in the lobby. Self-guided tours of the huge operation are continuous and last about 45 minutes. Lots of historical information. No cameras or videos allowed. Free. Hours: 9-4:30, Mon.-Sat. Telephone. 215-597-7350.

FAIRMOUNT PARK HISTORIC HOUSE TOURS: Fairmount Park cuts a wide swath through Philadelphia on both sides of the Schuylkill. It includes, within its many acres, not only the usual playgrounds, pools and tennis courts, but also such major attractions as the Philadelphia Zoo and the Philadelphia Museum of Art.

In the 18th Century, the park was a center for country homes of the gentry who wanted to escape the epidemics of the crowded city. Eight of these homes have been restored and are now open to the public. They include John Penn's *Solitude*, Robert Morris' *Lemon Hill*, and such Georgian classics as *Woodford* and *Mount Pleasant*. The houses, which are scattered throughout the park, are furnished with authentic antiques and hark back to the time when Philadelphia was the most important colonial town in the world.

Guided tours for groups can be arranged beforehand to emphasize history, decorative arts or gardens. In early December, a special Christmas tour features the houses decorated in the manner of the 18th and early 19th centuries. Public hours and fees vary. There is also a special trolley-tram which stops at several places in Fairmount Park, including the historic houses. The trolley can be boarded at the Visitor's Center at 16th and JFKennedy Boulevard and other major stops. It covers most tourist spots and you can get on and off at will. The Philadelphia Museum of Art administers most of the Fairmount Park house tours. Telephone: 215-236-SHOW.

For general Information on Philadelphia write:
Philadelphia Convention and Visitors Bureau,
1515 Market St, Suite 2020, Philadelphia, PA 19102
or call 215-636-1666.
Also try www.phillyvisitor.com for general information.

See Also: Lambertville and Chester in the chapter on" Flea Markets and Outlets".

WHERE WASHINGTON
SLEPT, ATE AND FOUGHT

Photo: Courtesy NJ Travel & Tourism

In This Chapter You Will Find:

Jockey Hollow, NJ
Washington's Headquarters (Ford Mansion,
    Revolutionary War Museum), NJ
Dey Mansion, NJ
Wallace House, NJ
Old Dutch Parsonage, NJ
Rockingham, NJ
The Old Barracks, NJ
Washington Crossing State Park, NJ
Washington Crossing Historic Park, PA
Fort Lee Historic Park, NJ
Valley Forge, PA
Monmouth Battlefield State Park, NJ
Covenhoven House, NJ
The Proprietary House, NJ
Red Bank Battlefield, NJ
Indian King Tavern, NJ
Boxwood Hall, NJ
Buccleuch Mansion, NJ
Von Steuben House, NJ
Other Revolutionary War Sites, NJ

JOCKEY HOLLOW

The winter of 1779-1780 was the coldest in a century. On December 1, 1779, General George Washington entered Morristown and took up residence at the house of Mrs. Jacob Ford, Jr.

Meanwhile, four miles away at Jockey Hollow, 10,000 men chopped down six hundred acres of oak, walnut and chestnut trees to build hundreds of huts along the slopes of the "hollow". Severe snowstorms hindered their work and delayed the supply of meat and bread they needed to survive. Starvation confronted the army, which also suffered from inadequate clothing, disease and low morale. So terrible was the winter of the Morristown encampment that many troops finally mutinied.

But the history books only tell you about Valley Forge. Why? Because New Jersey has simply never had a very good public relations man. Not until recently, anyway.

Today there are several reconstructed huts on the site which is administered by the National Park Service. However, the Visitor's Center gives full information about the encampment. If you go beyond the main desk you find a mini-theater where an eleven-minute film begins at the touch of a button. The story of typical foot soldiers huddled in a simple hut waiting for the rations and money that took so long in coming is unfolded. After the film, you can move on to the mock-up of the soldiers hut and see the straw beds, muskets and clothing used at the time.

From the Information Center, proceed out the back door to the **Wick Farm**, where a Park Service employee is usually in residence. The farmhouse was occupied by both the Wick family (owners of the farm that included Jockey Hollow) and General Arthur St. Clair and his aide. A vegetable and herb garden, a well and a horse barn surround the wooden cottage.

Inside the smoky cabin, a Ranger dressed in Colonial garb will be cooking, melting down candles or just answering questions. A tour through the house shows the little bedroom of Tempe Wick, the General's office and bedroom.

From the Wick house, you can drive to the open slopes of the winter encampment. There the simple soldier's huts and some hiking trails await. On special weekends there are often demonstrations or musters. A section of the Morristown National Historic Park.

ADMISSION: Adults: $4.00 (includes all of MNHP). Under 17 free.
HOURS: 9-5 Daily. Closed major holidays.
LOCATION: Take Rte. 202 to Tempe Wick Road (south of Morristown). Follow signs.
TELEPHONE: 973-543-4030

WASHINGTON'S HEADQUARTERS
MORRISTOWN

For another look at the details of the Morristown encampment go to **Washington's Headquarters** (The Ford Mansion and Museum) which is part of the overall site called **Morristown National Historic Park**. It's a short drive away. You enter through the museum and here you will find military paraphernalia such as surgeon's tools, mess kits, muskets and cleaning rods that accompanied the troops. Another exhibit emphasizes the role of the citizens of Morristown and how they reacted to the soldiers in their town.

Don't miss the movie shown periodically in the auditorium. A professional film which was shot on location both here and in Jockey Hollow, it contrasts the warmth and food available to officers at the mansion with the hungry, freezing men camped four miles away. A lively ball scene was filmed in the central hall of the Ford Mansion.

The Mansion itself is a solid frame Colonial house — by no means a mansion in the modern sense. As you enter the long central hallway, you notice how well such halls were suited for line dances such as the Virginia reel. The house was offered as headquarters to Washington by Mrs. Ford, a widow with four children. The Ford family lived in two rooms while the General and his staff occupied the rest of the house. The furnishings are authentic to the period and many are true Ford family pieces. Beds include the canopied master bed used by Washington. Highboys, chest-on-chests, wall maps and lots of straw mattresses are all to be noted. The mansion is shown by regular tours. National Park Service people, usually in colonial dress, take you through.

Despite the rigors of the Morristown encampment the Ford Mansion looks like a warm, yet comparatively elegant abode for the Chief of Staff. From here, Alexander Hamilton, (who was Washington's Aide de Camp at the time) courted Betsey Schuyler who was staying at the nearby Schuyler-Hamilton house. The historic park also includes other sites such as Fort Nonsense.

        HOURS: 9-5 Daily. Closed major holidays.
  ADMISSION: Adults: $4.00 (Includes all sites in MNHP). Under 16 free.
  DIRECTIONS: Route 287 to Exit 36 or 36A to Morris Ave. East
                     Follow signs to Washington's Headquarters.
  TELEPHONE: 973-539-2085 / www.nps.gov

DEY MANSION

A solid Dutch farmhouse built in the early Georgian style, the Dey Mansion was Washington's headquarters for three months during the summer and fall of 1780. Furnishings reflect the status of the Dey family who were quite well to-do. An unusual feature of this northern house is the separate kitchen. (There is a breezeway between it and the main house for use during the colder months.) According to the guide, the separate kitchen was practical, for if the hearth caught on fire, it would not take the rest of the house with it

After an inspection of the well-stocked kitchen, you may tour the house which has two floors of well-kept furnishings and many family portraits. The third floor attic is used partly as a museum with varying exhibits of 18th and 19th century artifacts. The Bergen County Militia offers special reenactments here (although the house is maintained by the Passaic County Parks Department.)

HOURS: Wed. - Fri.: 1-4. Sat. & Sun.: 10-12 & 1-4.
ADMISSION: Adults: $1.00. Under 10 free.
LOCATION: 199 Totowa Rd., Wayne, Passaic County, (in Preakness Valley Park).
TELEPHONE: 973-696-1776

WALLACE HOUSE

Washington's headquarters during the winter encampment at Middlebrook (1778-79) is a two-hundred and twenty-five-year-old clapboard colonial house in Somerville. The guide who administers the Wallace House also takes care of the Old Dutch Parsonage across the street. So if you knock and nobody answers, wait a while - he might be at the other house. He will usually leave a sign advising you of the fact. On busy days, there are usually volunteers who help out

The headquarters itself is a nine-room, solidly built wooden structure with wide plank floors that creak curiously under modern weight. Although the furnishings are not those actually used by Washington and his staff, they are all of the period. A four-poster bed stands in the room where Washington probably slept, where typical toiletry articles abound. The house is refurbished to reflect its state when the Wallace's lived there, after the war.

The formal parlor does not look large, but it is said up to thirty people ate there when General and Mrs. Washington entertained. It must have been awfully crowded. The Wallace House may have been the best home in the area, but the rooms are small and cramped compared to the high, airy drawing rooms at Mount Vernon. However, the house has an office, four bedrooms and two parlors, so there was ample room for entertaining.

The winter of 1778-79 was rather mild, much more pleasant than those at Valley Forge or Morristown, and the encampment at Middlebrook faced less disasters. Food, however, was never plentiful, so when the Washington's entertained, they did so sparsely. The house may be undergoing renovations. Free

> **HOURS:** Wed.-Sat: 10-12 & 1-4. Sunday: 1-4.
> **LOCATION:** 38 Washington Place, Somerville, Somerset County.
> **TELEPHONE:** 908-725-1015

THE OLD DUTCH PARSONAGE

This house was the home first of Pastor Frelinghuysen, minister of the Dutch Reformed Church. Later it became the home of Rev. Jacob Hardenburgh who married Frelinghuysen's widow. Hardenburgh was one of the "Fighting Pastors" of the Revolutionary War who condemned the British from the pulpit. He founded Queens College which later became Rutgers University. He was a frequent host to General and Mrs. Washington when they lived close by during the Middlebrook Encampment. The house has since been moved so it is now across the street.

The displays at the parsonage are meant to reflect the life and times of this Dutch pastor. Although there have been Dutch artifacts and some handsome furniture on display here, it seems that renovations go on forever— so call first.

> **HOURS, ETC.,** Check Wallace House entry.

ROCKINGHAM

A little beyond the quaint town of Rocky Hill, which in itself looks like it has slept since the Revolution, lies Rockingham. It was here that Washington stayed in 1783 while the Constitution was being hammered out at nearby Nassau Hall in Princeton. Actually, both George and Martha stayed here and entertained extensively. It is best known as the house where the "Farewell Address to the Armies" was composed.

A medium-sized colonial with front porch, the house was once part of a fine estate of 350 acres with barns, stables, coach house and granary. It has since been removed from its original site (because of dynamiting in a nearby quarry) and is set a little way off Route 518. Surprisingly, the pillared porch of this colonial is in the back, and the vista from that side is quite pleasing. A nice kitchen garden, flowering trees and some out-buildings skirt the house.

There are two stories of period rooms and some historical exhibits. Of course rooms were never huge in these New Jersey homes, but the ten rooms in Rockingham are good sized. The furniture is handsome. Period pieces include Chippendale sets, burnished bureaus, canopied beds and antique tea services. The Blue Room study where the Farewell Address was composed is left with the inkstand and green cloth still on the table. There is a special children's area plus traveling exhibits, such as a display of handmade quilts, on hand. Free.

> **HOURS:** Wed.-Sat: 10-12 & 1-4; Sun.: 1-4.
> **LOCATION:** Route 518 (Off Rte. 206) Rocky Hill, Somerset County
> **TELEPHONE:** 609-921-8835

THE OLD BARRACKS

Set in the midst of bustling downtown Trenton, The Old Barracks, with its red-painted porches is an authentic reminder of the past. This is the only standing barracks of the type used by the British to house foreign troops in colonial America. It is also the place where Washington and his troops surprised the Hessian soldiers after he crossed the Delaware on Christmas night, 1776, and turned the tide of the Revolution.

This U-shaped fieldstone building has quite a history. Just before it was saved from demolition, the rooms were being used as a "Home for the Relief of Respectable, Aged and Indigent Widows and Single Women". The Barracks were originally built in 1758 during the French and Indian War because American colonists objected to the billeting of British troops in private homes. In 1776, the British and Hessian mercenaries used it until the Americans gained control, when it then became a hospital for the wounded. After the war, the building went through a series of ups and downs until the Old Barracks Association saved it in 1899. Nowadays, interpretative history, with costumed guides, is emphasized.

A recent restoration has opened up plenty of space in the building. The long barracks room, an officer's apartment and a room dedicated to General Washington are all on view. Costumed docents depict various "characters" such as a farmwoman, a volunteer soldier, or a Hessian mercenary. They tell you their stories or show you how to load a musket or care for the wounded. There are also maps and displays. The Barracks hosts an annual recreation of The Battle of Trenton on the weekend after December 26 with lots of cannons and reenactors in the streets.

HOURS: Tues. - Sat: 11-5; Sun.: 1-5. Closed major holidays.
ADMISSION: Adults: $6.00; Seniors & children: $3.00. Under 5 free.
LOCATION: Barracks St. at West Front St., Trenton.
(Take Willow St. Exit from Route 29S).
TELEPHONE: 609-396-1776 / www.barracks.org

WASHINGTON CROSSING
STATE PARK (NJ)

This popular park, covering 807 acres that stretch from the banks of the Delaware in Titusville, commemorates the crossing that led to the most important victory of the war's early years. On Christmas night 1776, General Washington crossed the icy Delaware with 2,400 men, plus artillery and supplies. The crossing took nine hours and the men and officers converged on this spot on the Jersey side. The ensuing surprise attack gave a sweet taste of victory to the discouraged American troops.

The Visitor Center is filled with information on this and other early battles of the Revolutionary War, plus the uniforms and muskets of the time. There are a variety of exhibits and audio-visuals, including the extensive Swan collection of armaments.

Outside there are open fields for Frisbee throwing, an excellent nature center, and an open-air amphitheater for summer shows. There are many picturesque picnic groves here also. Near the Delaware River there is a monument marking the spot where the troops disembarked, and two historic houses set in the greenery. One of these, the **Johnson Ferry House,** a refurbished inn, offers guided tours at specific times (Call 609-737-2515). Nearby, the Nelson house is even closer to the river.

Admission to the park is free, but there is a parking fee on summer weekends.

HOURS: Visitor Center. Wed. - Sun.: 9-4:30.
Shorter winter hours. Park open all the time.
LOCATION: Routes 29 & 546, Titusville, Mercer County.
TELEPHONE: Park: 609-737-0623; Visitor Center: 609-737-9303.

WASHINGTON CROSSING
HISTORIC PARK (PA)

Across the river, the site of the embarkation is the focus for a large park that stretches up the Delaware River and includes several sections. In the first section, a modern Visitor's Center offers brochures, a theater for a film about the crossing and tickets for the historical buildings within the park. Some of these buildings are within easy walking distance. The first is the **McKonkey Ferry Inn** where Washington and his staff met and ate just before the crossing. It is fixed up as a travelers' inn with tables set with pewter and a bar and grill. In this section of the park there are two other historic houses plus replicas of the longboats that were used for the crossing.

Traveling north you come upon another section of the park which includes a wildflower preserve, the high observation tower on Bowman's Hill and the **Thompson-Neely House** (which is an original structure built of Delaware River ledgestone and looking as authentic as all get out). Tickets for all historic houses are reasonable and of course you get a guided tour through each.

You'll find lots of picnic pavilions, walking paths and driving roads throughout the park and in the autumn the foliage is perfect. The visitor Center, movie and self-guided walking tour are free. An annual Recreation of the crossing takes place every Christmas Day.

HOURS: Tues.-Sat: 9-5, Sun.: 12-5.
ADMISSION: Guided Tour: Adults: $4.00; Seniors: $3.50;
Children: $2.00; Under 6, free.
DIRECTIONS: Take bridge from Titusville, NJ, drive north on PA 32
for other sections of park.
TELEPHONE: 215-493-4076

FORT LEE HISTORIC PARK

Set in the scenic Palisades Interstate Park with a view of the Hudson, the George Washington Bridge and Manhattan, Fort Lee commemorates a defeat, not a victory. The park is only 33 acres but is contains a handsome, modern Visitors Center, meandering roads, a picnic area, reconstructed gun batteries and an authentic 18th century soldiers hut. The park is actually a quarter mile east of the original Fort Lee (which was named after General Charles Lee who helped in the defense of New York City).

Washington planned Fort Lee as a bulwark against British control of the Hudson River by its strong navy. With forts on either side of the river and sunken ships in the river channel, the British ships could be kept at bay. However, the British, under General Howe, forced the American Army out of Long Island and then New York City. In November 1776, an orderly retreat from Fort Lee was planned. But before it could take place, General Cornwallis struck first— ferrying over 6,000 men across the Hudson, north of the fort. Washington ordered an immediate retreat before his men could be cut off. Unfortunately, the cannon and other military supplies had to be left behind in this hasty retreat. This devastating blow ushered in the darkest days of the Revolution.

Nowadays, you can see replicas of the abandoned cannon in the park, and view the story on plexiglas panels in the Visitors Center. A short film and displays of muskets are also on view. Down at the soldiers hut costumed guides interpret colonial life on summer weekends and for school groups. Because the historic site is part of the larger interstate park, there are plenty of good hiking trails and scenic outlooks nearby.

HOURS: Visitor Center: Wed. - Sun.: 10-5.
ADMISSION: $4.00 parking fee.
DIRECTIONS: Hudson Terrace, Fort Lee. Take Palisades Int. Parkway to last exit before GW Bridge. Turn left on Hudson Terrace.
TELEPHONE: 201-461-1776

VALLEY FORGE

It is known as "The Crucible of Victory" because the 10,000 men who emerged from the harsh winter had coalesced into an efficient, well-trained fighting force. The encampment lasted from December 19, 1777 to June 19, 1778. It is now commemorated at this huge park, which is so vast you must start with a map or a bus tour.

The modern Visitor Center, where you can procure both, also offers a movie and a small exhibit of Revolutionary swords and military equipment. It is here that you can board the buses that operate during the warm weather only. The bus tour, which stops at key sites, features a taped narration as you go along. Even better, you can rent or buy a tape for use as you drive along yourself. Among the important sites you will pass on the scenic drive are: The Memorial Arch, the earthen fortifications, the parade ground where Von Steuben reviewed the troops, and of course, the soldiers' huts.

When you get to **Washington's Headquarters,** costumed soldiers are at hand to welcome you. There is a small admission fee here in season. There are often costumed personnel stationed at the soldier's huts also. They help to point out the hardships the soldiers endured.

For modern-day visitors there are also picnic grounds, bicycle trails, a snack bar and souvenir shop and lots of beautiful scenery. The park is free, but there is a fee for bus tours, tapes and entry to some historic houses.

> **HOURS:** Daily except Christmas, 9-5. For buses: Warm weather only.
> **LOCATION:** Visitor Center Junction of PA 23 & 363, Valley Forge, PA. Take Exit 24 from PA. Tpke.
> **TELEPHONE:** 610-783-1077 / www.nps.gov

MONMOUTH BATTLEFIELD STATE PARK

Although it was not a complete victory, still the Battle of Monmouth proved that American troops, honed by the winter at Valley Forge, could hold their own against British soldiers. Today's park was the scene of a hot day's battle with a general who ordered a retreat (and was later reprimanded by Washington) and a lady named Molly "Pitcher" who became a heroine according to legend.

The fields of rolling hills are now empty at Monmouth Battlefield, but a large Visitors Center gives you the necessary information. There are relief maps of the battle and television screens showing a reenactment of the fight.

Here you can also pick up a map of the battlefield and other historic sites in the area. Also a refreshment counter and a picnic area are part of the building. If you drive around following the map you will find the **Craig House** (which may or may not be open, depending on staffing) where the wounded were cared for; **Tennant Church,** a good-looking, shake-sided Colonial edifice which was close to the battle, and **Molly Pitcher's Well.** Free. Once a year, the last weekend in June, a live reenactment of the battle takes place.

> **HOURS:** Daily 8-4, Winter. 8-7 Summer (Park only)
> **LOCATION:** Route 9 to Route 33, Manalapan, Monmouth County.
> **TELEPHONE:** 732-462-9619

COVENHOVEN HOUSE

One of the four historic houses administered by the Monmouth County Historical Association, it is significant for its role in the Battle of Monmouth. Henry Clinton, commander of the British troops at the battle, stayed at the home from Friday, June 26 until Sunday, June 28, 1778. After the battle, he and his troops left Freehold and returned to New York.

The main section of the home is in Georgian style and is furnished according to a 1790 inventory of William A. Covenhoven, the well-to-do farmer who owned the property. A mural depicting a sea-battle and walls decorated in a blue-and white Delft pattern were discovered in one bedroom during the restoration of the house. Extremely authentic and well-done - an interesting house to visit

> **HOURS:** May-Sept.: Tues.,Thurs., Sun.: 1-4; Sat: 10-4.
> **ADMISSION:** Adults: $2.00; Seniors: $1.50; Children: $1.00; under 6 free.
> **LOCATION:** 150 West Main St., Freehold.
> **TELEPHONE:** 732-462-1466

THE PROPRIETARY HOUSE

This mansion is a true Palladian villa, known as high Georgian in America. It was built in 1763 for the last Royal Governor of New Jersey (who was Benjamin Franklin's "natural" son, William). However, Franklin did not move in until 1774. When the Revolutionary War began, he was arrested - for unlike his famous father, he chose the Tory side. Benjamin Franklin made two visits in 1775 but could not talk his son into switching allegiance.

The house suffered much damage during the war and succumbed to fire in 1792. After that it had as many ups and downs as a soap opera heroine. It was a popular seaside hotel, and then was sold at a sheriff s auction. There were "rich" years as a merchant's abode, and then a downward slide. The house became in turn a widow and orphan's home, an apartment house and a rooming house. Restoration began some years ago and is still ongoing. There are special exhibits on view throughout the year.

Although the house is sparsely furnished, during a tour one can get a feel for its dimensions. The true Palladian windows, the high ceilings and the Adamesque fireplace are evident. The Governor's drawing room, also called the "Great Parlour" is dramatic. The fully restored upstairs bedroom features a housekeeper's typical furniture. The most charming room in the building is the downstairs vaulted wine cellar constructed of red brick.

HOURS:	Wed.: 10-4. Sun. by appt.
ADMISSION:	Adults: $2.00; Children: $1.00. Under 12 free.
LOCATION:	149 Kearny Ave., Perth Amboy, Middlesex County
TELEPHONE:	732-826-5527

RED BANK BATTLEFIELD

A small but decisive battle to defend Fort Mercer took place here on October 19, 1777. The Hessian army received many casualties at the hands of the American Army, which, up until this point, had known mostly defeat. Since the Fort guarded the Delaware River and prevented British ships from entering occupied Philadelphia, the freedom of Fort Mercer was quite important. Although British ships eventually went through, the Red Bank victory helped France decide to join America in her fight against the British. The picturesque park contains old cannons and monuments and some remains of Fort Mercer. The historic Whitall house, where the wounded were cared for, is open at specific hours. Picnic areas. Free.

HOURS:	Daily, 9-5. House: Wed.-Fri.: 9-12 & 1-4: Weekends: 1-4. Closed weekends in winter
LOCATION:	100 Hessian Ave., National Park, Gloucester County.
TELEPHONE:	856-853-5120

INDIAN KING TAVERN

Set in the little town of Haddonfield, which looks as if it stepped out of the past, this public house, or tavern, was the site of frequent meetings of the New Jersey State Legislature during the Revolutionary War. Among the rooms the guide shows off are the colonial kitchen, the toy room, and the bedroom where Dolly Madison slept. (Her uncle was at one-time the owner of the tavern). Groups by appointment only. Children under 12 must be accompanied by an adult.

Guided tours for individuals are ongoing. You must wait at the door for the next tour if there is one in progress at the moment. Free.

HOURS: Wed.-Sat: 10-12 & 1-4; Sun.: 1-4
LOCATION: 233 Kings Highway, Haddonfield, Camden County.
TELEPHONE: 856-429-6792

BOXWOOD HALL

Also known as the Boudinot Mansion, this very nicely furnished colonial house is not far from the main drag in Elizabeth. Built in 1750, it was the home, during the Revolution, of Elias Boudinot, president of the Continental Congress. George Washington had lunch here on the day he embarked for New York and his inauguration as President. House furnishings include both the Colonial and later Empire style. State Historic Site. Call first. Free.

HOURS: Mon.-Sat.: 9-12 & 1-5.
LOCATION: 1073 East Jersey St, Elizabeth (off Routes 1 & 9).
TELEPHONE: 973-648-4540

BUCCLEUCH MANSION

A handsome Georgian mansion which was recently refurbished. The surrounding gardens are very impressive. The house is set inside Buccleuch Park on a tree-lined street that is practically part of the Rutgers Campus in New Brunswick. Originally built in 1763, White House Farm, as it was then known, was sold to an English army officer in 1774.

The house was confiscated by the Americans in 1776, but by December the British troops reoccupied New Brunswick. The banister still retains the marks of the soldiers' musket barrels from the time of this occupation, which lasted until 1777. After the war, Colonel Charles Stewart, Commissary General of the Revolutionary Army, became the owner. At this time, White House Farm was visited by Washington, Hancock and Alexander Hamilton, who all loved the setting.

Much of Buccleuch Mansion's furnishings today are of 19th century origin. Of particular note is the striking wallpaper in the downstairs and upstairs hallways. Rooms include a Victorian parlor and a drawing room with Queen Anne pieces. You can also inspect the bedrooms (including the one where Washington slept), a toy room, and a craft room with spinning wheel. Free (donations accepted). Groups tours by appointment. Although visiting hours are very limited, the surrounding park and well-tended gardens are open.

> **HOURS:** June-Oct.: Sun. 2-4.
> **LOCATION:** Easton Ave. to Buccleuch Park, New Brunswick, Middlesex County.
> **TELEPHONE:** 732-745-5094

STEUBEN HOUSE

A Dutch Colonial home built in 1695 with a further addition in 1752, this home is an example of early architecture in New Jersey. The house was confiscated by the Americans during the Revolutionary War because the owners (the Zabriskie family) were loyal to the British crown. Its position on the Hackensack River made it a strategic prize for both sides. (The house literally sits on the river's edge). Washington headquartered here in September 1980. The house was later presented to Baron von Steuben for his aid in drilling the troops during the war.

One thing you notice in the furnishings here is the emphasis on local craftsmen, and on the Dutch influence in Bergen County. Some fine specimens of the local Colonial craft include a New Brunswick kas and an old settle. There are also Indian artifacts, dolls and toys. The house is part of **Historic New Bridge Landing** an eighteen-acre park that includes other historic buildings. Among these are the Campbell-Christie House, the Demarest House, an out-kitchen and a barn. Free.

> **HOURS:** Wed.-Sat: 10-12 & 1-4
> **LOCATION:** 1209 Main Street River Edge, Bergen County (take River Edge exit from Route 4).
> **TELEPHONE:** 201-487-1739

OTHER REVOLUTIONARY WAR SITES

Among the many other historical sites and buildings associated with the Revolutionary War are:

PRINCETON BATTLEFIELD STATE PARK: A short decisive battle was fought here on January 3, 1777, just a week after the famous crossing of the Delaware. General Hugh Mercer was mortally wounded during this battle. Within the park, you can visit the Thomas Clarke House, a refurbished colonial home used as a hospital following the battle, when it is open. Hours: 9 AM to dusk. *Location:* 500 Mercer St., Princeton. *Telephone.* 609-921-0074.

BRANDYWINE BATTLEFIELD STATE PARK- This battle was a defeat for Washington's forces. It took place on September 11, 1777, and is commemorated by dioramas and audio-visuals at the Visitors Center. There are also two historic houses within the park. One was Washington's headquarters and the other was used by The Marquis de Lafayette. Free (fee for houses). *Hours.* Tues.-Sun.: 9-5. May 30-Labor Day. *Location:* Route 1, Chadds Ford, PA. *Telephone.* 610-459-3342.

DRAKE HOUSE: During the battle of the Watchung Mountains, Washington used this house as his command headquarters. Although there is a colonial bedroom where he is supposed to have rested, the house was later remodeled. It now reflects the Empire and Victorian styles as well as the basic colonial. *Hours:* Sun.: 2-4. Small admission fee. *Location:* 602 West Front St, Plainfield, Union County. *Telephone:* 908-755-5831.

HANCOCK HOUSE: Scene of massacre of thirty unarmed Quakers by attacking British Rangers, this 1734 house has period furnishings. Call for hours. Free. *Location:* Route 49 at Hancock's Bridge, 5 miles south of Salem, Salem County. *Telephone:* 856-935-4373.

ALLEN HOUSE: Since this 1750 house was operated as the Blue Ball Tavern during the Revolutionary War, two major rooms here have been furnished in that manner. Tables are set with pewter, there is a bar and grill with whiskey jugs and so forth. Upstairs, there are changing exhibits. *Hours:* May-Sept.: Tues., Thurs., Sun., 1-4; Sat.: 10-4. Small admission fee/ under 6 free. *Location:* Route 35 & Sycamore Ave., Shrewsbury, Monmouth County. *Telephone:* 732-462-1466.

See Also: Nassau Hall, Morven, Independence Hall and several of the colonial homes mentioned in the chapter "Restored Villages and Homes"

HOMES OF THE RICH
AND FAMOUS

Photo by Barbara Hudgins

In This Chapter You Will Find:

Nemours, DE
Winterthur, DE
Kykuit, NY
Hyde Park, NY
The Vanderbilt Mansion, NY
Ballantine House, NJ
Edison National Historic Site, NJ
Grover Cleveland Birthplace, NJ
Lambert Castle, NJ
Ringwood Manor, NJ
Lyndhurst, NY
Sunnyside, NY
Boscobel, NY
Maccoulloch Hall, NJ
Drumthwacket, NJ
Bainbridge House, NJ
William Trent House, NJ
Kuser Farm Mansion, NJ
Walt Whitman House, NJ
Craftsman Farms, NJ
Pennsbury Manor, PA
Andalusia, PA
Pearl S. Buck Home, PA

NEMOURS

The fabulous homes of the super-rich are America's equivalent of the palaces and castles of Europe. And no home is more palatial than Nemours, the former residence of Alfred 1. DuPont. It is located outside Wilmington in the popular Brandywine Valley area.

The mansion, built in 1909, is a modified Louis XVI French chateau. The landscaped gardens are in the French formal style and include marble statues, cascading fountains and a series of terraces and stairways to please the eye. In fact, the hand of Louis XVI seems to he everywhere in Nemours - a tribute as much to the Gallic origins of the DuPonts as to the possibility that American millionaires in 1910 must have known the era of conspicuous consumption was about to end. A few years later the income tax and World War I helped destroy any notion of an American aristocracy.

Once you enter the chateau, you are led by a tour guide into a home of vast elegance. The gold and white dining room boasts ornate moldings on walls and ceilings, Rococo style paintings and a chandelier worthy of the Phantom of the Opera. The reception room, living room and other public rooms are equally fabulous with inlaid ceilings, marble tiled floors, rich oriental rugs and carved walls. Furniture includes both genuine antiques like George Washington's chair and fine copies of Louis XVI furnishings.

You rarely see the kitchens of "great homes," but at Nemours there's a downstairs tour of the restaurant-sized cooking area with its empty pantry and huge pots. Also downstairs is the bowling alley, the billiard room (with a table the size of a bowling alley) and the furnace room (ingeniously set up by Alfred himself, who was an engineer).

After the house tour you may either board a mini-bus for a tour of the gardens or walk around yourself. Fountains and pools, colonnades and balustrades, marble Cupids and Dianas, velvet lawns and clipped hedges create a mini-Versailles here.

Nemours doesn't exactly admit hordes of people. Tours are limited in number and reservations are highly suggested. No children under 16.

HOURS:	May-Nov.: Tues.-Sat.: tours at 9, 11, 1 & 3.
	Sunday tours: 11, 1 & 3.
ADMISSION:	$10.00
LOCATION:	Rockland Road (inside Alfred I. DuPont Institute)
	Wilmington, Delaware.
TELEPHONE:	302-651-6912 / www.nemours.org

WINTERTHUR

Henri DuPont, grandson of the founder of the DuPont empire, was a great collector of American decorative arts. Winterthur is his crowning achievement. Although he actually lived in this mansion, inherited from his family, he turned it into a veritable museum. Not only china and furniture, but whole rooms were transported into the house. The main mansion contains 175 rooms, many of them decorated in a pre-1860 style. So you will find dining rooms, kitchens, (including walls, ceilings and fireplaces) placed panel by panel inside the mansion. Several style periods are shown: Seventeenth Century, William and Mary, Queen Anne, Chippendale, Federal, Empire and Victorian.

Each piece is documented, so that the Duncan Phyfe room, for instance, had its architectural elements removed from a specific house in New York where Phyfe furniture was used. You can find a striking plantation dining room removed in its entirety from a South Carolina home, a New England kitchen, a Shaker bedroom, a New York parlour, and a flying staircase copied from an estate in North Carolina. One oft-photographed room features authentic 18th Century Chinese wallpaper that covers both the walls and the ceilings.

After the guided tour, you can visit the museum galleries on the other side of the main building. These include displays of furniture, china and silver, and explanations of their social significance. In a separate gallery, you will also find the wonderful collection of tureens from the Campbell Soup Collection that was once in Camden.

Besides the museum, there are extensive gardens at Winterthur- -sixty acres of greenery, dotted with woods and copses. During spring, flowering displays include azaleas and dogwoods. A special tram takes you through the gardens. It leaves from the main Visitors Center which is also where you buy tickets, pick up maps, eat at the cafeteria or check out the extensive book and gift shop. For those who want to engage in serious shopping, there are rugs, chairs and china for sale at the Gallery and Plant Shop, a luxurious little building located across from the main house.

General admission includes the galleries, gardens and "touch-it" rooms, but not the mansion tour.

> **HOURS:** Mon.-Sat: 9:00-5; Sun.: 12-5. Closed major holidays.
> **ADMISSION:** $13.00 (45-min. tour) Gen. Admission: $8.00
> **LOCATION:** NJ Turnpike to 295 & Delaware Mem. Bridge, then north on 1-95 to Route 52 (Exit 7) then left to Winterthur.
> **TELEPHONE:** 800-448-3883 / www.winterthur.org

KYKUIT

You may never be as rich as Rockefeller, but at least you can visit the family estate in Pocantico Hills, near Tarrytown, New York. While reservations are no longer required at this popular outing, if you're coming from New Jersey it's best to book beforehand. You can get there by land or by sea.

The mansion was the country home of four generations of Rockefellers: John D., his son, John D. Jr., Nelson and Nelson's children. The furnishings inside and the magnificent terraced grounds show the influence of the first three generations. John D. Rockefeller, who started the fortune, did not believe in conspicuous consumption. The original stone house, called "Kykuit" which is Dutch for "lookout" was not particularly ornate. It was later remodeled in the Renaissance Revival style.

Inside the house you'll find rooms decorated in various ways including a beautiful Adamesque side room. The most spectacular is the two-floor music room (it once housed an organ) which now has graceful balconies rimming the oculus - an oval ceiling opening. 18th and 19th century furniture along with Chinese vases from various dynasties are found in the first floor rooms.

What made Kykuit unique is the incorporation of modern paintings and sculptures into classic and Victorian surroundings. Both Nelson Rockefeller and his mother, Abby Aldrich Rockefeller, were strong collectors of modern art. So you will see a modern work or folk art mixed in with traditional furnishings. However, most of the modern paintings, rugs and lithographs are found downstairs in a separate, air-conditioned art gallery. Kandinsky, Picasso, Motherwell and a number of "Op Art" pieces from the 1960s are on display.

Once outside, you really get a feel for the opulence of the place. The magnificent gardens, originally landscaped by William Bosworth in the Italian Villa style, are built in a series of terraces that drop down the hill. The view of the rolling hills, the Hudson River and the Palisades beyond is spectacular. The terraces include a stone teahouse, a rose garden and a nine-hole golf course. And that's not all. There are also all those modern sculptures placed around the greenery. Some blend in beautifully. Others may take you back a bit.

Last stop on the tour is the coach and carriage house where the men can admire the 1916 Crane Simplex or the 1939 Cadillac convertible along with a number of pony carts, halters and horse stalls.

The Visitors Center at Philipsburg Manor is where you begin the tour, run by *Historic Hudson Valley*. You are asked to sign in, get a "badge" and watch an introductory film. Tours are limited to 18 people at a time. The tour takes about 2 hours and much of that is walking. A separate tour, which concentrates only on the outside gardens and sculpture, is available on a limited basis.

Not far from Kykuit is **The Union Church of Pocantico Hills,** a community church where the Rockefeller family worshipped. The small stone structure is famous for its stained glass windows created by two modern masters. Henri Matisse designed the rose window above the altar, while the side windows and the huge Narthex panes were painted by Marc Chagall in strong colors and swirling images. Tours are conducted by *Historic Hudson Valley* also and cost $3.00 (use telephone number below). The church is located on Route 448, east of Route 9 in North Tarrytown.

HOURS:	Apr.-Nov.
ADMISSION:	Adults: $20.00; Seniors: $19.00; Students: $18.00
LOCATION:	See Philipsburg Manor listing
TELEPHONE:	914-631-8200. Day Cruises: 800-53-FERRY / www.hudsonvalley.org

HYDE PARK

For people who lived under Franklin Delano Roosevelt's administration, there is either a deep love for the man who dominated the White House from 1932 to 1945 - or an abiding hatred. As president during the great Depression and World War II, Roosevelt was both blamed and praised for cataclysmic changes in American life. And Roosevelt's charming boyhood home has always been identified with the man.

Now a National Historic Site, the Hyde Park complex consists of the family home, the beautiful grounds on a high, green hill overlooking a clean Hudson River and the **Roosevelt Library and Museum.** You enter from a parking lot, which is lined with apple trees still bearing fruit. The white, classically proportioned country house called "Rosewood" is not overly large and can accommodate only a limited number of people at a time. Currently, access is by guided tour only.

Upon entering the main hall, you see the heavy furnishings that characterized a country home of the 1890's. Further on, the pretty Dresden Room is brightened by the colorful floral drapes and upholstery picked out by Sara Roosevelt in 1939 shortly before the King and Queen of England visited. The whole house, in fact shows much more the influence of Franklin's mother, Sara, than of his wife.

The upstairs, section which contains FDR's boyhood bedroom and other family rooms is under re-construction until the summer of 2000. Some of the rooms are only partially furnished.

Next to the house is the FDR Library. The museum section contains gifts from foreign rulers, cartoons, photographs, and a passing picture of both the Depression and World War II. Special exhibits on both Franklin and Eleanor are here, plus the wooden wheelchair Roosevelt used. You can peruse this building at your leisure, since it is self-guided.

Outside on the quite green lawn next to the rose garden are the graves of both FDR and Eleanor. And, in another section of the estate, **Val-Kill,** The Eleanor Roosevelt Historic Site, is open to viewers from a separate road.

HOURS: Daily: 9-5.
ADMISSION: Adults: $10.00; Under 16 free.
LOCATION: Hyde Park, N.Y. Take Garden State Parkway to NY Thruway to Exit 18. Cross Mid-Hudson Bridge, then Route 9N for 7 miles. Follow signs.
TELEPHONE: 914-229-9115. 800-967-2283 (advanced regis.) / www.nps.gov

VANDERBILT MANSION

If the Roosevelt home radiates quiet wealth, the Vanderbilt Mansion exudes conspicuous consumption. A marble palace in the style of the Italian Renaissance, it is set on large estate grounds where swans paddle about in a meandering stream. Inside, the mansion's furnishings are closer to French Rococo than Italian Renaissance. The huge marble reception hall opens to both the dining room and drawing room. The dining room, which seated thirty, and the beautifully furnished drawing room were the scene of gala balls. A small side room called the Gold Room was the gathering place for guests to sip sherry before dinner. This room attracts tourists to its ceiling painting, which depicts scantily clad maidens floating in an azure sky.

If the downstairs chairs all look like thrones, then the upstairs bed-rooms of Mr. and Mrs. Vanderbilt were certainly fit for a king and queen. Walls of embroidered silk and a bed with a marble gate around it are fea-tures copied from a French queen's bedroom to outfit the one Mrs. Vanderbilt used. As for Mr. Vanderbilt - he merely had a canopy with a crown above his bed and true Flemish tapestries hanging on the walls. It all goes to show what you could do if you had money in the pre-income tax days.

The mansion with its marble floors and the formal gardens of the heavily treed grounds all help to recreate the splendor of a bygone era. Tours begin at the Visitors Center where you can buy tickets and pick up brochures and postcards. A film about the estate is shown here. It's a short walk over to the mansion, which is open only by guided tour at this point. You can walk around the grounds yourself for free, however. Advanced registration during the popular foliage season is recommended.

HOURS: Wed.-Sun. 9-5 Closed major holidays.
ADMISSION: Adults: $8.00; Under 16 free.
LOCATION: Use Hyde Park directions.
TELEPHONE: 914-229-9115, 800-967-2283 (adv. Regis.)

EDISON NATIONAL HISTORIC SITE

Edison National Historic Site consists of the **Edison Laboratories** in downtown West Orange and **Glenmont**, the home of Thomas Edison situated two miles away in the private enclave of Lewellyn Park. Since you must buy the tickets for Glenmont at the Park headquarters at the laboratories, and those are closed until the spring of 2001, both sites are unavailable to the public at this time. Glenmont is a rambling, Queen Anne style house, where Edison resided with his second wife, Minna, after he moved north from Menlo Park. Here he entertained visitors from around the world — but it is also a warm family home where his children grew up. The house is filled with carved oak woodwork, oriental rugs, wild animal skins, stained glass windows, and features a sunny enclosed porch. It was closed several years ago for refurbishing, so it should be in the same shape when the Historic Site reopens again. New hours and prices will be announced.

TELEPHONE: 973-736-0550 / www.nps.gov

GROVER CLEVELAND BIRTHPLACE

Grover Cleveland, the only United States president to be born in New Jersey, spent his early childhood in this pleasant Manse. The clapboard house was built in 1832 for the pastor of the First Presbyterian Society. Two years later, Reverend Richard F. Cleveland obtained that position.

44

Grover was born in 1837, but soon after, the pastor retired and moved his family to Buffalo.

The house, which is a State Historic Site, therefore boasts a mélange of furniture. The open-hearth kitchen reflects the earlier 1830 period when life in the country was fairly simple. However, a number of later pieces from Cleveland's presidency reflect the richer, more ornate world of the 1880's. A large chair from the White House term plus several other pieces show both Cleveland's girth and his station in life.

A picture of Mrs. Cleveland, a beautiful young woman whom he married when she was 21 and he 49 adorns the house. Frances was Grover's ward, and she turned down his marriage proposal several times before she finally said yes. She was the youngest First Lady ever and their first baby, Ruth, became the namesake of a still popular candy bar.

After his second term (Adlai Stevenson was his Vice-President), Cleveland retired to Princeton where he served as lecturer and trustee. He became friends with Woodrow Wilson, then president of the university. They are both buried, incidentally, in Princeton Cemetery.

Recent refurbishing endeavors to return the house to its original look. Much of the memorabilia and photographs about Cleveland and his administration will be in a separate museum area. The Manse, by the way, is set on a busy street in Caldwell and is easy to miss since it's not really very large. Free.

HOURS: Wed.-Fri.: 9-12 & 1-5. Sat: 9-12 & 1-5; Sun.: 1-6. Call first
LOCATION: 207 Bloomfield Ave., Caldwell, Essex County.
TELEPHONE: 973-226-1810

THE BALLANTINE HOUSE

One of the pleasures of visiting the Newark Museum is the presence of the Ballantine House right next door. You enter this opulent late Victorian townhouse from an interior passageway in the museum proper. And while you cannot go completely into the rooms, you can see perfectly when you enter partially. It is a marvelous job of restoration with the colors brighter and the furniture cleaner than it probably ever was in its heyday.

The Ballantines were a Scottish family who rose from poor immigrants to wealthy beer barons within the span of two generations. But this three-story Renaissance Revival townhouse also typifies the manners and aspirations of the Victorian upper class in the 1880s.

45

In the high Victorian period, the term "interior decoration" was taken literally and every inch of space is covered, plastered, paneled, draped, or otherwise prettified. The dining room, for instance, features oak and cherry parquet floors, mahogany woodwork, a ceiling of molded papier-mache panels between painted plaster beams, and walls of leather-looking paper. Add to that a brick and wood fireplace, small stained glass windows, tapestried chairs and a table sparkling with white linen and you get a scene of solid bourgeois luxury that was meant to impress the guests.

Other rooms include the delicate French-style drawing room and the somber reception room. A magnificent stained glass window with its rising sun presides over the stairwell. On the second floor the bedrooms and exhibits of china and silver are on view. A film and interactive displays are also set up. The Ballantine House provides not only insights into Victorian living, but its legacy of manners and mores as well.

> HOURS: Wed.-Sun.: 12-5
> LOCATION: (Enter through Newark Museum) 49 Washington St, Newark.
> TELEPHONE: 973-596-6550

LAMBERT CASTLE

Situated high on a bluff in the Garrett Mountain Reservation overlooking Paterson, Lambert Castle is most impressive. Built by silk manufacturer Catholina Lambert in the heyday of 19th Century opulence, it appears as a medieval castle with rounded towers and crenellated turrets — just perfect for longbow archers to repel the invading hordes.

However, it was not the invading hordes that undid Lambert, but the silk strike of 1913 together with a decline in the American silk trade. Bankruptcy loomed and many of Lamberts prize possessions— European paintings and fine furnishings were sold to pay debtors. He retained the house, though, until his death in 1923.

The view from Lambert castle is spectacular, encompassing both the city of Paterson with its many church domes and spires and the mountains beyond. However, the castle has been closed during a long-term restoration, except for a few events. Plans are to open the refurbished building in the autumn of 2000. Call for information

> LOCATION: Valley Road, Garrett Mountain Reservation. Paterson, Passaic County.
> TELEPHONE: 973-881-2761

RINGWOOD MANOR

If they ever film a Chekov play in New Jersey, Ringwood Manor would make a perfect setting. This rambling manor house set on a rise overlooking a small lake where ducks paddle about is a prime example of the Victorian country house. Actually the house goes back to colonial days when it was the residence of Martin Ryerson, an ironmaster. One section of the house has been restored to reflect that period and relics of the old iron forge days still dot the landscape. Short cannons and iron chains are placed near the entrance.

But it is the expanded manor with a porte-cochere designed by Stanford White that gives Ringwood its high Victorian look. As the country home first of Peter Cooper, the industrialist and philanthropist who founded not only Cooper Union but also the short lived Greenback Party as well, and then of his son-in-law Abram S. Hewitt, Ringwood became a pleasant haven filled with antiques, and cottage furniture. Approximately 17 rooms are open to the public (the house contains many more) and bedrooms with lace curtains, parlors filled with paintings, heavy oak stairways and bronze chandeliers create a pleasant ambience.

Outside on the grassy lawn and beyond, visitors picnic or meander around the wide grounds with its gardens and playgrounds. The manor is one corner of a huge state park high in the Ramapo Mountains. Each section of the park has its own tollgate and parking fee (during the summer season). Shepherd's Lake has a lovely swimming, canoeing and picnic area and therefore is by far the most popular area of the park, filling up early on weekends.

Another historic section of *Ringwood State Park* is **Skylands,** a 44-room mansion in the Tudor style, that looks like an English castle. Skylands is best known for its gardens (see chapter on Gardens). At the moment the mansion is being restored and refurbished.

> **HOURS:** Park - daily. MANOR HOUSE: Memorial Day - Labor Day-
> Wed. - Sun.: 10-4
> **ADMISSION:** Parking fees, $3/ in season
> **LOCATION:** Route 17 past N.Y. State line to Sloatsburg Road
> **TELEPHONE:** 973-962-7031 or 7047

LYNDHURST

Just a few minutes south of the Tappan Zee Bridge and run by the National Trust for Historic Preservation, this Gothic Revival "castle" was the summer home of Jay Gould. The crystal greenhouses were once the foremost indoor gardens in America although they are now empty. The house, with its turreted towers and manicured lawn, is often used in commercials and advertisements as an example of the good life.

Visitors are taken through the home by tour guides and are shown, among other things: an ornate dining room with enough carved woodwork to fill a Gothic church, the butler's pantry, and the huge drawing room with its many landscape paintings, its stained glass windows and view of the Hudson. Much of the interior is wood or plaster painted to look like stone to enhance the medieval effect. This is not unusual in homes built in the Gothic Revival style.

The renovated carriage house now offers a lunchroom where you can buy light salads and sandwiches. The gift shop and a museum gallery are housed in a former garage. This affords a chance to walk around the gorgeous grounds. On summer weekends there are often concerts and fairs here. Specific times for guided tours vary—call first. Self-guided audio tour also available.

HOURS: Mid-Apr.-Oct.: Tues.-Sun. 10-5 Nov.-Apr.: Weekends 10-4.
ADMISSION: Adults: $10.00; Seniors: $9.00; Students: $4.00; under 12 free.
LOCATION: Route 9, Tarrytown, N.Y., 1/2mile south of Tappan Zee Bridge.
TELEPHONE: 914-631-4481 / www.lyndhurst.org

SUNNYSIDE

Home of Washington Irving, America's first internationally famous author. Built in a whimsical manner to suit Irving's individual taste, the reconstructed house is a mélange of the Dutch, the Spanish and the quaint. It is built on the banks of the Hudson with several acres of lovely grounds, including an ice house and swan ponds. At the Visitor's Center a charming film on the Legend of Sleepy Hollow is shown.

The house is shown by guided tour only and because the rooms and hallways are small, the tour takes time. You see the canopied bedchamber, the parlor and so forth. It is modestly furnished but hosted many a famous visitor. Picnicking is allowed on the grounds and there is a café for light bites on weekends. The Sleepy Hollow Church and graveyard are nearby.

HOURS: Apr.-Dec.: 10-4 daily except Tues. Weekends in March
ADMISSION: Adults: $8.00; Children: $4.00; Seniors: $7.00; Under 5 free.
LOCATION: Take Tappan Zee Bridge to Tarrytown, NY, then
Route 9 south to Sunnyside Lane.
TELEPHONE: 914-631-8200/www.hudsonvalley.org

BOSCOBEL

A stately Federal mansion set on the banks of the Hudson River (it was moved 15 miles from its original location), Boscobel was begun by Morris Dyckman in 1804. Dyckman, who made his money as an arms dealer, was able to afford the best furnishings. Although he died before it was finished, his wife moved in and furnished it most elegantly. The house is completely restored and refurbished (in fact it was refurbished twice!) and reflects an authenticity of period.

A large central hall, sweeping stairway, patterned wallpaper, Duncan Phyfe furniture, china, glass, silver and a bevy of whale oil lamps reflect an era of early and gracious wealth. The wide lawns, the elegant rose garden and the view of West Point across the river all add to the air of quiet gentility. Guides take you through the home, but you may peruse the outdoor vistas, including the rose garden, on your own. A small gift shop is located in a separate building. Scene of a Shakespeare festival in summer.

HOURS: Daily except Tues. Tours: 9:30-5. Closed Jan.-
Mar, Nov & Dec.: 9:30-4
ADMISSION: Adults: $8.00; Children 6-14: $5.00; Seniors: $7.00
LOCATION: Garrison, N.Y. on Route 9D, 8 miles north of Bear Mt Bridge.
TELEPHONE: 914-265-3638/www.boscobel.org

MACCULLOCH HALL

This 1908 Federal-style structure has furnishings that are quite handsome. These include oriental rugs, huge crystal chandeliers brought over from the millionaire Twombly estate (now Fairleigh Dickinson campus), and an original portrait of Washington by Rembrandt Peale. There is no attempt to furnish each room according to a specific period but you will see quality cupboards, china, and crystal of the 18th and 19th Century throughout the house.

Besides its eclectic collections, Macculloch Hall has a museum section for temporary exhibits. These may vary from teapots to quilts. A permanent gallery is dedicated to Thomas Nast, the famous cartoonist whose vitriolic cartoons helped to topple the corrupt Boss Tweed regime in New York. Nast was a Morristown resident whose drawings became classics. His depiction of Santa Claus has become the standard and he also created the donkey and the elephant as symbols of the political parties.

Although the house is open for limited hours, you may wander through the English garden behind it, daily. The mansion is specially decorated for Christmas and offers special exhibits other times of the year.

HOURS: Wed., Thurs. & Sun. 1-4
ADMISSION: Adults: $4.00; Seniors & Students: $3.00. Under 12 free
LOCATION: 45 Macculloch Ave., Morristown, Morris County
(2 blocks west of South Street)
TELEPHONE: 973-538-2404

DRUMTHWACKET

On any Wednesday you can visit Drumthwacket, the Governors Mansion in Princeton, and get a tour of the gracious Greek Revival building that has been refurbished to the hilt. The governor will not be in, of course. For two hours, this white-columned house belongs to the people who pay for its maintenance - namely New Jersey citizens.

The mansion, with its two-story high Ionic columns and wide veranda will remind many of the plantation houses of the deep south. Indeed, Charles Olden, who built it in 1835, had spent nine years in New Orleans and was impressed by southern architecture.

The entrance hallway includes several historic paintings. A docent explains the history of the building as you move from room to room. Moses Taylor Pyne bought the estate from Olden's widow in 1893. Pyne named the house Drumthwacket – which is Celtic for "Wooded hill." He added two wings. One of these includes a striking wood-paneled library. This room boasts a Gothic Revival stone fireplace mantel that would be worthy of a Dracula film.

The dining room is most impressive. The extra-long table is often set with sterling silver candelabra, an ornate punchbowl and gold-trimmed Lenox china with the green seal of New Jersey. Across the hall in the comfortably furnished living room a special exhibit of New Jersey porcelains from the studios of Cybis and Boehm are displayed. Outside, you can meander through the lovely formal terraced gardens behind the house. Free.

HOURS: Wed.: 12-2. Group tour by reservation.
LOCATION: 354 Stockton Street, Princeton, Mercer County.
TELEPHONE: 609-683-0057/www.drumthwacket.org

BAINBRIDGE HOUSE

This small brick building is wedged between stores and movie houses on the well-traversed Nassau Street and stands practically opposite the iron gates of Princeton University. The one-time home of Captain William Bainbridge, a hero of the War of 1812 and a commander of the U.S.S. Constitution, it serves now as headquarters for the Princeton Historical Society. Luckily, this particular historical society keeps its house open to the public much longer than most. A typical small home of the well-to-do family of the late 18th Century, it features period furnishings, and a history of Princeton, but is given over mostly to changing exhibits.

There is also a small souvenir and bookshop here. The Historical Society conducts tours of Princeton from here—they should be reserved beforehand. Anyone can join the Sunday walking tour at 2 p.m. Self-guided tour maps are also available.

HOURS: Tues.-Sun.: 12-4. Closed Jan., Feb. except weekends.
ADMISSION: Free (donations accepted)
LOCATION: 158 Nassau Street Princeton, Mercer County
TELEPHONE: 609-921-6748

WILLIAM TRENT HOUSE

The founder of Trenton, so to speak, because his house and property were known as "Trent's Town", William Trent built his stately home in 1719. It was later the residence of four governors. "A genteel brick dwelling house, three stories high, with a large, handsome staircase and entry", according to an early observer, it is one of the best restorations in New Jersey. In Georgian style with 18th Century English furniture and many early American pieces. Some of the William & Mary and Queen Anne furnishings here are equal to what you would find in Colonial Williamsburg, and the kitchen with its old-fashioned gadgets is really worth the tour. Guided tours by knowledgeable volunteers.

HOURS: Daily 12:30-4
ADMISSION: Adults: $2.50; Students & Seniors: $2.00; Children: $1.00
LOCATION: 15 Market Street, Trenton.
TELEPHONE: 609-989-3027

KUSER FARM MANSION

The country home of the Kusers was built in 1882 as both a vacation home and a working farm. The family had financial interests in hotels, beer, cars and more, but are best known for their connection with 20th Century Fox. The elder Kuser had helped William Fox start his motion picture company with a $200,000 loan. The connection continued for years with the Kusers showing movies at a specially constructed screen in their dining room well into the 1960s.

While the house here is not a place of super luxury (it was meant for casual summer entertaining and family get togethers) it is one of meticulous craftsmanship. Specially trained German craftsmen worked on the ornately carved mantelpieces throughout the house. Double floors, heavy woodwork, stained glass windows and a bedroom featuring a Delft tile fireplace are among the details to be noted. The 45-foot dining room features the heavily ornate table and chairs that were the hallmark of the Victorian age.

The Kuser Mansion and surrounding farm were sold to Hamilton Township in the late 1970s to be used as a public park. The outdoor area includes a gazebo and many picnic tables, and has a pleasant, quiet atmosphere. Last tour begins one half-hour before closing. Free. Christmas open house and other special events.

HOURS: (House) May-Nov., Thurs.-Sun.: 11-3.
LOCATION: 390 Newkirk Avenue, Hamilton Twp., Mercer County
(take Kuser Road exit from 1-295)
TELEPHONE: 609-890-3630

WALT WHITMAN HOUSE

A narrow row house in Camden contains the rooms where the poet who sang of America lived out the last eight years of his life. Accumulations of furniture (much of it the landlord's which Whitman took over along with the house), photographs and memorabilia are here. Whitman had had a paralytic stroke and much of what is in the house was given to him by friends during this invalid period. A bathtub kept in the bedroom is typical of the many gifts his friend collected for him. A settee there was for his visitors.

Actually, this is a rather "poor" house. It has only a few rooms on each floor. Whitman spent the money collected by friends on an elaborate mausoleum in a cemetery two miles away. The house has been returned to its original looks, with mustard-colored walls, wallpaper and fading furniture.

Space has been expanded by the purchase of the house next door. This is slated to be a museum area for the books, manuscripts and photographs that have piled up. (Whitman was the most photographed writer in America in his time). This area was not open at the time I visited. A guide will show you around the house. Call first. The house is across the street from a prison, but it's perfectly safe and close to the Camden waterfront area and the Benjamin Franklin Bridge. Free.

> **HOURS:** Wed.-Sat: 10-12 & 1-4; Sun.: 1-4.
> **LOCATION:** 330 Mickle Blvd., Camden.
> **TELEPHONE:** 856-964-5383; 856-726-1191

CRAFTSMAN FARMS

No it's not a farm. And there usually are no craftsmen. This is the home of Gustav Stickley, a well-known furniture designer of the early 20th century. He was also the foremost American spokesman for the Arts and Crafts movement. His large, wooden, somewhat chunky furniture is often referred as "Mission" style.

Stickley also published a journal called "The Craftsman" (hence the name of the Farm) which printed his house designs. Although he was not a trained architect, his plans appealed to those who disliked the overly ornate houses of the Victorian age. Since local builders used these plans, there are many Craftsman style houses in New Jersey. They are typically two story, with large overhanging eaves, a porch supported by round, wooden columns and windows that are grouped together. When styles changed, and his furniture and house plans were no longer popular, Stickley went into bankruptcy. Craftsman Farms was saved from developers a few years ago. Nowadays, Stickley furniture is back in vogue.

There are 26 acres left of the original 650 acre tract. The main house - a large log cabin with a stone chimney - was intended as a clubhouse for a boy's farm. This explains the huge kitchen and the fifty-foot-long living room and dining room. The home features rounded ceiling beams and hammered copper fireplace hoods and of course, Stickley furniture. Tours take about an hour and include a short walk around the sloping acreage. An interesting gift shop sells books on the Arts and Crafts Movement. Many special events plus brown-bag Wednesday lectures.

HOURS: April-mid-Nov.: Wed.-Fri.: 12-3; Sat.: 10-4; Sun.: 11-4
ADMISSION: Adults: $5.00; Seniors & students: $4.00; Children: $3.00. Under 6 free.
LOCATION: Route 287 to Route 10 West to Powder Mill Estates, Parsipanny, Morris County. Follow signs.
TELEPHONE: 973-540-1165

PENNSBURY MANOR

Here is a complete recreation, on the original site, of the beautiful Manor House built by William Penn on the banks of the Delaware. Located 25 miles above Philadelphia in what was then a wilderness, the estate includes many outbuildings such as a bake and brew house, a smoke house, icehouse and stable. Although everything was built from scratch in the 1930s, great care was taken to follow the letters and journals of Penn regarding this self-sufficient estate.

There are two striking things about Pennsbury Manor. One is the earliness of the period. The house was built in the late 17th Century (Penn lived there only from 1699 to 1701), so the furnishings reflect the heavy Jacobean hand. The other is the surprising elegance of this Quaker household. Although nothing is lavish, the furnishings are richer than one would expect of a Quaker leader.

As the guide points out, although William Penn was a great believer in the equality of men, he was still the Proprietor, entitled to receive an annual fee from each settler for each parcel of land sold. He had, after all, received the Charter of Pennsylvania from King Charles II. He also came from a wealthy background and apparently relished good furniture.

After a tour through the bedrooms, parlors and counting rooms of the Manor, a tour through the grounds is in order: first to the barge-landing, then the herb garden, the barnyard with its peacocks and hens, and the orchards. A brew/bake house where great vats of ale were mixed and huge ovens baked loaves is also on the estate. There are four tours a day.

HOURS: Apr.-Nov.: Tues.-Sat.: 9-5; Sun: 12-5. Call for winter hours.
ADMISSION: Adults: $5.00; Seniors: $4.50; Students: $3.00; Under 6, free.
LOCATION: 400 Pennsbury Manor Road, Morrisville, PA.
TELEPHONE: 215-946-0400 / www.pennsburymanor.org

ANDALUSIA

Nicholas Biddle was one of America's first millionaires, and the Biddle name still connotes a sense of grace, polish and "old money" in the Philadelphia area. Andalusia came to him through marriage. He transformed it in 1834 from a Regency mansion to its present form as one of the outstanding examples of Greek Revival architecture in the Northeast. Indeed, its facade of startling white pillars and "Greek temple" architrave will remind you of many antebellum Southern mansions built in the same style.

The house faces the Delaware River and its large sloping green lawn runs down to the edge of the water. On this lawn you will find both a billiard room and a Gothic "ruin". The "ruin", a crumbling tower, was built that way. This was not uncommon in the 1830s, when the romantic novels of Sir Walter Scott, plus tales of excavations in the mid-East, had Americans crazy over anything Medieval, Greek, Turkish or Egyptian.

Inside the mansion, furniture varies from splendid, polished Regency buffets to odd shaped Greek-style chairs. The music room, with its delicate pianoforte and whale oil lamps brings visions of genteel ladies offering an evening musicale to an assemblage of local gentry.

Outside again, there are extensive grounds, which include a hedge walk, a grape arbor and another huge house, which is not open to visitors. Tours of Andalusia are for groups only, but one can go through with a minimum of seven people for a set price. For groups of twenty or more there is a package called "Mansions Along the Delaware". Call Pennsbury Manor for this.

HOURS: By reserved tour only.
LOCATION: Bensalem Twp., Bucks County, PAL
TELEPHONE: 215-245-5479

PEARL S. BUCK HOME

Bucks County, Pennsylvania, was a haven for writers in the 1930s. Most of the literary celebrities of that time moved on to other pastures. But Pearl S. Buck, who reached the zenith of her fame during the pre-World War II period, (she won the Nobel Prize in 1938) remained here in her lovely country home until her death in 1963.

The stone and wood house seems to typify the Hollywood picture of a writer's country retreat: a huge floor-to-ceiling brick fireplace, great expanses of polished wood flooring, overstuffed sofas and walls lined with books. Add to this a collection of Oriental lamps and tables, screens and sculptures, and you get a picture of Pearl S. Buck, author and admirer of Chinese culture. At one point there were also nine adopted Amerasian children in the house, which explains the generous dimensions and open spaces of the home.

Visits to the home are by guided tour only. The tour includes a look at the room where her awards and prizes are displayed and the study where Ms. Buck wrote her works (sitting in a most uncomfortable looking straight-backed Chinese chair). Outside there is a lovely old-fashioned patio, lots of green rolling hills, and a separate shop where you may purchase Oriental pieces and other souvenirs. The Pearl S. Buck Foundation, dedicated to helping Amerasian children abandoned by their fathers, is located in the big red barn not far from the house. A film about the Foundation often precedes the tour. Chinese luncheon available for groups of 25 or more.

> **HOURS:** Tours are given Tues.-Sat.: 11:00, 1:00 & 2:00; Sun.: 1:00 & 2:00, Mar. 1 - Dec. 31. Closed Jan. & Feb.
> **ADMISSION:** Adults: $6.00; Seniors, students: $5.00; Under 6, free.
> **LOCATION:** Perkasie, PA Take 202S to 313W to town of Dublin, PA. Turn left at Maple Ave. (which becomes Dublin Road) then one mile.
> **TELEPHONE:** 215-249-1330 ext. 170

See Also: *Longwood* and *Duke Gardens* (The Garden Variety) and specific homes of the prominent in the chapter on "Walking Tours".

RESTORED AND RECONSTRUCTED COLONIAL, FEDERAL & VICTORIAN VILLAGES, FARMS, MILLS & HOMES

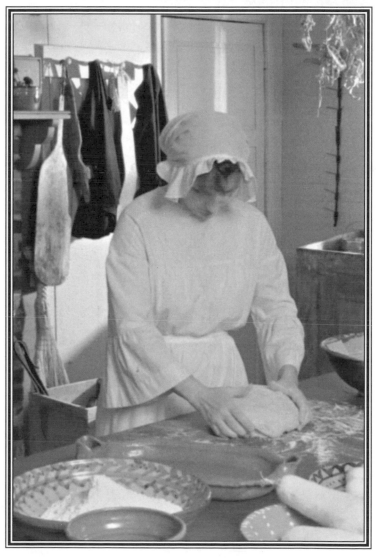

Courtesy: Historic Cold Spring Village

In This Chapter You Will Find:

Waterloo Village, NJ
Van Cortlandt Manor, NY
Philipsburg Manor, NY
Wheaton Village, NJ
Hunterdon Historical Museum, NJ
Batsto Village, NJ
Allaire Village, NJ
Historic Cold Spring Village, NJ
Tuckerton Seaport, NJ
East Jersey Olde Towne, NJ
Historic Speedwell, NJ
Millbrook Village, NJ
Historic Towne of Smithville, NJ
Longstreet Farm, NJ
Fosterfields, NJ
Howell Living History Farm, NJ
Israel Crane House, NJ
Miller-Cory House, NJ
The Hermitage, NJ
Other Restorations in New Jersey
The Hagley Museum, DE

WATERLOO VILLAGE

The largest restoration in New Jersey, Waterloo offers homes and mills scattered along the woodsy terrain next to the Musconetcong River. The village complex covers over 5000 acres and includes buildings ranging from a tiny 1740 duplex to a solid 1870 mansion. Since Waterloo prospered both during the Revolutionary War and the later era of the Morris Canal and Sussex Railroad, the houses reflect the Colonial, Federal and Victorian styles. Guides are dressed according to the period. A blacksmith and a potter are usually on hand at their workplaces.

The speeches the guides give to school and scout groups are often the most interesting aspect of a restored village. The hostess in the Canal House, for instance, demonstrated the wooden-knobbed weasel that used to draw the wool yarn into a skein. Every time the weasel made a full skein, it would go "pop", thus explaining the childhood song about thirty years too late for me.

A favorite for children is the gristmill where stones grind the corn, which the guide upstairs pours between the stones. Then you troop downstairs where the waterwheel is creating a loud whoosh. Here you discover the cornmeal pouring out the spout, while another guide explains the process.

There's a lot of walking to do here - several homes, the General Store, a sawmill and the Canal Museum. The 1859 Methodist church looks like it's straight out of Vermont. Wear good shoes—a long walk up the hill takes you to a complete Indian village, as it would have been in the 1600s. A long house, animal skins, and the accoutrements of tribal life are here, together with a guide who explains the customs.

Food is available at the Picnic Pavilion or you can bring your own to eat outdoors. The quaint stone tavern serves cheese, crackers and wine when it's open. During concerts other eating areas may be open. The big pop and rock concerts take place in a field a mile away from the village.

HOURS: Mid-April - Mid-Nov.: Wed.-Sun.: 10-6
ADMISSION: Adults: $9.00; Seniors: $8:00; Children: $7.00; Under 6: Free.
LOCATION: Byram Twp., Sussex County. Take 1-80 to Route 206N, Left at Waterloo Road.
TELEPHONE: 973-347-0900/www.waterloo.org

THE VAN CORTLANDT MANOR

Set on a rise overlooking both the Hudson and Croton Rivers, Van Cortlandt Manor is a prime example of the strong influence of the Dutch in the New York-New Jersey area. At one time in the late 1700s, the estate extended as far as Connecticut. The Manor House is now one of the better colonial restorations in the area, and is one of several sites run by *Historic Hudson Valley.*

Tours begin at the reception center where accurately costumed guides take groups of people through several buildings. Our group stopped first at the *Ferry House.* The ferry once plied the Croton River and travelers would stop here for food, drink, and lodging. The building is not large, but travelers would sleep three or four to a bed so they all managed.

At the other end of a long brick walk, lined with rows of tulips, is the *Manor House* itself. While not as elegant as the Southern Colonial mansions, it is impressive for this area — three stories high with a two-story porch wrapped around it. A heavy Dutch door opens to the main floor where the atmosphere is one of burnished wood and quiet elegance. Delft tiles line the fireplaces. Chippendale and Queen Anne furniture fill the rooms, and English china rests in the practical Dutch cupboards whose doors could be closed at night.

The ground floor kitchen is a magnet for groups. Here the guide shows the original Dutch oven (a heavy iron kettle with a closed lid), the beehive oven in the back of the fireplace and the gridiron for baking steaks.

Van Cortlandt Manor also includes a smokehouse, icehouse, tenant house and a blacksmith forge. The tours are geared for adults and school age children. There is a picnic area available.

> **HOURS:** Apr.-Oct.: 10-4 daily except Tues. Weekends only Nov.& Dec.
> **ADMISSION:** Adults: $8.00; Seniors: $7.00; Children: $4.00 Under 6 free
> **LOCATION:** Croton-on-the-Hudson, N.Y. Take Tappan Zee Bridge to
> Route 9N to Croton Pond Ave., one block east to
> South Riverside Ave., turn right and go 1/4mile to entrance.
> **TELEPHONE:** 914-631-8200/www.hudsonvalley.org

PHILIPSBURG MANOR

A large farm and gristmill, a wood-planked bridge that spans a tranquil stream, an old stone manor-house and a huge modern reception center filled with exhibits are all a part of this **Historic Hudson Valley** restoration. The estate is set up as it would have been from 1680 to 1750, with authentic furnishings and authentically garbed guides. You begin with a movie about the Philipse family who once managed 90,000 acres and shipped flour and meal down the Hudson. Unfortunately, they backed the losing side during the Revolutionary War and lost their holdings as a result

Guided tours of the manor, a demonstration of the gristmill, and a walk around the large property and through the barn are part of the outing. You can see sheep and lambs gamboling about as you traverse the property. The Visitors Center includes a large, well stocked gift shop and a glass enclosed cafe that offers light lunches (closed on Tuesdays). This is also the embarkation point, in season, for tours of the Rockefeller estate, Kykuit.

HOURS: Apr.-Dec.: daily, except Tues. 10-4. Weekends only in March
ADMISSION: Adults: $8.00; Seniors: $7.00; Students: $4.00; under 6 free.
LOCA17ION: Upper Mills, North Tarrytown, N.Y. Take Tappan Zee
Bridge, then Route 9N for 2 miles. Look for signs.
TELEPHONE: 914-631-8200/www.hudsonvalley.org

WHEATON VILLAGE

Set around a green, with buildings styled in 1888 gingerbread, Wheaton Village is a nice, clean spot in the middle of a small industrial town called Millville about 35 miles west of Atlantic City. The village is dedicated to the glass industry that still flourishes in this corner of New Jersey and its main attraction is the **Museum of American Glass.**

The museum is housed in an elegant Victorian building and includes glass items that go back to Jamestown. Collectors will probably enjoy the world's largest bottle, plus paperweights, medicine bottles, and exhibits of contemporary glass. You'll learn everything you ever wanted to know about bottles, Sandwich glass, and cut and pressed glass.

Another attraction is the glass factory where visitors can watch from a gallery above while gaffers plunge their rods into the blazing furnaces and then shape them into wine glasses, bottles and paperweights. At these "shows" an announcer with a mike explains just what the gaffer is doing. This is hot work and even from the gallery you can feel the intensity of the furnace. Nowadays, Wheaton Village allows visitors to make their own paperweights. For a fee, you and a qualified gaffer can make an individual creation. Call to reserve for this offer.

Other buildings include a craft arcade where you can see weavers, potters and printers going about their work. The craftsman's handiwork plus glasswork can be purchased in the stores on the village green. *The Down Jersey Folklife Center* exhibits the diverse ethnic crafts of the region such as Japanese origami, Puerto Rican music or Ukrainian embroidery

For kids there's a small play area on the green, an 1876 schoolhouse to peek at, and an 1897 Train Station with a miniature train ride (extra fee). The General Store sells penny candy from an old-fashioned glass jar, but for real food go to the restaurants outside the gates. Special event weekends feature everything from art glass demonstrations to fire engine musters.

> **HOURS:** Daily: 10-5. (Reduced schedule Jan.-Mar.)
> **ADMISSION:** Adults: $7.00; Students: $3.50; Seniors: $6.00. Under 5 free. Reduced winter rates.
> **LOCATION:** 1501 Glasstown Rd., Millville, Cumberland County. Exit 26 off Rte. 55.
> **TELEPHONE:** 609-825-6800/www.wheatonvillage.org

HUNTERDON HISTORICAL MUSEUM

An old red mill with a churning water-wheel sits by a 200-foot wide waterfall to create the picturesque environment for this museum village. In fact, the red mill is one of the most photographed structures in New Jersey. It is this mill that is the hub of the "village". The other buildings are smaller and scattered along the banks of the river. You can find a log cabin, a little red schoolhouse, a general store/post office, a blacksmith shop, a quarry with stonecrusher and an information center in the small complex.

As for the mill, the 18th century structure offers several floors of exhibits. The agricultural development of the region is followed with a series of displays of tools and country life. Everything from barrels to baskets is shown, with the whoosh of the water "buckets" from the wheel always within earshot. The gift shop has a pleasant country store ambience. The museum also runs a series of specials to attract the crowds. These include summer concerts, craft days and a harvest jubilee. (Special events may cost extra). Special Haunted House for Halloween weekend.

Across the river, the large stone building facing the mill houses the **Hunterdon Museum of Art,** which is certainly worth a visit. Exhibits of prints, painting, and sculpture are always on hand. Take a camera along for a shot of the picturesque dam.

From the art museum you can walk up the main street of the small country town of Clinton. Some nice boutiques and luncheon spots make for pleasant browsing.

HOURS: April-Oct 31: Tues.-Sat.: 10-4; Sun.: 1-5.
ADMISSION: Adults: $4.00; Seniors: $3.00; Children: $1.00; Under 6, free.
LOCATION: 56 Main Street, Clinton, Hunterdon County
(Exit 15 off Rte. 78).
TELEPHONE: 908-735-4101

BATSTO VILLAGE

What was once a self-contained community lies within the Wharton Tract (a huge State forest within The Pine Barrens). Tall trees, open lowlands, lakes with clusters of campgrounds are all part of this unusual region which reminded me of the North Carolina tidelands.

As for Batsto Village itself, it was once the center of the bog iron industry in New Jersey. Later, glass was manufactured here, then lumbering and cranberry farming were tried. As you approach, you find a handsome farm surrounded by split- rail fences with horses and ducks in view. The huge farmhouse has a late Victorian tower rising eight stories from its center, giving the place a "haunted mansion" look. The rooms inside are filled with the furniture of the well-to-do families that lived there, and the wall-to-wall library of James Wharton, the financier who once owned the place, is most impressive. The tour takes 45 minutes and is very comprehensive.

The first stop at Batsto is the Visitors Center. If you want the mansion tour, buy your tickets immediately for they admit only 15 people at a time. But there are other things to see at Batsto. A walk-through museum at the Visitors Center features old time tools and plenty of information about the region. A General Store, a Post Office, a barn with farm animals, a large lake where fishing is allowed, a sawmill, and refurbished workers houses can be perused on your own. During the summer, the houses usually have some craftsmen inside -a weaver or a potter may be at work. The sawmill is open on Sunday afternoons.

The farm with its unusual main house, surrounding barns and wide

63

swept fields all in the middle of the untouched Pine Barrens has the true look of the haunting past. A nature center, a full nature trail and a picnic area are also part of the grounds. Mansion visitor days vary. Call first.

HOURS: Mem. Day-Labor Day: 10-6; rest of the year: 11-5.
Closed major holidays.
ADMISSION: (to Mansion) Adults: $2.00; Children 6-11: $1.00.
LOCATION: Route 9 to 542 West or Garden State Parkway, to New Gretna Exit to 9S to 542.
TELEPHONE: 609-561-3262
PARKING: $3.00 weekends.

ALLAIRE VILLAGE

Set inside the greenery of Allaire State Park, this complex was once an active workers community during the 19th century. The huge brick furnace is one left over from the bog iron days when James P. Allaire bought the ironworks in 1822 and sought to establish a sort of ideal, self-contained community. Since this was the age of Utopian communities, such a worker's paradise did not seem unusual. In fact, as long as the ironworks transformed local bog into pig iron, everything prospered. But after twenty-five years, competition from the high-grade iron ore brought economic ruin to the region. A well documented display on the ironworks can be found in the clean, air-conditioned Visitors Center.

Historic Allaire Village, as it is now called, is operated by a separate non-profit organization. They do not get their money from New Jersey State, which runs the park. During the warm weather weekends (including Fridays) you will find docents, dressed in 1830s costumes, standing in the various buildings. They will talk about village life, and perhaps there will be a blacksmith or pattern maker about. You can view the church, which has a unique feature — its steeple was erected on the wrong end! There's a lot of hilly walking here, with a pond, a bakery, and a gift shop plus several other houses. The well-stocked gift shop is open from Wednesday to Sunday.

If you visit during the week, the Visitors Center may not be open and the docents may not be around, but you can walk around the grounds and take pictures. Groups, of course, can reserve tours. On summer and fall weekends there are always lots of activities including craft and antique fairs. There are lantern tours of the village in November and December (extra fee for these).

While visiting Allaire Park, be sure to ride on **The Pine Creek**

Railroad, a narrow-gauge rail line that runs a short trip for visitors on both diesel and steam locomotives. For information on this call 732-938-5524. The State Park also offers nature trails, bicycle trails and picnic areas. At the parking lot there is a concession that offers hot dogs and ice cream when it is open.

HOURS: Park: 8-8. Village: May-Oct.: 10-4
ADMISSION: Weekends: $3.00, (Parking). Mem. Day - Labor Day.
LOCATION: Allaire State Park, Monmouth County. Take Exit 98, Garden State Parkway, go 2 miles west.
TELEPHONE: 732-938-2371 (Park) 732-938-2253 (Village)

HISTORIC COLD SPRING VILLAGE

A delightful little restored village has sprung up among the pine trees on a quiet stretch of road not far from the hubbub of the Wildwood motels. Historic Cold Spring Village has much charm. It's not so large as to be exhausting, nor so small that it might disappoint.

The buildings are set around a village green that has a mid-19th century look to it. Most of them have been moved here from elsewhere. They range from an ancient colonial to the large Grange Hall, which dates back to 1897. Inside the various structures, you'll find a printer at his shop or an 1820s school complete with resident schoolmistress, or a tinsmith punching holes in tin. These are docents and craftspeople who explain what they are doing while they work.

There are bits of country nostalgia here such as old-fashioned water pump (the water is undoubtedly from the cold spring), a farm enclosure with animals, and walkways made out of crushed clamshells. A horse-drawn carriage, on hand the day I visited, was a big hit with the children. In the large Visitors Center, a Marine Museum offers displays on the whaling industry and other facts. For those who get hungry, the village offers an ice cream store and bakery. Full meals are available at the Grange Hall where superior American fare is featured. Weekends there are often special events such as singers at the gazebo on the green, contests and so forth. A special excursion train run at the adjacent Cold Spring Station to and from Cape May is available in summer.

HOURS: Father's Day - Labor Day: Daily 10-4. Weekends: June, Sept.
ADMISSION: Adults: $5.00; Children: $3.00; Seniors: $4.00. Under 5 free.
LOCATION: 720 Route 9, Cold Spring, Cape May County. Take G.S.P. Exit 4A to Route 9S.
TELEPHONE: 609-898-2300 / www.hcsv.org

TUCKERTON SEAPORT

Do you know what a sneakbox is? If you don't, you can find out all about clammers, and the fishermen who lived and worked in the shallows of the bays and tidal creeks along the Jersey shore at this new seaport village. Hunting for waterfowl, dredging for oysters, building boats and carving decoys was a way of life that has just about disappeared. The founders of Tuckerton Seaport hope to memorialize the baymen and create a tourist destination at the same time.

An outgrowth of the **Barnegat Bay Decoy and Baymen's Museum**, Tuckerton Seaport opened in May of 2000 with thirteen buildings. Many of the artifacts and decoys that were in the Baymen's Museum are now ensconced in Tucker's Island Lighthouse. This lighthouse is the cornerstone of the village and looks more like a colonial house with a light on top than the more familiar tall structures. The hunting shanty that used to house the Baymen's Museum is now the ticket and information center.

Other buildings include a houseboat, a decoy carving shop, the Perrine Boat Works, a sawmill, an instructional clam house and a few residential homes. There are docents to help out and plenty of pictures of the old days in the museum portion. Of course you can't have a seaport without offering seafood, so *Skeeters*, a replica of a summer cottage, will offer fried clams, fried oysters, French fries and even a hamburger or two.

The seaport is about 15 miles south of Long Beach Island and skirts the Pine Barrens. More structures will open in the future. In the meantime, special events such as a Classic Boat Festival in July and the well known Decoy and Gun Show in the autumn will attract visitors to the place.

HOURS: 10-5 daily
ADMISSION: Adults: $8.00; seniors: $6.00; children: $4.00; under 6 free
LOCATION: 120 Main St., (off Route 9) Tuckerton, Ocean County.
TELEPHONE: 609-296-8868 / www.tuckertonseaport.org

EAST JERSEY OLDE TOWNE

Set on twelve acres in Johnson Park, this is a collection of restored colonial houses set around a pretty village green. Most of them have been moved from other localities in central Jersey. For a long time this village was ignored, but now a large money grant has renewed the place. At least two residences are open to guided tours on particular days. One of the open buildings is the Smalleytown Schoolhouse, where students learned their lessons in the mid-1800s or faced wearing a dunce cap or, even worse, corporal punishment with a paddle. The FitzRandolph house was a typical farmhouse of the Raritan valley. The Vanderveer house represents a wealthier landowner.

The Church of the Three Mile Run is a typical Dutch structure with a pyramid roof and an interesting history. A tavern and a barracks are also on the green and may be opened to the public in the future. The whole village has pretty white picket fences and brick pathways. It is now administered by the Middlesex County Cultural and Heritage Commission and seems headed back to becoming a first-class restoration. Free

HOURS: Tues.-Fri & Sun.: 8:30-4:30. Tours: 11:30 & 1:30 weekdays; Sun.: 1:30
LOCATION: River Road (Route 18) at Hoes Lane, Piscataway.
TELEPHONE: 732-745-4489 or 732-745-3030.

HISTORIC SPEEDWELL

Every 19th Century technological breakthrough led to further inventions. And Historic Speedwell in Morristown is the scene of one of the most important American achievements. It was here that Samuel Morse and Alfred Vail spent years perfecting the electromagnetic telegraph. And that invention gave rise to the later inventions of radio and television.

One thing you learn from a visit to this green and pleasant village compound: you do not have to be a scientist to be an inventor. Samuel Morse was a portrait painter by profession. At the **Vail House** (the main building of the complex), you can see the portraits Morse painted of the senior Mr. and Mrs. Vail. Other rooms in the house show a modest early Victorian lifestyle.

The original Vail money came from their Iron Works. One of the buildings is devoted to an exhibit concerning the making and molding of iron machinery and to the ironworkers themselves. The foundry was best known for its early steam engines. In fact the first Transatlantic steamship was built here.

At the Factory building, originally built for cotton weaving, you will find an exhibit about the telegraph. Vail and Morse held the first public demonstration of this new wonder here in 1838. An exhibit of documents, models and instruments illustrates the invention and development of the telegraph.

Historic Speedwell is situated on the old homestead of the Vail family across from a picturesque dam where a Vail factory once stood. There are several historic buildings on the grounds and plenty of walking areas. Special Christmas events and summer history camp available.

HOURS: May-Oct. Thurs. & Sun.: 1-5
ADMISSION: Adults: $5.00; Seniors: $4.00; Children 5-16: $3.00
LOCATION: Route 202, at Cory Road, one mile north of Morristown
TELEPHONE: 973-540-0211 / www.speedwell.org

MILLBROOK VILLAGE

One of New Jersey's best-kept secrets is this authentic 19th century village set in the Kittatiny Mountains. It is run by the National Park Service as part of the Delaware Water Gap Recreation Area. On weekends, guides dressed in period costumes of the 1860-1880 era, lead tours. When guides are not available, you may walk around the village yourself, although the houses will not be open.

The original Millbrook Village was a small enclave of houses and stores clustered around a gristmill that opened in 1832. Since the mill served grain farmers in the surrounding countryside, the town became the social and commercial center of the community. A hotel with taproom, a smithy, a general store and a simple white-steepled church are among the buildings that surrounded the original mill by the brook.

Millbrook reached its zenith between 1870 and 1885. The village declined after 1900 and by mid-century it was a ghost town. What you see here now is a recreation of Millbrook at its height. A village green, lovely, well-kept homes and a church within walking distance are part of the scene. If only the Park Service could keep it humming Free.

HOURS: May - Mid October: 9-5.
Staffed - Fri., Sat. & Sun.
LOCATION: Sussex County. Take Route 80 west to the last exit in NJ. (Millbrook exit). Turn right, follow Old Mine Road 12 miles north.
TELEPHONE: 908-496-4458

HISTORIC SMITHVILLE

Set around Lake Meone, and only 12 miles from Atlantic City, this shopping "towne" started out as a colonial village combined with boutique shops adorned with brick walkways and planted flowers. Way back in the 1970s and early 1980s, there were costumed "colonials" spinning yarn in tiny restored houses on one side of the lake, and charming shoppes on the other. Now the two sides of the lake are called Historic Smithville and The Village Green and together they comprise 60 shops and restaurants.

No more colonial spinners. But this is still a pleasant spot and parking is free. The lake and walkways give an old-time ambience to the village. The bakery, ice cream shop, and some boutique stores are on hand. The Smithville Inn, a true 18th century building, has reopened and serves meals. In season there are miniature train rides, a carousel and paddleboats on the lake. They even had a Town Crier dressed up in colonial attire last time I visited.

LOCATION: Smithville on Route 9 & Moss Mill Road, Atlantic County.
TELEPHONE: 609-652-7777

LONGSTREET FARM

For those who want to recapture the sights and smells of an era not so long past, a visit to Longstreet Farm fills the bill. Although the farm is kept to the 1890 to 1900 era, the machinery here was used well into the 1920s and may being back memories to those born on a farm. Old-fashioned combines and tractors, an apple corer, and other antique contraptions are kept in a series of barns and sheds. Of course, animals are present although not in profusion. There are pigs lying in the mud, horses swatting flies, cows, chickens, and flies, flies, flies.

Open-slatted corncribs that allow the air to circulate are on view. The milking shed is fitted out in the old way - with slots for the cow's head and buckets for hand milking. The carriage house contains a variety of buckboards. Since Longstreet is a living historical farm, the workers dress in casual 1890s clothes as they go about their usual farm chores. (During summer they have a historical camp for children and let the kids help out). The main farmhouse has tours at specific times. It contains the furniture and artifacts of a late Victorian home.

The farm is just one portion of the beautiful **Holmdel Park,** which provides much lovely scenery. Across the street, a sheltered picnic area offers tables and a snack bar. In a hollow below the shelter, a pond allows ducks to swim by gracefully. And beyond the pond, a cultivated arboretum presents a colorful view of flowering crabapples, rhododendrons and hundreds of shade trees. The park also provides a nature trail that winds among the beech, oak and hickory trees. Wildflowers and blueberry bushes are other plusses at this abundant county park. Free.

HOURS: 10-4 daily. Weekends only in winter.
LOCATION: Longstreet Road, off Holmdel Road. Take Garden State Arts Center Exit off GSP, follow Keyport Road, look for signs.
TELEPHONE: 732-946-3758

FOSTERFIELDS

Another old-fashioned farm that dates from the turn of the century in American agriculture, Fosterfields is run by the Morris County Park Commission. The large farm has many farm implements on display and a variety of farm animals visible in various enclosures along the walkway. There are also barns and various outbuildings. The main house, **The Willows,** has been restored. It is a handsome Gothic Revival farmhouse with many original furnishings intact. Tours of the house show you what it was like for a young woman growing up in the early 20th century, as Caroline Foster did.

On weekends, from the spring to fall season, there are demonstrations of farm tasks such as ploughing, sowing seed or threshing. Perhaps the women at the farmhouse will be washing clothes and setting them out to dry. Or someone will milk a cow. Often, the audience is allowed to get involved.

The Visitors Center has farm displays and also offers a short film on the history of Fosterfields. Here is where you can pick up brochures, book tours of the Willows and get information on special activities - whether it's a Fourth of July picnic or a Saturday devoted to hay racking.

HOURS: Apr.-Oct.: Wed.-Sat: 10-5; Sun.: 12-5.
ADMISSION: Adults: $4.00; Children 6-16:$2.00; Seniors: $3.00.
LOCATION: Route 510 & Kahdena Rd., Morris Twp., Morris County.
TELEPHONE: 973-326-7645

HOWELL LIVING HISTORY FARM

Yet another active farm set in the turn of the century mode. What you find here is farm life that is pre-computerized. Various stages of mechanization are shown — the reaper reaps and binds mechanically, but it does not thresh. The wheat is bound by machine but the machine is pulled by a plodding draft horse, not a yellow Caterpillar. The wagon that picks up the bound sheaves is also available for hayrides. We were lucky enough to get a hitch in this wagon - great fun if you don't have back trouble or allergies.

There's plenty of acreage at the farm and you're part of the bucolic atmosphere from the moment you leave the parking lot and walk down the dirt road to the farmhouse. You pass sheep, pigs and geese - all safely behind fences. The farmhouse itself is a simple one. School groups are welcome here to weave burlap, make corn husk dolls, and help out in other ways. On Saturdays, a professional farmer is on hand to guide the draft horse in ploughing, sowing and reaping.

There are several Saturdays devoted to such things as a Spring Market and a Fall Festival. Special events, such as a maze in a cornfield, are held in season. Free.

HOURS: Tues.-Sat: 10-4; Sun.: 12-4. Closed Dec.-Jan.
LOCATION: Howell Twp., Mercer County. Take Rt. 29 to Belle Mtn. Ski Area turnoff (Valley Rd.) then 2 miles east
TELEPHONE: 609-737-3299

ISRAEL CRANE HOUSE

A handsome house built in the Federal period and then remodeled in the Greek Revival style, the Crane house was moved from its original site to the present location by the Montclair Historical Society. Costumed docents give guided tours throughout the three-story building with its furnishings in the Federal and Empire style.

Behind the main house is a two-story kitchen building reconstructed to resemble the 1840 kitchen that once existed. One unique feature of the Crane House is that the docents do allow you to sample the cooking. Just a tiny piece, but you can taste bread from the beehive oven, while the chicken simmers over the open hearth. Docents are quite good at explaining about the cooking utensils (such as the lazy-back which eased cooking chores for wives).

Beyond the kitchen building is a pleasant backyard planted with flowers and herbs in 18th Century fashion. And beyond that, the Country Store. Although the items in the store are just wooden models and not for sale, you do get the sense of an old-fashioned post-office/store as the social center for a town.

HOURS: Mid- Sept- mid-June: Sun.: 2-5
ADMISSION: Adults: $3.00; Children: $1.00
LOCATION: 110 Orange Rd. (Off Bloomfield Ave.) Montclair, Essex County.
TELEPHONE: 973-744-1796

MILLER-CORY HOUSE

Every Sunday during the school season, volunteers cook, spin or perform seasonal tasks in and around this 1740 farmhouse. The everyday, humdrum tasks of colonial life — from soap making to herb-drying are emphasized here. The house, the adjacent Visitor Center, and a separate kitchen comprise a small enclave of colonial life. In pleasant weather, wool spinners and other workers may be found outside and the separate kitchen is the scene of soup and bread making.

Guided tours of the house proper take about half-an-hour. The tour is most thorough and includes everything from how to tighten the rope springs on a bed to how to make utensils from a cow's horn. School children and adults will find the house tour highly educational while pre-schoolers may be content to simply mosey around the grounds. They can tour the herb garden, visit the small gift shop, or watch the outdoor volunteers at work.

HOURS: Sept-June: Sun.: 2-5; Jan.-Mar.: Sun.: 2-4.
ADMISSION: Adults: $2.00; Children: $.50.
LOCATION: 614 Mountain Ave., Westfield, Union County
TELEPHONE: 908-232-1776

THE HERMITAGE

Known primarily as an example of 19th century Gothic Revival architecture, the original Hermitage was a two-story brownstone erected in 1750. During the late 18th century it was owned by Lt. Colonel Prevost and his charming wife, Theodosia. At that time, it was host to James Monroe, Alexander Hamilton, General Lafayette, and Aaron Burr among others. When Colonel Prevost died, Burr wooed his widow. In 1782, Burr and Theodosia married in the parlor of the Hermitage.

Twenty-five years later Dr. Elijah Rosencrantz bought the house (which his family retained for 160 years). In 1847 the structure was remodeled into the picturesque Gothic Revival home it is today. Steep gabled roofs trimmed with carpenter's lace and diamond-paned windows give it the mid-Victorian look we often associate with Charles Dickens. In fact one of the several programs given at the house is a performance of "The Christmas Carol."

The Hermitage owns a large collection of antique clothing (448 women's gowns alone) that includes fans, handbags, and handmade lace. There is also original furniture, old maps, letters and photographs in the collection. The house was bequeathed to the State in 1970 and is administered by the Friends of the Hermitage. Special events include a costume exhibit from June to September and two Craft Boutiques that last four weeks each.

HOURS:	Summer: Wed. & Sun. 1-4.
	Otherwise: Wed. & 1st & 3rd. Sun. 1-4.
	Special hours & prices for craft show in fall and spring.
ADMISSION:	Adults: $3.00; Under 12, free.
LOCATION:	335 N. Franklin Tpke., Ho-Ho-Kus, Bergen County.
TELEPHONE:	201-445-8311

OTHER HISTORIC RESTORATIONS

The number of historic houses and sites in New Jersey is so large it would take an entire volume just to list them. Here are a few: (Please note that besides their regular hours, many of these offer special Christmas viewing hours or host special festivals.)

COOPER MILL: An 1826 mill where you can see corn ground into meal before your eyes. Guided tours upon request. Open Fri.-Tues.: 10-5, July & Aug. Weekends only in May, June, Sept & Oct. Located on Route 513, Chester, Morris County, one mile west of Rte. 206. *Telephone:* 908-879-5463.

BELCHER-OGDEN MANSION: A well-respected restoration on a historic street in Elizabeth. Tours by appointment only. *Location:* 1046 E. Jersey Ave., Elizabeth. *Telephone.* 908-351-2500.

GREENFIELD HALL: This well-furnished, handsome Georgian building features personal items belonging to Elizabeth Haddon, and includes a doll collection. Headquarters of the historical society in a charming town. Open Fri.-Sun.: 10-4. Call for library hours and guided tour. *Location:* 343 King Highway, Haddonfield, Camden County. *Telephone.* 856-429-7375.

KEARNY COTTAGE: Picturesque four-room cottage near Raritan Bay, was once the home of poet Elizabeth Lawrence Kearny, (half sister of James Lawrence, the War of 1812 hero). *Hours:* Tues. & Thurs. afternoons (but call first). *Location:* 63 Catalpa St, Perth Amboy. *Telephone:* 732-826-1826.

SHIPPEN MANOR: Part of the Oxford Furnace Historic District, this Georgian mansion is constructed of stone walls two feet thick and features three immense chimneys. Built by the well-known Philadelphia Shippen family in 1754, the house was a center for an iron manufacturing area. Original iron firebacks in chimneys, period furniture and cellar kitchen are featured. Tours are given by costumed docents on the 1st & 2nd Sun. of every month. *Location:* 8 Belvidere Ave., Oxford, Warren County. *Telephone:* 908-475-6204.

HISTORIC WALNFORD: The gristmill at this 250-year-old farm has been restored and is now open to visitors. Other buildings and sites are in various stages of restoration, including a house, a barn, and a millpond. Located in the beautiful 1046-acre Crosswicks Creek Park and managed by the Monmouth County Park system. Call for tour hours. Park open daily. *Location:* Upper Freehold Twp. Walnford Rd. off Rt. 539, Monmouth County. *Telephone:* 732-842-4000.

MARSHALL HOUSE: One-time home of James Marshall who discovered gold at Sutter's Mill, California, but never made any money from the find. Built in 1816. Prize possession is a friendship quilt. Headquarters of Lambertville Historical Society and start-off point for seasonal walking tours. *Location:* 60 Bridge Street, Lambertville, Hunterdon County. *Telephone.* 609-397-0770.

VAN-RIPER-HOPPER HOUSE: Dutch Colonial farmhouse with period furnishings, local history display, herb garden. Open Sat, Sun 1-4. Small admission fee. *Location:* 533 Berdan Ave., Wayne, Passaic County. *Telephone.* 973-694-7192.

SOMERS MANSION: Oldest house in Atlantic County has unusual roof shaped like upside-down ship's hull. Nice furniture and local memorabilia. A State Historic Site. Tours given by Historical Society next door. Call for hours. *Location:* Route 52 to Shore Rd., Somers Point. *Telephone.* 609-927-2212.

ACORN HALL: Mid-Victorian home in the Italianate style with many original furnishings in its two parlors. Children's toys and gadgets. Well-kept lawn with huge oak and Victorian garden with gazebo. *Hours:* Thurs. 11-3; Sun.: 1:30-4, spring through fall only. Small admission fee. *Location:* 68 Morris Ave., Morristown, Morris County. *Telephone.* 973-267-3465.

THE OLD MONROE SCHOOLHOUSE: Hand-hewn stone schoolhouse with wooden desks, hand slates and pot-bellied stove. Picnic facilities. Open 1st Sun. June-Oct., 1-4. Small admission fee. *Location:* Route 44 between Hamburg and Newton, Sussex County. *Telephone:* 973-827-9402.

TOWNSHIP OF LEBANON MUSEUM: A white 1823 schoolhouse with all its desks, textbooks and inkwells in place. Reserved school tours are booked and classes taught. Lots of special exhibits and events. *Hours:* Tues., Thurs.: 9:30-5; Sat: 1-5. Free. *Location:* Musconetcong River Road, New Hampton, Hunterdon County. *Telephone:* 908-537-6464.

BARCLAY FARMSTEAD: Federal period Quaker farmhouse with 19th century furniture. Several outbuildings (such as a blacksmith shop) and a kitchen garden. Costumed docents interpret life of the period. Free. *Hours:* Tues.-Fri.: 9-4. *Location:* Barclay Lane, Cherry Hill, Camden County. *Telephone.* 856-795-6225.

DR WILLLAM ROBINSON PLANTATION: Restored 1690 farmhouse with artifacts, maps and pictures in its museum section. Guided tours by costumed docents. *Hours:* April-Dec., first Sunday of month: 1-4. *Location:* 593 Madison Hill Road, Clark, Union County. *Telephone.* 732-381-3081.

HAGLEY MUSEUM

Another Dupont complex and a huge one at that. The acreage includes homes, offices, barns and the black powder apparatus of the original gunpowder mills that was the foundation of the DuPont fortune. The "museum" section offers exhibits that trace industrial development throughout the 19th Century. From there you take a small bus to visit the other sections, such as the original DuPont home. The bus goes through a steep wooded area along the banks of the Brandywine River, passing machine shops, roller mills and other stops of interest.

The original DuPont residence, called *"Eleutherian Mills"* is a handsome Georgian structure surrounded by gardens. Nearby is the office where the company began. It still contains the old desks and ledgers. There are guided tours at both these places, but you are free to roam around the gardens, the barn (which contains a Conestoga wagon and antique carriages) and the cooper's workshop.

Also on the premises, along the bus stops, are an early schoolhouse where children of the workers could learn their ABCs and a worker's home that now houses a good coffee shop. A picnic area and several vending machines are on the grounds also, while the gift shop is near the Visitors Center.

HOURS:	Mid-March to Dec.: Daily 9:30-4:30. Jan.-Mar.: Reduced.
ADMISSION:	Adults: $9.75; Seniors, students: $7.50; Children 6-14: $3.50; Under 6, free. Family rate: $26.50
LOCATION:	Greenville, Delaware, off Route 141
TELEPHONE:	302-658-2400

See Also: Pennsbury Manor (Homes of the Rich and Famous), *JockeyHollow* (Where Washington Slept, Ate and Fought), *New Jersey Historical Museums* (Museums of All Kinds) and such tours as *Bordentown* and *Mt. Holly* in the "Walking Tours" chapter.

MUSEUMS OF ALL KINDS

Photo by Ricardo Barros / Courtesy: Grounds for Sculpture

In This Chapter You Will Find:

New Jersey - Art & Science Museums

Liberty Science Center, New Jersey State Museum, Newark Museum, Montclair Art Museum, Morris Museum, Zimmerli Museum, Grounds for Sculpture, Other Museums of Art and Science.

New Jersey – Children's Museums

NJ Children's Museum, Garden State Discovery Museum, Monmouth Museum, Other Children's Museums

New Jersey - Specialty Museums

Yogi Berra Museum, Vietnam Era Educational Center, Franklin Mineral Museum, The Golf House, NJ State Police Museum, NJ Aviation Hall of Fame, Edison Memorial Tower Museum, American Labor Museum, Other NJ Specialty Museums.

New Jersey - Historical Museums

Museum of Early Trades and Crafts, Ocean County Historical Museum, Hopewell Museum, Ocean City Historical Museum, Cape May County Historical Museum, New Jersey Historical Society, Monmouth County Historical Association, Camden County Historical Society, Paterson Museum.

New Jersey Planetariums

New York Museums

Metropolitan Museum of Art, American Museum of Natural History, The Cloisters, The Frick Collection, Museum of Modern Art, Forbes Galleries.

Pennsylvania Museums

Franklin Institute, Please Touch Museum, Philadelphia Museum of Art, Rosenbach Museum and Library, The Barnes Foundation, The Mercer Mile, Brandywine River Museum.

LIBERTY SCIENCE CENTER

Perhaps you've seen the gleaming white building with its campanile style tower and spherical hump as you pass Exit 14B on the Turnpike. That's the science and technology museum in the forefront of the interactive, get-the-kids-to-like science centers. Set in the middle of Liberty State Park, the modern building is surrounded by grasslands and offers a view of New York Harbor from its outside deck.

As you enter the building, the first thing that strikes your eye is the aluminum Hoberman Sphere which expands and contracts as it hangs in the 90-foot atrium in the center of the building. This fascinating ball lets you know you have come to a place where technology is king.

Exhibits are housed on the three levels that circle the atrium. There are distinct areas: Environment, Health and Invention. This covers everything from fish tanks on the top floor to pink-toed tarantulas over at the bug zoo, to the playful doodads on the bottom floor. There are always interesting traveling exhibits (which often outshine the permanent ones).

Some of the permanent attractions are: a virtual reality basketball game where you play "hoops" against a video "pro"; a large touch tunnel where children navigate a pitch-black maze using only their tactile senses; and a mini-wall for rock climbing. Down on the Invention Floor there are plenty of goodies including a sound booth, where you can mix high-tech electronics to compose music, and the Discovery Room where guests can build their own structures assisted by staff members.

As for the IMAX Theater – it is housed in a geodesic dome (which helps give the Science Center its unique appearance) and features an eight-story-curved screen. Movies produced in the Imax format are twice as large as feature films and use a six-channel sound system. This gives an all-surrounding feel to the films (and vertigo to some). Nature films are popular here—best to reserve when you come in (or even ahead of time).

Although the 3-D shows are in a separate theater and are an extra expense, they are usually very good. There is a large gift shop on the middle floor and The Laser Lights Cafe offers sandwiches and salads and a very nice view.

HOURS: Tues.-Sun.: 9:30-5:30
ADMISSION: Adults: $9.50; Seniors, children 2-18: $7.50
Extra fee for IMAX & 3D show.
LOCATION: Exit 14B, NJ Turnpike, turn left, Follow Liberty State Park signs, take Burma Road to Center.
TELEPHONE: 201-200-1000 / www.lsc.org

NEW JERSEY STATE MUSEUM

It stands in Trenton, pristine and white against the backdrop of the Delaware River, the very model of a modern, well-kept museum. There is no admission charge. The adjacent Museum Theater offers a well-proportioned stage and comfortable seating. The Planetarium, housed in its own section, seats 150 people. The restrooms are well maintained and plentiful. The State Museum seems to have everything.

Set up as a family museum, with exhibits to interest both children and adults, the museum offers a balance between its art and science sections. On the upper floor galleries, paintings and decorative arts range from 17th century urns to 20th century cubist canvasses. The natural science section offers an excellent collection of stuffed animals posed within their natural habitats. Another large display is devoted to life around the seashore with relief dioramas depicting the chain of tidal life from worms to higher life. There are also exhibits on insects, minerals and the solar system. The first floor is devoted to changing exhibits of art and sculpture.

As for the **Planetarium,** (extra fee), public shows are given on weekends and also weekdays during summer. Check for appropriate children's ages. The seats are comfortable and the simulated sky has great depth once the stars get moving around. Laser concerts, scheduled on Friday and Saturday nights, are highly popular with teenagers. There is a gift shop outside the planetarium with science items. Another gift shop upstairs has a larger selection.

For people living within easy driving distance of the museum, this is a bargain not to be missed. For those farther away, it is a worthwhile stop when you are in the area. Parking may be a problem on weekdays, so try for a weekend. Free.

> **HOURS:** Tues.-Sat. 9-4:45; Sun. 12-5.
> **LOCATION:** 205 West State Street, Trenton. Use Route 29 along Delaware River or Route 1 into State Street.
> **TELEPHONE:** 609-292-6464

NEWARK MUSEUM

A few years ago, the Newark Museum was expanded. Now it is not only twice its previous size, it has also been completely redesigned so that it is open, airy, convenient - a first class museum that is worth every penny that was put into it. There is room to show off the collection - American paintings, Tibetan statues, African masks, - plus plenty of space for the special exhibits that come and go. The center court is open for light lunches and teas. The well-designed corridors make for easy walking.

The Asian Galleries on the third floor include not only the museum's fine Tibetan collection but Indian, Chinese and Korean treasures as well. Here, as in the other galleries, the exhibits are well mounted and the explanatory material easy to read. The second floor includes both 19th Century American art and lots of contemporary painting.

In another wing of the second floor there is the Junior Gallery and mini-zoo with its terrariums and aquariums. Nearby is the Native American Gallery with its large collection of costumes and artifacts. And of course there is a program hall for all the school classes that come to the museum.

It may be a little confusing at first, moving from one wing to another, but floor plan guides are available. The 50- seat **Dreyfuss Planetarium** is on the left hand side at the garden entrance. This facility offers sky shows to the general public on weekends and holidays (there's an extra fee for this). The museum also includes a pleasant garden complete with several modern sculptures. A tiny one-room schoolhouse that dates back to 1784 and a Fire Museum are also part of the garden scene. Attended parking is available in the adjacent parking lot (corner of Central & University Avenues). Have your parking ticket stamped at the Information Desk. *The Ballantine House* (q.v.) is next door. You enter through the museum. Free.

> **HOURS:** 12-5 Wed.-Sun., except major holidays.
> **LOCATION:** 49 Washington St., Newark (facing Washington Park).
> **TELEPHONE:** 973-596-6550. Planetarium: 973-596-6609

THE MONTCLAIR ART MUSEUM

A true art museum nestled in a town that was once an artists' center, the Montclair Museum reflects a high level of community support. Built in the early 20th century, this is a solid, stone neoclassical edifice dedicated to the showing of painting and sculpture. The major collection is of American paintings covering a period of three centuries. Many familiar names such as Edward Hopper, Mary Cassatt, and George Inness are represented here, along with many modern artists. The paintings in the permanent collection are used as part of the constantly changing exhibits, which are themed for a certain point of view. Special traveling exhibits are shown also and there are sculptures outside.

A permanent Native American collection is of interest to the kids. Costumes and artifacts include those of the Plains and Southwest Indians with good displays of Sioux and Navajo dress. This is quite an active museum what with classes and gallery talks. Currently undergoing renovation, it will soon double its size.

> **HOURS:** Tues.-Sat.: 11-5; Sun. 1-5.
> **ADMISSION:** Adults $5.00; seniors & students $4.00; under 12 free. Free Sat.: 11-2
> **LOCATION:** 3 South Mountain Ave. (at Bloomfield Ave.) Montclair, Essex County.
> **TELEPHONE:** 973-746-5555 / www.montclair-art.com

THE MORRIS MUSEUM

On rainy days, empty weekends or just any day, there's nothing like a quick trip to a local bastion of culture to uplift the spirit, educate, and get the kids out of the house all in one fell swoop. The Morris Museum of Arts and Sciences has long been one of these bastions (although changes in administration has meant changes in direction). Housed in a lovely old mansion surrounded by great trees, it is small enough not to be to exhausting to young children and still have some adult appeal.

One permanent fixture is the rock and mineral exhibit (which comes complete with a dark room for viewing fluorescent rocks.) The natural sciences are represented by glass-encased exhibits of stuffed animals. For adults there is always one art exhibit on display that is changed every few months: this might be a watercolor exhibit or a showing of favorite New Jersey artists. As for kids: there is often one large exhibit geared toward the younger set. In warm weather, the outside deck is used to extend this—(usually an interactive exhibit using such structures as a baseball diamond or whiffleball court.)

Upstairs, where classes often visit, one room is devoted to the North American Indian. Another room contains the mock-up of a 19th century one-room schoolhouse. A collection of unusually dressed dolls, a good-sized dollhouse, and a special "touch and feel" room for two-to-seven year olds are also on the second floor.

Downstairs there is still a small model railroad. And last, but not least, is the Gift Shop with an interesting range of gifts. The museum also includes a comfortable 300-seat theater which is the scene of many special events and shows.

HOURS: Mon.-Sat 10-5; Sun.: 1-5; Thurs. until 8.
ADMISSION: Adults: $5.00; Seniors & Children: $3.00. Thurs. 1-8: Free
LOCATION: 6 Normandy Heights Road off Columbia Tpke., Morristown, Morris County.
TELEPHONE: 973-538-0454 / www.morrismuseum.org

ZIMMERLI ART MUSEUM

Under construction for a new wing at press time, The Jane Voorhees Zimmerli Art Museum keeps growing all the time. Once a small collection, there are now over 50,000 works (paintings, lithographs, drawings, photographs) stored in this museum. The building stands on the Rutgers Campus in the middle of New Brunswick. Even before expansion, the place offered large open spaces for its shows. A spiral ramp takes you to the lower level where a maze of walls offer different views of the art world - prints, paintings, fabric hangings, murals and posters.

The permanent collection includes Japanese prints, American landscapes and Russian artwork. In fact, The George Riabov collection of Russian art shows a wide variety of formats, including folk prints, lithographs and stage designs. New Russian exhibits will include Soviet propaganda posters and other works from the 1930s and 40s. Collection of original illustrations for children's books of interest to kids. Special traveling exhibits, the museum shop and the small café will undoubtedly reappear when construction is finished. Call for new hours and admission prices.

LOCATION: 71 Hamilton St. (at George St.), New Brunswick
TELEPHONE: 732-932-7237

GROUNDS FOR SCULPTURE

For those who like to stroll on lush lawns and inspect large works of sculpture at leisure, there is now a venue in New Jersey! Located on the former fairgrounds of the New Jersey State Fair, the 22-acre site includes two large buildings dedicated to indoor exhibitions, and an expanse of well-tended greenery that serves as a backdrop for the large sculptures.

Although there are many abstract pieces, you will also find "lifelike" forms, by artists such as W. Seward Johnson, who specialize in plaster renditions of real people.

Walkways throughout the site are made of concrete and pebble, but there is no prohibition against walking on the grass. A large lake serves as backdrop for the grounds. One of the pleasant aspects of this place is the number of benches and Adirondack chairs where you can sit and contemplate the "scene" (a combination of green lawn, ornamental trees and heroic-sized sculptures). In fact, the grounds have so many plants and flowering bushes, it is as attractive to garden groups as it is to art lovers.

The Domestic Arts Building includes large spaces for rotating exhibits, a small cafe for light sandwiches, and a museum shop. The cafe offers both indoor space, and an outdoor courtyard where you can sit at a bistro-style table next to bamboo trees and a three-dimensional rendition of a French café scene. A formal Water Garden which features reflecting pools, concrete walkways, plantings, and outdoor "rooms" of sculpture is on the far side of the building. Please note: It's no longer free and prices and hours seem to change haphazardly. Call first!

HOURS: Tues. - Sun.: 10-9
ADMISSION: Varies by day.
LOCATION: 18 Fairgrounds Road, Hamilton Twp., Mercer County.
TELEPHONE: 609-586-0616 / www.groundsforsculpture.org

OTHER MUSEUMS OF ART AND SCIENCE

JERSEY CITY MUSEUM: Located on the top floor of the Jersey City main library, the museum is a combination of rotating exhibits of contemporary art (usually one-person shows) and a permanent gallery of 19th century paintings and furnishings. Free. *Hours*: Wed.: 10:30-8; Tues.-Sat.: 10:30-5. No Sat. in summer. *Location*: 472 Jersey Ave., Jersey City. *Telephone*: 201-547-4514.

RUTGERS GEOLOGY MUSEUM: A super-large room ringed by a balcony comprises this science museum located on the second floor of the Geology Hall on the Rutgers campus. A reconstructed mastodon, charts of geological periods, small fossils, mineral display, etc. Interesting lectures and demonstrations for school groups. The small gift shop offers minerals for sale at reasonable prices. Free. *Hours:* Mon.: 1-4; Tues.-Fri.:

9-12; Sun.: 12-4, Sept-June. Call for summer and holiday hours. *Location:* Hamilton St.& College Ave., New Brunswick. *Telephone:* 732-932-7243.

PRINCETON ART MUSEUM: Mentioned in the section on Princeton but worth another look here since it is one of the nicest art museums in New Jersey. Expanded and now beautifully laid out: modern, well-lit, and with a collection that encompasses European and Oriental art as well as American and contemporary. Highlights Tour at 2 p.m. on Sat. Free. *Hours:* Tues.-Sat: 10-5; Sun.: 1-5. *Location.* Princeton Campus, Nassau St. & Witherspoon, Princeton, Mercer County. *Telephone:* 609-258-3788.

NOYES MUSEUM: A striking beach-style museum set on the edge of a wildlife refuge which specializes in changing exhibits of contemporary painting, photography, and sculpture. A well-mounted collection of duck decoys is also on display. The building overlooks a lilypad lake and is quite pleasant *Hours:* Wed.-Sun., 11-4. Admission fee (free on Fridays). Under 12 free. *Location:* Rte. 9 south to Lily Lake Road, Oceanville, Atlantic County. *Telephone:* 609-652-8848.

MIDDLESEX COUNTY MUSEUM: Set in a handsomely restored 1741 Georgian mansion (known also as the Cornelius Low House) the museum offers changing exhibits of local history and special themes. A one-theme exhibit often takes up the entire house. Entrance is most easily attained through the Busch Campus of Rutgers University.The interpretive path from the back parking lot here offers a history of the local area. Free. *Hours.* Tues.-Fri. & Sun.:1-4. *Location:* 1225 River Road, Piscataway. *Telephone:* 732-745-4177.

TRENTON CITY MUSEUM: Housed in the Victorian Italianate building known as Ellarslie, the museum offers a combination of changing art exhibits and a permanent collection of local historical material. Also exhibits of Trenton's porcelain sculptors such as Boehm and Cybis. Ellarslie is set inside of Trenton's Cadwalader Park, which was designed by Frederick Law Olmstead. Free. *Hours.* Tues.-Sat.: 11-3; Sun.: 2-4. *Location:* Cadwalader Park, Parkside Ave., Trenton. *Telephone:* 609-989-3632.

HUNTERDON MUSEUM OF ART: Housed in a 1836 stone gristmill across a picturesque dam from the Hunterdon Historical Museum. Rustic wood interior is backdrop for changing exhibits by New Jersey and other artists. Paintings, sculpture, prints, art classes, gift shop. *Hours:* Tues.-Sat.: 11-5. Admission by donation. *Location:* 7 Lower Center St. , Clinton. *Telephone:* 908-735-8415.

NEW JERSEY CHILDREN'S MUSEUM

This museum is dedicated to the proposition that children learn through play and experience. Set in a reconditioned industrial building in Paramus with 15,000 square feet of space, the museum is 100 percent hands-on. Children from 3 to 8 can touch, climb, put on clothes, and play-act to their hearts content

The walls are brightly painted, the floor is carpeted, and it may remind you of a giant nursery school. But the exhibits are far more expansive than what you would find at your local preschool. There is a real helicopter, for instance. It has been simplified so that a child can climb inside and pretend to fly. There is a genuine backhoe with a hard-hat to match. And most popular of all -the fire engine that comes complete with fire hose and bell.

There are forty interactive exhibits. These include a fantasy castle, a prehistoric cave where kids can scribble their own "cave paintings" on a blackboard, and a garage where they can repair a jeep. The huge space is divided into sections devoted to dance, music, medicine and so forth. The "office" has real computers and the pizzeria has the kids busy for hours.

The museum is not meant as a drop-off spot. Parents must supervise their children, but they are welcome to join in the play. There are assistants around to help. No food allowed, but you can duck outdoors to a nearby fast food place.

> **HOURS:** Mon.-Fri.: 9-5; Weekends: 10-6.
> **ADMISSION:** $8.00. Under one, free.
> **LOCATION:** 599 Industrial Ave., Paramus. Call for directions.
> **TELEPHONE:** 201-262-5151

Valley Health Plaza

GARDEN STATE DISCOVERY MUSEUM

This interactive children's museum serves the southern part of the state. The two women who run it have filled the 15,000 square foot center with painted murals on the walls and a number of interesting and innovative exhibits. The theme is New Jersey, so included is a Jersey diner complete with chrome and red vinyl seats, and a kitchen where

A young hardhat at the backhoe in The New Jersey Children's Museum

kids can whip up plastic hamburgers. A "Down the shore" exhibit lets kids fish off a boat or send rubber ducks down a stream.

Other areas include a rock-climbing wall and the one-hundred -seat theater where the kids can put on costumes and act. A flowered Volkswagen "bug", and house construction complete with gravel pit and junk musical instruments are also on hand. One section is devoted to the science of sports. The museum directors have wisely included a snack area where you can eat your own sandwiches and augment them with vending machine items. There are also kiddie-size picnic tables outside and a gift shop inside. Geared for childen up to 10 year olds — and parents must accompany. Family membership available.

HOURS:	Tues.-Sun.: 9:30-5:30. Sat. until 8:30 p.m.
ADMISSION:	$6.95; Seniors: $5.95; Under 12 mos., free.
LOCATION:	16 N. Springdale Road, Cherry Hill, Camden County, Not far from NJ Tpke Exit 4. Call for directions.
TELEPHONE:	856-424-1233 / www.discoverymuseum.com

MONMOUTH MUSEUM

Although this is a three part museum with one section an art museum devoted to revolving displays, it is best known for its children's museums. *The Becker Junior Museum* is geared toward 7 to 12-year-olds. It mounts major exhibits on a particular theme (such as the western frontier) that run for two years. It is open to the public after 2:30 p.m.(earlier hours reserved for groups). The third section, *The Wonder Wing* is designed for the three- to-six set. It contains a treehouse, a waterfall and all sorts of touch and feel things but is on the small side.Limited hours here. If you plan to visit the museum, call first, since section hours vary or they may changing from one major exhibit to another. And be aware that although The Monmouth Museum is located inside a public college campus, it is a private institution.

HOURS:	Tues.-Sat: 10-4:30; Sun.: 1-5. (Adult section).
ADMISSION:	Adults: $4.00; children & seniors: $2.50
LOCATION:	Exit 109, Garden State Parkway, then west on Newman Springs Road (Route 520) to entrance of Brookdale Community College, Lincroft, Monmouth County.
TELEPHONE:	732-747-2266

OTHER CHILDREN'S MUSEUMS

They're popping up all over the place, and whether you call them Children's Museums, Discovery Museums, Discovery Centers or whatnot, they certainly appeal to double-income working parents who feel they have to do something important with their kids on the weekend. Also popular with grandparents and (probably) divorced fathers. Birthday parties and other group functions are usually available.

IMAGINE THAT!! A discovery center with 35 hands-on activities. Ballet room, computers, art, music, drama, shadow play, play pirate ship, real Piper plane. Food is available at the in-house cafe. There are two of these franchises in New Jersey. One is at 200 Route 10 in East Hanover, Morris County *(Telephone:* 973-952-0022) and the other is located at Route 35N and Harmony Road, Middletown, Monmouth County *(Telephone:* 908-706-9000). *Admisslon:* $7.99 for kids (under one free); $2.00 for adults. Open daily except for major holidays.

DISCOVERY HOUSE: Over 100 activities include a live-action TV news show, huge kaleidoscopes, large spin-art table, crafts, magic castle, a Volkswagen "Beetle" (non-moving of course) in 8,000 square ft. space. Allow two hours at least. Closed Mondays and major holidays. Located at 152 Tices Lane, East Brunswick, Middlesex County. *Admission:* $6.50 for kids and adults; under 18 mos.free. *Telephone:* 732-254-3770.

THE JERSEY EXPLORER CHILDREN'S MUSEUM: Inside the East Orange Library, this non-commercial museum is dedicated to bringing the Afro-American heritage alive for children. Open to groups only, by reservation: Tues.-Fri. Open to the public: Saturday. 10-3. Includes Time-traveler Theater, arts and crafts, interactive storytelling, and some exhibits. Located at 192 Dodd St, East Orange. *Admission:* $3.00 for adults and kids, under 2 free. *Telephone:* 973-673-6900.

Note: Be sure to check out the **PleaseTouch Museum,** the granddaddy of them all, under the *Philadelphia Museums* listing.

YOGI BERRA MUSEUM

He was a famous catcher for the New York Yankees and a famous coach for the New York Mets. And he's just as famous for his funny sayings that rank up there with those of Reverend Spooner and Samuel Goldwyn. So here's an interesting, well-done museum that adjoins the Yogi Berra Stadium right on the campus of Montclair State University. Did I mention that Berra lives in Montclair, which is a major reason that a New York baseball player is honored in New Jersey?

The museum and learning center not only has loads of memorabilia about Berra, but lots of general baseball lore as well. An exhibit on the evolution of the catcher's glove was on display when I visited. Also cases of trophies, rings, bats and newspaper clippings are on view in the well-lighted space. In the 125-seat auditorium you can watch a movie about the glory days of the Yankees. The front area allows for unobstructed viewing from wheelchairs.

The center is open late on days when a baseball game is on and you can visit the souvenir shop then also. From a special "group" area you can overlook the 3500-seat stadium where the Montclair State baseball team and the minor-league New Jersey Jackals both play. If you have a kid who memorizes baseball statistics or a relative who remembers the 1961 World Series—take them here.

> **HOURS:** Wed.-Sun.: 12-5 (til 7 p.m on. NJ Jackals game nights)
> **ADMISSION:** Adults: 4.00; Students & children: $2.00
> **LOCATION:** 8 Quarry Road, Little Falls (Montclair State campus)
> **TELEPHONE:** 973-655-2377 / www.yogiberramuseum.org

VIETNAM ERA EDUCATIONAL CENTER

The New Jersey Vietnam Veterans Memorial is set on a green hillock only a short way from the PNC Arts Center and features a circular black wall engraved with the names of the fallen. A short distance behind it stands *The Vietnam Era Educational Center* a beautifully constructed building that is easily accessible from the site.

The Education Center is a revelation: it is dedicated to the whole

Statue at The New Jersey Vietnam Veteran's Memorial in Holmdel. Behind the memorial, The Vietnam Era Educational Center is a cutting-edge museum.

Vietnam era—not just the war. It was designed by the same firm that created the Holocaust Museum in Washington, and refurbished Ellis Island. The museum is able to capture the tempo of the 1960s and early 1970s without taking sides in the great debate. It is an even-handed presentation of the events behind the war. The history of Vietnam, the history of Communism, the French colonization of Indo-China and the Japanese occupation in World War 2 are all covered.

A double timeline runs along the walls of the circular building. On top there is a diorama composed of montaged photos of the culture of the era. Scenes from 1950 television shows, pictures of Marilyn Monroe and JFK, Elvis and the Beatles, the 1970s disco era, presidential conventions and moonshots are featured. Below that are pictures and text on our growing involvement in their war. The French defeat at Dien Bien Phu, the Red scare in this country— anyone remember the Domino Theory?

For a personal touch, there are the hand-written letters to mothers, wives and sweethearts back home—many from soldiers who never returned. Interactive TV sets allow you to call up a scene from a specific year— the murder of a Vietnamese official, or a college anti-war rally. The tone of the TV narration changes over time—from brisk reports to "up close and personal" views of battle scenes and burning villages.

Outside, the **New Jersey Vietnam Veteran's Memorial**, is dedicated to the men and women who lost their lives during the conflict. A hillside amphitheater is surrounded by a wall of black granite panels with the names of over 1000 New Jersey residents carved inside. The parking lot has plenty of handicapped parking spaces and everything is accessible to wheelchairs.

HOURS: Tues.- Sat.: 10 – 4.
ADMISSION: Adults: $4.00: Seniors/students: $2.00. Under 10 & veterans: free.
LOCATION: Holmdel. Exit 116 on GSP to PNC Arts Center. Follow signs.
TELEPHONE: 732-335-0033 / www.njvvmf.org

FRANKLIN MINERAL MUSEUM

New Jersey is both the zinc mining and fluorescent rock capital of the world. While this may not be on the same level as a financial or entertainment capital, it does provide one mecca for rock-hounds -Franklin Borough in Sussex County. Here, you will find both the Franklin Mineral Museum and the Sterling Hill mine (check separate listing).

Children seem to have a fascination with rocks - as any mother can attest. At the Franklin Mineral Museum you can dig for rocks with pick and shovel at the adjacent Dump. The museum itself is divided into several sections: a fluorescent rock display, a general exhibit on zinc and other minerals, and a replica of an actual mine.

As part of the tour you are ushered into a long, narrow room where you face a row of gray, ordinary rocks behind a glass case. The guide flicks off the lights, and lo and behold- -the rocks turn into an extraordinary array of shining colors. Green, purple, blue luminous rocks with unusual patterns glow behind the glass. Next is a tour of the mine replica, which is a plaster labyrinth. You can also check out a roomful of dinosaur footprints and Indian artifacts. At the gift shop you'll find a good selection of rocks, gemstones and necklaces.

But for many, the highlight of the trip is the chance to go prospecting in the rock dump at the back of the museum, although chances of finding a true specimen are slim. Check with the museum about equipment and age requirements.

> **HOURS:** Mon.-Sat.: 10-4; Sun.: 12:30-4:30.
> **ADMISSION:** Adults: $4.00; Children: $2.00. Same rate applies for dump.
> **DIRECTIONS:** Route 80 to Route 15 Sparta, then Route 517 to Franklin then one mile north on 23. Museum is on Evans St
> **TELEPHONE:** 973-827-3481 / www.franklinmineralmuseum.com

THE GOLF HOUSE

Set among the posh country estates of Far Hills, the Golf House includes a stately house-museum, an administration building and an interesting research lab, and a gift shop. There are two floors of exhibit space, which include a history of the game itself, plus rooms devoted to golfing costumes, golf clubs, and the evolution of the golf ball.

A short movie about different golf celebrities is shown in a small theater. There is a special exhibit on women in golfing and another on rules of the game. Some of the well-prized mementos are the golf clubs of presidents Wilson, Franklin Roosevelt and Eisenhower. Also on view is the Moon Club used by Alan Shepard to play on the lunar surface.

The house contains a magnificent flying staircase, paintings and sculpture and a library of 8000 volumes. But also be sure to visit the

Photo by Barbara Hudgins

Women have their place in every museum nowadays. This display is at the Golf House.

Research and Testing Center, which is in a separate building behind the main house. Here there are plenty of whizbang interactive displays such as one on velocity tests. You can even watch a machine that tests golf balls (nicknamed "Iron Byron') on the greens outside the Center. Free.

> **HOURS:** Mon.-Fri. 9-5; Weekends: 10-4. Closed holidays.
> **LOCATION:** Route 512, east of Route 202, Far Hills, Somerset County
> **TELEPHONE:** 908-234-2300

NEW JERSEY STATE POLICE MUSEUM

For mystery buffs, the exhibits in this two-million dollar edifice offer information about the role of the State Police as well as insights into crime detection. In fact you'll feel like Sherlock Holmes just trying to locate the place — the museum is inside the grounds of the New Jersey State Police Headquarters.

The museum buildings include a refurbished log cabin that once was the dormitory for State Troopers. It now houses a 1930 Buick touring car, and other exhibits of early transportation. You learn that the State Police only began in 1921 and that Colonel H. Norman Schwarzkopf was the first Superintendent.

The main building is full of interactive exhibits and easy- to- read posters. The 911 exhibit for instance, lets the viewer decide whether to send an incoming call to the police, fire or medical emergency unit. Most interesting is the exhibit called "Scene of the Crime". Through a glass window you see a murder scene. A man is lying on the floor of a kitchen in a pool of blood. Flour is spilled on the counter. Is the dead man the owner of the premises, or is he an intruder? He was shot, but where is the murder weapon? An overhead video walks you through the preliminary investigation and the procedures for collecting and preserving evidence.

But the "piece de resistance" of the museum is its exhibit on the Lindbergh case. The kidnapping of the baby son of Charles and Anne Lindbergh took place in 1932 from an estate just outside of Hopewell. The State Police played a major role in the investigation and some of the evidence used to convict Bruno Hauptmann of the crime is on display. You can see the baby sleeping suit that was sent to the Lindbergh's, along with a ransom note. Reward posters, pictures and memorabilia of the "trial of the century" which took place in Flemington in 1935 are here. Free. (A State Trooper will check you in.)

HOURS: Mon. – Sat.: 10 - 4
LOCATION: Route 175 (River Road) West Trenton (near Exit 1 on Route 95).
TELEPHONE: 609-882-2000 Ext. 6400

NJ AVIATION HALL OF FAME

Located on one edge of Teterboro Airport, is a museum filled with aviation memorabilia with a focus on the Garden State. There are loads of model airplanes, a section devoted to women pilots, and photos of all sorts of early air machines. Hanging from the ceiling are models of satellites and astronaut uniforms. There is also a small helicopter you can try out, and a balloon basket that children can climb in. At the 60-seat theater you watch a film on the history of aviation in New Jersey. In the tower room you can listen in to pilot-control tower conversations.

Outside, you can climb aboard an old-fashioned propeller plane, and see how the folks in the Forties and Fifties used to ride. (At least the seats were wider then -and only two across!). And behind the building, a Bell helicopter and a M.A.S.H. unit along with jeeps and a truck re-create a Korean War scene. There is even a mess tent (you can eat lunch there).

For those who remember when a Sunday afternoon outing with the kids was a jaunt to the airport, and for Air Force veterans, this is a fun place to visit.

HOURS: Tues.-Sun.: 10-4 year round
ADMISSION: Adults: $5.00; Children and seniors: $3.00.
LOCATION: 400 Fred Wehran Dr., Teterboro Airport, off Route 46, Bergen County.
TELEPHONE: 201-288-6344 / www.njahof.org

EDISON MEMORIAL TOWER AND MUSEUM

The tower is shaped like an electric light with a bulb on top and commemorates the site of Edison's Menlo Park laboratory, birthplace of the incandescent bulb. The original laboratory was moved to Greenfield,

Michigan, by Henry Ford for his Americana Museum. At the moment the tower itself is not open to tourists. However, there is a small museum adjacent to it, which is filled with light bulbs, phonographs, and other mementos of Edison's achievements. Free.

HOURS: Wed.- Sat: 10-4: Sun.: 12:30-4:30.
LOCATION: Christie St, Menlo Park, (off Rte. 27) in Edison State Park, Middlesex County.
TELEPHONE: 732-549-3299

AMERICAN LABOR MUSEUM

Also known as **The Botto House**, this is a combination historic house/museum with an emphasis, for a change, on the working class. This family home of an Italian immigrant worker became a rallying place for striking union members during the 1913 Paterson Silk strike. Since Haledon had a Socialist mayor at the time, and Paterson itself had banned group assemblies, workers gathered here to hear John Reed and Big Bill Hayward during the bitter strike.

The Botto House is a sturdy, well-built wooden structure smack-dab in the center of a middle-income neighborhood in a suburb of Paterson. It has been restored to the era of 1903-1913 and kept to reflect the time when Italian immigrants lived here. There is even a bocce court in the yard.

The museum section of the Botto House offers a video and displays about the early American labor movement. These include photographs of the unsafe and unsanitary working conditions in turn-of-the century factories, and the 1913 silk strike. Temporary exhibits cover the whole spectrum of the history of labor unions and immigrant life in the United States.

HOURS: Wed.-Sat: 1-4.
ADMISSION: Adults: $1.50; Children under 12, free.
LOCATION: 83 Norwood St, Haledon, Passaic County. Call for directions.
TELEPHONE: 973-595-7953.

OTHER NEW JERSEY
SPECIALTY MUSEUMS

WHIPPANY RAILWAY MUSEUM: Set in an old boxcar of Erie Lackawanna vintage, the museum includes a model railroad set, lots of lanterns, badges, posters and other memorabilia. Open weekends in warm weather. On holidays such as Christmas and Easter there are special train excursions (by reservation). Small fee for museum.. *Location*: Depot yard, Route 10 and Whippany Road, Whippany, Morris County. *Telephone*: 973-887-8177.

AFRICAN ART MUSEUM: Run by the S.M.A. Fathers and set inside a church complex, this museum highlights West African art and artifacts. Masks, beadwork, sculpture, religious symbols from Ghana, Mali, etc. Tours for school groups. Free. *Location*: 23 Bliss Ave., Tenafly, Bergen County. Call for hours. *Telephone*: 201-894-8611.

VOLLENDAM WINDMILL AND MUSEUM: Inside this replica of an authentic 60-foot-high Dutch windmill is a small museum, which includes tools and millstones. Set way out in a rustic area of the state, the seven-story structure boasts sail arms that are 68 feet long. Interior is currently closed for restoration. *Location*: 231 Adamic Hill Road, near Milford, off Route 519, Hunterdon County. *Telephone*. 908-995-4365.

U.S. BICYCLING HALL OF FAME. 135 West Main St., Somerville (it recently moved from its digs across the street). The museum features the jerseys, photos and memorabilia of famous cyclists and mementos of the Velodrome in Newark. This was a BIG sport in the old days. Somerville still holds a well-known race every Memorial Day. Admission by donation. *Telephone*: 908-722-3620.

AFRO-AMERICAN HISTORICAL AND CULTURAL MUSEUM: Concentrates on Afro-American experience in America. Exhibits on the Civil Rights movement, athletes, black dolls, quilts, typical kitchen, African artifacts. Over 4000 square feet on 2nd floor of Greenville library. Free. *Location:* 1841 Kennedy Blvd., Jersey City. *Hours*: Mon.-Sat: 10-5. Closed Sat in summer. *Telephone.* 201-547-5262.

BARNEGAT BAY DECOY AND BAYMAN'S MUSEUM: Now part of the Tuckerton Seaport (q.v.).

TOMS RIVER SEAPORT MUSEUM: Devoted to boat restoration and maritime memorabilia, especially in Ocean County. Several boat sheds, specialized library. *Hours*: Tues., Thurs., Sat.: 10-2. *Location:* Water St & Hooper Ave, Toms River. *Telephone.* 732-349-9209.

HIRAM BLAUVELT WILDLIFE MUSEUM: First art museum to concentrate on wildlife and sporting art exclusively. Also includes prehistoric and extinct specimens of birds and animals. Housed in mansion. Free. *Location:* 705 Kinderkamack Road, Oradell, Essex County. *Hours:* Wed.-Fri.: 10-4; Sat. & Sun.: 2-5. *Telephone.* 201-261-0012.

HUNGARIAN HERITAGE CENTER: Used as a meeting place for programs and activities for Hungarian-Americans, the center includes 10,000 feet of exhibition space. Folk art, and immigrant life plus special exhibitions by Hungarian artists are featured here. *Hours:* Tues.-Sat: 11-4, Sun.: 1-4. *Location.* 300 Somerset St, New Brunswick. *Telephone.* 732-846-5777.

NEW JERSEY MUSEUM OF AGRICULTURE: Early farming equipment, 17th century trading post, tractors, buggies, kitchen work, plus displays of land-clearing, etc. This is a large museum with everything from egg laying to cow milking carefully depicted. *Hours:* Tues.-Sat: 10-5; Sun.: 12-5.Small admission fee. *Location*: Off Route 1 and College Farm Road, Cook College, New Brunswick. *Telephone:* 732-249-2077.

HERITAGE GLASS MUSEUM: Dedicated to local glassblowing industry with, blowing tools, and displays of bottles, vases, and other glassware. Also lots of local memorabilia. *Location*: High & Center Streets, Glassboro. Call for hours. *Telephone*: 856-881-7468.

New Jersey Historical Museums

MUSEUM OF EARLY TRADES AND CRAFTS

Housed in a handsome Richardson Revival building that once was the Madison Public Library, this museum serves two purposes. The refurbished building is now shown in its circa 1900 glory, with brilliant stained glass windows, bronze chandeliers, and wrought iron balcony. It's an architect's delight. Meanwhile, downstairs, a collection of tools for the 34 trades that existed in New Jersey in 1776 are on revolving display.

Major exhibits in the museum concern particular trades such as coopering (barrel-making), printing and so forth from the colonial period forward. The development of local businesses from their early origins is traced. For instance, the town funeral home is still owned by a family whose patriarch was a carpenter. He made coffins as a sideline, but when funeral parlors came into vogue, he expanded his business. Docents are on hand and there is a children's "activity" room downstairs.

HOURS: Tues.-Sat.: 10-4; Sun.: 12-5. Closed major holidays.
ADMISSION: Adults: $3.50 Children & Seniors: $2.00.
LOCATION: Main Street (Route 124) and Green Village Road, Madison, Morris County
TELEPHONE: 973-377-2982

OCEAN COUNTY HISTORICAL MUSEUM

Basically a historic house with rooms set up in comfortable 19th century fashion. A music-library room, and a well-set dining room set the tone. The Victorian kitchen is of particular interest since it is chock full of useful gadgets that have since been deemed nonessential. A gizmo for softening corks had the curators mystified until a tourist told them what it was.

Upstairs a child's bedroom is all set up and a small schoolhouse impresses the youngsters. Downstairs, in the basement, there are museum-type memorabilia including pictures of Lakehurst during the age of dirigibles. In the main house there are now changing exhibits. A separate wing is dedicated to Ocean County industries such as cranberry production and houses a research library with 8000 volumes of history.

HOURS: Tues.-Thurs.: 1-4; Sat.: 10-4.
ADMISSION: $2.00 (donation).
LOCATION: 26 Hadley Ave., Toms River, Ocean County
TELEPHONE: 732-341-1880

HOPEWELL MUSEUM

Again, a combination historic house/museum with rooms done up in particular periods. The house itself is Victorian, but the rooms display Colonial, Empire and Victorian furnishings. An 1880 organ and a Joseph Bonaparte sideboard are prized possessions here. In the back of the mansion, an addition houses a large collection of Indian artifacts and a great many costumed mannequins. The costumes include ballgowns, wedding dresses and other finery worn in the 19th century. Upstairs there are even more decorated rooms since this house is much larger inside than it seems from the exterior. Guided tour. Free. (Donations accepted).

OCEAN CITY HISTORICAL MUSEUM

Life in the 1890's is graphically depicted in this small historical museum, which is now housed in the Community Cultural Center along with the library and art museum. Mannequins in costumes and photos hark back to the heyday of the Jersey shore when Victorian families headed for Ocean City, the quiet and sober neighbor of Atlantic City. Indian artifacts and a complete exhibit devoted to the wreck of the Sindia (a famous maritime disaster) are here. Free. The museum also administers a typical Victorian seaside cottage on a different site, which is open only in the summer.

HOURS: Mon.-Fri.: 10 -4.; Sat.: 1-4. Call for winter hours
LOCATION: 1735 Simpson Ave., Ocean City, Cape May County.
TELEPHONE: 609-399-1801.

CAPE MAY COUNTY HISTORICAL MUSEUM

Housed in a well-preserved 18th-Century home, the museum includes an 1820 dining room all set up, a children's room with antique toys, and much glassware and china. Across the yard the well-stocked barn features harpoons from Cape May's whaling past, Indian artifacts and farm implements. Here also is the huge glass prism top to the old Cape May Lighthouse. Visits are self-guided with a brochure for regular admission. A one-and-one-half hour guided tour costs an additional fee.

The adjacent Genealogy Room is of interest to many historians because of the number of Mayflower descendents in the Cape May area. There is also a small gift shop in the museum proper.

HOURS: Tues.-Sat 9-4; From Dec.-Mar.: Sat only.
ADMISSION: Adults: $2.50; Under 12: $.50.
LOCATION: 504 Route 9, Cape May Courthouse.
TELEPHONE: 609-465-3535

NEW JERSEY HISTORICAL SOCIETY

In 1997 the Society moved into its new digs (a building which was formerly The Essex Club) which is only a short walk from the much publicized NJPAC (q.v.) There are now three floors of exhibits about the Garden State. An extensive collection of books and manuscripts are in the library. Permanent holdings include furniture, paintings, sculpture, and an incredible number of items covering three hundred years of history: music, quilting, shipmaking, and what-have-you.

Revolving exhibits emphasize different periods or themes based on New Jersey history. The opening exhibit in the new building was called "From Sinatra to Springsteen" and traced the evolution of teenagers in the Garden State from the 1940s to the 1980s. Another exhibit followed the life of Paul Robeson. Various interactive exhibits are geared toward school age children, to keep them involved. Free.

> **HOURS:** Tues.-Sat.: 10-5
> **LOCATION:** 52 Park Place, Newark
> **TELEPHONE:** 973-596-8500

MONMOUTH COUNTY HISTORICAL ASSOCIATION

Another combination of museum and society headquarters is housed in a handsome, 3-story Georgian colonial not far from the scene of the battle of Monmouth. Impressive collections of mahogany furniture, old china, glassware and paintings furnish the historical rooms of the "mansion" (it was actually built in 1931).

You can also find specialty rooms devoted to dolls, old boxes, and so forth, plus an attic filled with bicycles, pony carts, and other leftovers from the 18th and 19th centuries. Rooms devoted to "hands-on experience" allow children to try on period clothes. The association also administers several historic houses in Monmouth County.

> **HOURS:** Tues.-Sat.: 10-4; Sun.: 1-4. Shorter summer hours.
> **ADMISSION:** Adults: $2.00; Children: $1.00; Seniors: $1.50.
> **LOCATION:** 70 Court St, Freehold.
> **TELEPHONE:** 732462-1466

CAMDEN COUNTY HISTORICAL SOCIETY

Three sections include: a museum with early American glass, fire-fighting equipment military artifacts and the tools of early handicrafts set up in "shops" of cobblers, carpenters, coopers, etc.; a library with 19,000 books and pamphlets, manuscripts and newspapers; and Pomona Hall, an excellent example of early Georgian architecture furnished in both 18th and 19th Century fashion. Pomona Hall is a separate house, connected by a breezeway to the museum section. The guided tour will take you through many well-furnished rooms. Call ahead for appointment

> **HOURS:** Tues. & Thurs.: 12:30-4:30; Sun.: 1-5.
> Closed Aug. & major holidays.
> **ADMISSION:** Adults: $2.00; under 16 free.
> **LOCATION:** Park Blvd. & Euclid Ave., Camden.
> **TELEPHONE:** 856-964-3333.

THE PATERSON MUSEUM

Located a block from Paterson's Great Falls, in the one-time factory building of the Rogers Locomotive Company, the Paterson Museum takes up the huge first floor of the imposing red brick building. The museum contains a fascinating compilation of photographs, factory machines, old posters and early inventions. Among other things, you'll find the great wheels that spun silk thread and ribbons, model trains for children, a mock-up of the Botto House (q.v.) and reminders of the Colt factory. Although primarily a historical museum, there are other exhibits including a mineral exhibit.

Paterson seems to be the only community in New Jersey that does not equate the historical with the quaint. The great spinning machines, and the metal shell of the first submarine all testify to the fact that the dominant thrust of the 19th Century was the Industrial Revolution. The Rogers locomotive that stands outside the building was the Iron Horse that opened up the plains.

> **HOURS:** Tues.-Fri.: 10-4; Sat., Sun.: 12:3-4:30..
> **ADMISSION:** Adults: $2.00 (donation)
> **LOCATION:** 2 Market St, Paterson, Passaic County.
> **TELEPHONE:** 973-881-3839

NEW JERSEY PLANETARIUMS

Aside from the planetariums you find within major museums, there are a number of places star-seeking New Jerseyans can visit for sky programs. Children under six are sometimes not admitted to programs for good reason - once those doors shut in darkness, there is no escape. Luckily, many planetariums feature special "Stars for Tots" shows. Admission fees run about $5.00 for adults at college sites. Here's what is available.

OCEAN COUNTY COLLEGE: College Drive, Toms River. Robert J. Novins, Planetarium. Outside the main hurly-burly of Toms River on a large campus, this planetarium not only schedules public shows all year round but has a special astronomy curriculum for school grades 1-6 during the public school year. (And this attracts students from outside counties as well.) Public shows are well attended. They do shut down every once in a while to prepare a new show, so call first. The planetarium holds 117 people and is quite modern. Admission fee. Under 6 not admitted except for special "tot" shows. *Telephone:* 732-255-0342.

TRAILSIDE PLANETARIUM: Coles Avenue and New Providence Road in Mountainside, Union County. Part of the Watchung Reservation's Trailside Nature and Science Center, this simple "down home" building is worth tracking down (it's just down the hill from the big Nature Center). Although it seats only 35 people, it is rarely overfilled and offers the same slide presentations, manufactured by a scientific company, that you see anywhere else, plus their own local star show. Sundays at 2 and 3:30 p.m. Weekly after-school shows for groups - such as scouts - who reserve in advance. Admission fee. *Telephone.* 908-789-3670.

RARITAN VALLEY COLLEGE: Lamington Road and Rte. 28, North Branch, Somerset County. The newest planetarium in New Jersey seats 100 people. Many school shows plus public showings on Saturdays. Special pre-school shows. Uses both the "canned" slide shows, and their own give -and -take lecture style sky show. Nice little astronomy museum before you go in. Reservations required. Admission fee. *Telephone.* 908-231-8805.

MORRIS COUNTY COLLEGE: Route 10 & Center Grove Road, Randolph. This automated 80-seat planetarium offers not only several programs to the local citizenry but also courses for those who really want to delve into the subject. Shows for school and scout groups are scheduled during the week and early Saturday. Public showings take place on select weekends while the college is in session. Call first. Admission fee. *Telephone.* 973-328-5076.

New York Museums

METROPOLITAN MUSEUM OF ART

This huge Beaux Arts building that covers several blocks of New York's Fifth Avenue is still the Grande Dame of museums this side of the Atlantic. It is the repository of a European culture wafted to our shores by millionaires whose art collections were donated for reasons of either generosity or tax exemptions. At one time the Museum was so old-Europe centered that it admitted neither American nor "Modern" art. However, all that has changed.

With the American Wing you get a museum and a half. The "wing" is, in fact, equal to most medium-sized museums. The three floors encompass American furniture and decorative arts, recreated 17th and 18th Century rooms, paintings and sculpture. To view it chronologically you must take an elevator and start at the top, descend through the restored rooms, paintings of George Washington, pass the Frederic Remington sculptures and end up on the first floor with large canvasses by Whistler and John Singer Sargeant. To get back to the main museum, you cross the beautiful Englehardt Garden Court This courtyard contains purple willowed Tiffany screens, Louis Sullivan stairs and a wonderful 1900s ambience.

But to begin at the beginning - when you first enter the Metropolitan's huge marble lobby you may feel as if you've entered Grand Central Station by mistake. Milling crowds, a central information booth, ticket booths, coat-check areas, signs for the restaurant and rest-rooms, a bookshop and a jewelry counter doing booming business - this is a museum? Well, one traditional feature of the Museum is that from the front lobby its Greeks to the left, Egyptians to the right, and Europeans upstairs.

If you are with children you might as well go for the mummies and the Egyptian section. The Medieval armor on the first floor is another child's favorite. The second floor houses the European paintings, which start with the medieval period. From there you wander through Italian and Northern Renaissance, Dutch Masters, English portraits and French landscapes. There are whole wings devoted to modern art, New Guinea artifacts and fashion design.

For the exhausted, there's always lunch where you can wait on line for cafeteria food, or opt for the center restaurant. (Reserve for the restaurant at the Information Booth when you arrive.) Another stopping place is the roof garden (complete with sculptures), which is open in summer.

HOURS: Tues.-Thurs., Sun.: 9:30-5:15, Fri, Sat.: 9:30-8:45
ADMISSION: Suggested donation: Adults: $10.00; Students, seniors: $5.00. Children under 12, free.
LOCATION: Fifth Ave. between 81st and 84th Sts., N.Y.C.
TELEPHONE: 212-879-5500; 535-7710. www.metmuseum.org

AMERICAN MUSEUM OF NATURAL HISTORY

The big news at this museum is the reappearance of the Planetarium in a new and jazzed-up form: *The Rose Center for Earth and Space*, a seven floor, 333,500 foot wonder, opened in the spring of 2000. Its centerpiece is an 87-foot sphere that appears to hover within a cube of glass. This sphere houses both the planetarium upstairs and a space theater below where visual and audio effects simulate how the universe began.

There are lots of whiz-bang special effects inside but the look from the outside is breathtaking! The Hall of the Universe, and The Cosmic Pathway will usher you into 13 billion years of cosmic evolution by way of a spiral walkway . You'll discover four zones, which include the Black Hole theater, the Galaxies Zone and the Star Zone. When you get to the Planet Zone, you'll find the 15-ton Willamete Meteorite. Visitors can also walk to the Gottesman Hall of Planet Earth which has all sorts of rocks, astrophysics exhibits, videos of earthquakes and the usual interactive computers.

Since this is a completely new addition to the 125 year old museum, the Rose Center will offer some much-needed amenities. This includes a parking garage, more public space, and more eating facilities and museum shops.

As for the main part of the museum—save energy for a visit. You might want to go to the fourth floor to see the dinosaur collection first . The skeleton bones are arranged in poses that scientists now deem these ancient reptiles would assume. The dinosaurs seem to be poised for flight as if they were birds —shades of Jurassic Park! Then, on to the Hall of Peoples where you can visit almost any culture. On the first floor you'll find gems and minerals — a beautiful collection of quartz, sapphires, and jade . The museum also hosts an IMAX theater that shows those eight-story high movies.

While there are any number of museums in New Jersey that are cheaper or easier to reach, nothing reaches the sheer immensity of the American Museum of Natural History. But one thing that has really gone to the moon here is the prices! If you want the space show, book first (by phone or internet) before you leave New Jersey—The Rose Center is a hot ticket in town!

HOURS: Sunday-Thursday-10 a.m. -5:45 p.m. Fri-Sat: 10 a.m.-8:45 p.m.
ADMISSION: Combination Space Show & museum admission:
Adults: $19.00; Seniors & students: $14.00; children: $11.50.
(Regular museum admission is less)
LOCATION: Central Park West at 79th St., NYC
TELEPHONE: 212-796-5100 / www.amnh.org

THE CLOISTERS

High on a tree-covered bluff just minutes from the bustling streets of Washington Heights, there stands a world apart. The Cloisters, a museum built in the style of a 14th Century monastery, displays the art and architecture of the Middle Ages in a setting completely devoted to that single age. Unlike its mother museum (The Metropolitan Museum of Art) which tries to cover the span of art from antiquity to the present, this monastic replica covers only the 12th to 15th Centuries in Europe. The Cloisters includes both religious and secular art and geographical variety. The red tile roof of the building reflects the style of Southern Europe. But inside there are the stones of a Romanesque Chapel, and a Gothic Hall complete with arched ceiling and flying buttresses.

The Cloisters gets its name from the covered walkway around an enclosed garden that was typical of the medieval monastery. The main cloister at the museum is the one on the first floor, but there are several others downstairs. Of particular interest to gardeners is the herb garden where two hundred species of plants sprout among the espalier trees and arcades of a Cistercian cloister.

107

A star attraction here is the *Unicorn Tapestries*. Remarkable in their color, preservation and realism, these panels tell a story which you read by moving from one to the other. The story of the hunt, killing and resurrection of the Unicorn shows the life of the medieval aristocracy as well as the symbolism of the age. Other top exhibits include illuminated manuscripts and The Chalice of Antioch.

Since the Cloisters is built on a bluff overlooking the Hudson, be sure to drink in the view of Fort Tryon Park and the wild Palisades across the river in New Jersey. John D. Rockefeller Jr. paid for it all -the Cloisters, the park and the view, when he donated the whole shebang in 1938.

HOURS: Tues.-Sun.: 9:30-5:15. Nov.-Feb.: 9:30-4:45.
ADMISSION: Suggested donation: Adults: $10.00; Seniors, students: $5.00. Includes admission to the Met. Museum.
DIRECTIONS: George Washington Bridge to Henry Hudson Parkway North. Take first exit off Parkway to Fort Tryon Park. Follow signs.
TELEPHONE: 212-923-3700 / www.metmuseum.org

THE FRICK COLLECTION

This little jewel of a museum, housed in the former mansion of the coke and steel magnate is a must for art lovers. The European paintings and furniture display a heavy emphasis on both the Renaissance and Eighteenth Century. The Fragonard Room with panels painted for Madame Du Barry and the Boucher Room with panels commissioned by Madame de Pompadour have the appropriate French furniture and ambience to take you back to the reigns of the various Louises. Medieval paintings, enamels, Rembrandts and lots of 18th Century British portraits and landscapes abound.

Since this was once a home, the paintings are hung much as they would have been in the days of opulence. Gainsborough ladies and Turner landscapes decorate the comfortable halls, and a lovely inner courtyard provides an atrium for rest and contemplation. There is also a lecture hall for free talks.

Only the first floor is open, but this is a formidable collection, so allow at least an hour to browse through. Children under ten are not admitted and those under 16 must be accompanied by adults - they are serious about art in this place. No lunchroom available.

HOURS:	Tues.-Sat.: 10-6; Sun.: 1-6.
ADMISSION:	Adults: $7.00. Students, Seniors:$5.00
LOCATION:	One East 70th St. (At Fifth Ave.) N.Y.C.
TELEPHONE:	212-288-0700 / www.frick.org

MUSEUM OF MODERN ART

Although the MOMA was remodeled in 1984, it is still undergoing renovation, with more space being added to its wings. However, certain things will remain the same. Its position in the center of midtown means it is still a great place to meet. Its core holdings of Impressionists, post-Impressionists and modern greats will always attract a crowd, no matter how strange the rotating exhibits are. From Henri Rousseau to Monet and Matisse, large Picassos and 1920s abstracts, there's plenty to peruse here. Upstairs, a helicopter, downstairs, photographs and films. The sculpture garden provides chairs and coffee service. There's a bistro-style cafeteria inside for hot food. The bookstore is adjacent to the museum but if you want to get the latest in industrial design in everything from ice cream scoops to toys, the gift shop is across the street Remember, the museum is closed to the public on Wednesdays.

HOURS:	Sat-Tues. &Thurs.: 10:30-6. Fri.: 10:30-8:30.
ADMISSION:	Adults: $10.00; Seniors & students: $6.50.
	Children with adult free.
LOCATION:	11 W. 53rd St (between 5th & 6th Ave.), N.Y.C.
TELEPHONE:	212-708-9400 / www.moma.org

FORBES GALLERIES

Since Malcolm Forbes was one of New Jersey's most colorful residents, many Jerseyans enjoy a peek at the toys of this fabulous millionaire and his family. And toys they are - literally. For in one of the sections of this museum you will find 12,000 toy soldiers set up in dioramas or vignettes that include Indians circling cowboys, jousting knights, marching bands and so on.

In another section, called "Ships Ahoy", there are 500 toy boats on display. These are intricately wrought boats done in all sorts of materials. You will also see the glass panels from the grand salon of the old ocean liner, *The Normandie,* along with other art deco designs.

Other galleries include Presidential Papers (with documents emphasizing the personal side of the presidents) and a Trophy Room. One room is reserved for rotating exhibits often of "objects de luxe". And of course, since the Forbes collection is famous for them, you do get to see twelve of the jeweled Easter eggs and other ornaments created by the Imperial jeweler, Faberge, for the Russian Czars.

The galleries are housed inside the Forbes Magazine building in Greenwich Village. Thursdays are reserved for groups. Children under 16 must be accompanied by adult. Free.

> **HOURS:** Tues., Wed., Fri., Sat: 10-4.
> **LOCATION:** 62 Fifth Ave. at 12th St., N.Y.C.
> **TELEPHONE:** 212-206-5548.

Pennsylvania Museums

THE FRANKLIN INSTITUTE

The venerable Franklin Institute was always a pioneer in hands-on exhibits. Now it has a soaring modern, hi-tech addition to the original classical building. Architecturally it's like going from the 18th to the 21st century. As for exhibits - they range from the old hands-on favorites to new Disney World style contraptions. The museum has four main sections: The Science Center, The Mandell Futures Center, the Fels Planetarium and the Omniverse Theater. In addition there are computer terminals in the halls that can answer your questions about what is where. What you will find is:

The Science Center. This is the original museum, which still has many of its popular exhibits. There's the 36 times life-size heart you can walk through. The steam locomotive in the basement that chugs along for ten feet every hour. And the giant lever you can swing on. And the T-33 Air Force jet trainer you can "fly" plus lots of exhibits on physics, printing, and such.

The Fels Planetarium: The 340 seat planetarium is now outfitted with a state-of-the-art Digistar projection system that gives viewers a three-dimensional feel to their star-gazing. Special laser shows, also.

The Mandell Futures Center: This brave new world is divided into several permanent exhibits with names like FutureSpace, FutureEarth, and FutureComputers. Here you will find such things as a fiberglass model of a human cell one million times its actual size; a computer that let's you "age" yourself, a model of a NASA space station; a ten foot globe with fiber-optic lights to show population growth shifts; a man-made forest and displays involving cyberspace.

The Omniverse Theater. There are large reclining seats arranged in steeply angled rows. Above and around you is the movie screen, 79 feet across and four stories high - a hemispheric dome. Lots of loudspeakers to project the sound. This is the place for nature films that roar and soar.

The museum has underground parking and two restaurants, a huge atrium for resting and an outdoor science park (in summer). Expect to spend at least four hours here.

> **HOURS:** Daily. Science Center: 9:30-5. Futures Center: Call.
> **ADMISSION:** Science & Future Centers: Adults: $9.75;
> Children, seniors: $8.50: Under 4, free;
> Extra fee for Omniverse & planetarium.
> **LOCATION:** 20th Street and Benjamin Franklin Parkway, Philadelphia
> **TELEPHONE:** 215-448-1200 / www.fi.edu

PLEASE TOUCH MUSEUM

When visiting Philadelphia with younger children, this place is sure to hit the spot. One of the first hands-on, interactive museums to cater specifically to children under eight, it is also one of the most copied. Starting out in 1976, the museum has changed address several times. But it is now ensconced in a multi floored space right in the center of the city's museum district. In fact it is directly across from The Franklin Institute, which caters to the school age child (and grownups).

Since this is an urban museum, one display is set up to recreate a city's bus system - there's even the front of a bus on the floor. But there's also an outdoors "set" for boats that go down a river, and the standard kitchen and fruit market areas where kids can recreate grownup activities. A unique stop is the Russian nursery school, for an introduction to other cultures. Another exhibit is based on Maurice Sendak's most popular books: "Where the Wild Things Are", "In the Night Kitchen" and others. A giant bed, a giant mixing bowl, lost of pots and pans for creating a rumpus, and other scenes from the book are translated into play activities.

And during summer months visit Science Park, a joint venture with the Franklin Institute. It is a family centered, outdoor park with such interactive "elements" as a sky bike, Jumping Fountain, Bubbling Volcano and so forth (beginning to sound like Sesame Place, doesn't it?). Admission to the park is free with admission to either museum.

> **HOURS:** Daily, July 1 - Labor Day: 9-6; Rest of year: 9-4:30.
> **ADMISSION:** Adults, children: $6.95; Seniors: $5.00. Under one, free.
> **LOCATION:** 210 North 21st St (Across from Franklin Institute), Philadelphia.
> **TELEPHONE:** 215-963-0667 / www.pleasetouchmuseum.org

PHILADELPHIA MUSEUM OF ART

It is a Greek temple that surveys the town and the river from an imposing height, with a magnificent flight of steps leading up to its classical columns. The steps, in fact, are as famous as the museum ever since Sylvester Stallone ran up them in the movie, "Rocky".

But inside the pillared entrance (you can avoid most of the steps by parking in the back parking lot), one of the best collections of art in North America awaits. Galleries of European art include the Johnson Collection on the first floor, which is heavy in Renaissance paintings. Twentieth Century art comes next and includes Marcel DuChamps' famous "Nude Descending A Staircase." The variety of the museum is evidenced by the fact that there is a medieval cloister, an Indian temple, a Chinese palace hall and a Japanese teahouse all within these portals.

The kids will find the collection of armor, which includes swords, lances, maces, chain-mail and breastplates, to be fascinating. And one whole section, devoted to Americana, includes period rooms filled with Philadelphia style bonnet-and-scroll bureaus, secretaries and chests. There is plenty of early silverware, also.

Tours are offered by volunteer guides at no extra cost. They leave at specific times and originate in the West Entrance hall. Downstairs, there is a pleasant restaurant and gift shop. Admission price also allows entry to the nearby Rodin Museum, which houses a large collection of this master's works.

> **HOURS:** Tues.-Sun.: 10-5; Wed. to 8:45.
> **ADMISSION:** Adults: $8.00; Seniors, Students: $5.00. Under 5 free. Free on Sunday until 1 PM.
> **LOCATION:** Benjamin Franklin Parkway & 26th St., Philadelphia
> **TELEPHONE:** 215-763-8100

ROSENBACH MUSEUM AND LIBRARY

Located two blocks from Rittenhouse Square in a lovely section of Philadelphia, this townhouse was the home of rare book collectors. The books and furnishings of the Rosenbach brothers are at once a paean to the good life and a paradise for collectors. Since one brother searched for antiques while the other concentrated on books, the home is a treasure trove of decorative arts. It is also an important research library.

There are 130,000 manuscripts and 30,000 rare books, which range from medieval illuminated manuscripts to letters written by George Washington and Abraham Lincoln stored here. Lewis Carroll's own edition of *Alice in Wonderland* and the manuscript of James Joyce's *Ulysses* together with hundreds of first editions are shelved in what is essentially still a home with beautiful and delicate furniture.

The dining room where the brothers entertained wealthy guests features an Empire style table, Venetian Grand Canal scenes, and Chippendale chairs. A painting of Fanny Kemble by Thomas Sully and a scrolled fireplace adorn the cozy parlor. Upstairs, the museum displays illustrations by children's book author, Maurice Sendak, the personal papers of poet Marianne Moore and special exhibits.

Although the Rosenbach brothers lived in this house only from 1950 to 1952, when they were both old, the house seems to come out of some turn-of-the century novel by Henry James. It seems incredible that this cultured, even dandified atmosphere existed in the post-World War II period. Yet its all here - oriental carpets and Herman Melville's bookcase (stacked with first editions of *The White Whale*), 17th Century gold chests and delicate French parlors. The museum is a must for collectors, librarians, art historians and anyone who wants pointers on how to live with class. Not for children, but senior high school and college students are welcome.

HOURS:	Tues. - Sun.: 11-4. Closed August-mid-Sept.
ADMISSION:	Adults: $5.00; Students, Seniors: $3.00
LOCATION:	2010 Delancey Place, Philadelphia
TELEPHONE:	215-732-1600

THE BARNES FOUNDATION

The best collection of Impressionist and post-Impressionist paintings in America can be found in this museum, set in suburban Philadelphia.

But visiting hours to this Renaissance style mansion are extremely limited. And then there's the eccentric way the pictures are hung. It seems to be haphazard. Paintings cover some walls and even hang over a door transom. African statues and medieval ironwork are interspersed with 19th and 20th century art. For visitors conditioned to galleries based on geography and time line, this type of arrangement is disconcerting.

Dr. Barnes had his own ideas about art appreciation. Color and form are paramount. No biographical data, no dates. Luckily the name of the painter and the title of the painting are available. But that's all. Whether the artist was young or old, rich or poor, married or single, in a blue or pink period is considered irrelevant

However, the museum contains two floors of a formidable collection. More Matisses than you would expect - including a huge piece entitled *The Piano Lesson*. More Reniors than you can count— lots of pink cheeked children. Huge Navajo patterned baskets, Cezannes and El Grecos, African masks and wood sculptures. Downstairs, you can watch an orientation film and/or rent audio guides. And you can now visit the 13-acre arboretum that surrounds the museum. However, the Main Line neighbors have limited the number of visitors allowed. Reservations required.

> **HOURS:** Fri.-Sat.: 9:30-5.00; Sun.: 12:30-5.
> **ADMISSION:** $5.00. Audio tour: $5.00
> **LOCATION:** 300 North Latch's Lane (off City Line Ave.-Route 1) Merion, PA
> **TELEPHONE:** 610-664-7917/ 610-664-5191 / www.barnesfoundation.org

THE MERCER MILE

Three unusual museums in Doylestown are the legacy of Henry Chapman Mercer (1856-1930) a businessman, ceramicist, archaeologist, and apparently, an eccentric. The highly individual creations are known collectively as the Mercer Mile and are administered by The Bucks County Historical Society. They consist of:

THE MERCER MUSEUM: A sprawling, turreted structure of reinforced concrete, the museum houses a vast collection of America's pre-Industrial tools and crafts. Mercer was one of the first to collect early Americana (although everyone seems to be doing it now). He collected with the eye of an archaeologist, and all the minutae of everyday life - from kitchen utensils to hat making machines - are revealed here. Small objects are exhibited in rooms by craft (e.g., the evolution of butter making) while larger objects are left free-standing or are suspended. Visitors often gasp when they step into the main section of the museum and find Conestoga wagons, harpoons and whaling skiffs suspended from the ceiling. Six floors of exhibits surround the central hall. Gallows, hearses, prisoner's docks and the kitchen sink — it's all here. The Spruance Library of early Americana is also here.

HOURS: Mon. - Sat, 10-5; Sun.: 12-5; Tues. 5-9.
ADMISSION: Adults: $5.00; Seniors: $4.50; Students: $1.50
LOCATION: 84 Pine St., Doylestown
(Take Rte. 202 or Rte. 611 to Ashland St.)
TELEPHONE: 215-345-0210. www.mercermile.org

FONTHILL MUSEUM: The home of Mercer, it looks like a Spanish fantasy set on the quiet Pennsylvania landscape. Filled with the colorful Moravian tiles from his factory, the home has arches and winding stairways and uneven rooms and beautiful views. Guided tours only. Admission fee. Reservations advised. *Location*: East Court St. *Telephone*: 215-348-9461

MORAVIAN POTTERY AND THE WORKS: *A* short walk from Fonthill, the Tile Works shows the machinery and raw materials of the tile making process (workers are not always present) and also houses a gift shop where these unusual tiles may be bought. Hours. Daily 10-4:45. Small admission fee. *Location*: 130 Swamp Rd. *Telephone*. 215-345-6722.

THE BRANDYWINE RIVER MUSEUM

From the front, it's a century old gristmill; from the back it's a strikingly modern glass tower overlooking the Brandywine River, and altogether it is a most pleasant museum where the setting and structure are almost as interesting as the paintings within.

Inside the stone and glass structure, the atmosphere belongs to the Brandywine River artists (a group that formed around Howard Pyle and N.C. Wyeth) and to Wyeth's talented progeny, particularly Andrew and his son Jamie. Both Pyle and N.C. Wyeth were famous illustrators and many an older edition of *Treasure Island* or *King Arthur* contains their realistic action pictures. Although storybook illustrators have never reached the heights of adulation that "purer" artists enjoy, nevertheless they are among the most respected painters in America.

Howard Pyle began a summer teaching center in the Brandywine Valley in 1898. The artists from this center include Maxfield Parrish, Peter Hurd, and, of course, N.C. Wyeth. But it is Andrew Wyeth, whose painting *Christina's World* is world famous, who holds the most interest for viewers. The strong emotional impact of his canvasses dominates the collection here. You'll find a small number of Jamie's paintings in the permanent collection, plus special exhibits which emphasize other Brandywine artists.

After viewing the exhibits, you can lunch at the cafeteria and view the meandering river and wildflower garden below. This lovely preserve is part of the Brandywine Conservancy, which keeps 5,000 acres in a state of nature - a most poetic place that seems to attract strollers, readers and young romantics. As for children, there is a special Christmas display for them which runs throughout the month of December. It includes model trains, porcelain dolls and decorated Christmas trees.

HOURS:	Daily except Christmas, 9:30-4:30
ADMISSION:	Adults: $5.00; Seniors, students: $2.50; under 6 free.
LOCATION:	On Route U.S. 1 (at Route 100) Chadds Ford, PA.
TELEPHONE:	610-388-2700

See Also: Museums that are part of a larger entity are mentioned under the title of the larger attraction—e.g., *The Museum of American Glass* (Wheaton Village), *West Point Museum* (West Point).

THE CLASSICS

Photo: Courtesy NJ. Travel & Tourism

In This Chapter You Will Find:

United Nations Headquarters, NY
The Statue of Liberty
Ellis Island
World Trade Center, NY
Empire State Building, NY
West Point, NY
Independence Mall, Philadelphia, PA
South Street Seaport, NY

UNITED NATIONS HEADQUARTERS

The first thing you notice as you approach the United Nations complex is the line of colorful flags half-circling the entrance. All member nation flags are flown at the same height —only the UN flag is unfurled higher. The next thing you notice as you step through the iron gates is that this place is clean! No old newspapers, candy wrappers or soda cans litter the area. The United Nations may not police the world, but they sure know how to police the grounds!

Outside sculpture includes a gigantic abstract next to the circular fountain and the Japanese Peace Bell. In the spring be sure to check out the gardens which are in back of the buildings. Daffodils and cherry trees bloom early while the rose garden with its many varieties of tea roses blossoms in June.

Tours of the UN are still popular although nowadays you must enter the building through an airport-type security system. The tour combines a short history of the aims and activities of the United Nations with a description of the art and architecture you pass along the tour route.

The number of chambers you enter during the tour depends on whether the various councils are meeting or not. The General Assembly, which is usually open, is a huge hall with high-domed ceiling and more than 2,000 seats. The slatted back walls are interspersed with banks of windowed booths where translators, photographers and TV people sit. This is the hall most often seen on television when important meetings take place.

Most of these chambers were designed by Norwegian, Swedish and Danish architects and furnishings were donated by those countries. They display the vertical and horizontal lines and rich wood grains we associate with "Danish Modern." In fact, the whole complex has a definite Scandinavian look. A human thirst for color is seen in the gifts of other countries: such as a colorful tapestry from Senegal, or a crimson Peruvian ceremonial mantle.

The tour ends in the Public Concourse where you can proceed to the bookstore, gift shops and postal counter (a mecca for stamp collectors). Handicraft items from around the world, flags, and dolls of all nations are priced reasonably. The bargain is the fact that there is no sales tax anywhere in the UN complex! For hamburgers and french fries there's good coffee shop here. It is also possible to eat upstairs in the Delegates Dining Room, but you must reserve ahead for that.

HOURS: Daily: 9:30-4:45. No weekends Jan. & Feb.
ADMISSION: Free. For tours - Adults: $7.50; Students & seniors: $6.00;
grade school children: $4.00.
Children under 5 not admitted on tours.
LOCATION: 1st Ave. between 45th & 46th St, N.Y.C.
TELEPHONE: 212-963-8687 / www.un.org

STATUE OF LIBERTY

Don't wait until your Aunt Mabel comes to visit - go see this icon of American freedom for yourself. New Jersey residents can embark from Liberty State Park for the short ride over. Once aboard the Circle Line Ferry, (which stops first at Ellis Island) you get a view from all angles of the glistening lady as the boat turns to make port. As you disembark, the first building you see is the gift and souvenir shop. Here you can stock up on mugs, pennants and postcards.

Liberty Island is larger than you might expect. On its 12 acres there are administration buildings, a snack shop, a pleasant tree-shaded picnic area and esplanades rimming the island. Here you can savor the view of Manhattan's towers plus the wide expanse of the harbor with its bustling boats, or take a close-up picture of the "Lady With The Lamp".

Inside, there are lines for the pedestal, for those who want to walk to the crown, and sometimes even for the museum. The museum, just a short walk up a flight of stairs within the main lobby, is devoted to the building and restoration of the statue itself. It includes an incredible amount of displays and information. There are architectural mock-ups, and an audio-visual section. The museum that was devoted to American immigration has been transferred to Ellis island, which now rivals the statue in appeal.

As for those who actually walk the 22 stories up to the crown expect your calves to hurt for the next week. This is not for the frail or short-of-breath. You must walk all the way up since the elevator now goes only to the pedestal (where there is no access to the crown). For adults, the view from the fourth floor is just fine. On crowded summer days, access may be limited.

Both as a visit to a national shrine and as a pleasant day's outing on the water between two great ports, a trip to the Statue of Liberty is a must. Best to go in the spring and fall before the out-of-towners arrive.

HOURS: 9-5 Daily.
FERRY (Liberty State Park) Daily 9:15-3:45.
SCHEDULE: Schedule is expanded in summer, shortened in winter.
(Battery Park, N.Y.) Daily every half hour.
ADMISSION: Ferry fee: Adults: $7.00; Under 17: $3.00. Seniors: $6.00
LOCATION: Liberty State Park (take the NJ. Turnpike to exit 14B).
Parking fee for ferry
TELEPHONE: (Circle Line) 201-435-9499. (Liberty State Park) 201-915-3400.
(Liberty Island) 212-363-3200 / www.nps.gov

ELLIS ISLAND

If a visit to the Statue of Liberty is inspiring, a visit to its neighbor, Ellis Island, is absolutely fascinating. Since you get both islands for the same ferry price, it is best to allow enough time to explore both - up to five hours, if you stop at all the exhibits.

For Ellis Island is the basic museum which commemorates the peopling of America, not only those who set foot on this particular island (for that is only one section) but the story from the beginning, with emphasis on the late 19th and early 20th century. A movie, shown in two theaters, recounts the experience of those who left troubled homelands to take the sea voyage to the new land. First it was in wooden ships that took six weeks to make the voyage and left everyone sick. Later it was the steamship lines who filled up their steerage section with poor immigrants. If the immigrants were turned back because of sickness or other reasons, the steamship company had to pay for the return passage.

Earlier immigration sites, greed, corruption, and the one day processing of thousands of people are all covered in the movie as well as the displays. But there is also an amassing of hundreds of trunks, shawls, tickets, flyers and other mementos of the immigrant experience. Newspaper cartoons depict the rising tide of intolerance against the newcomers which finally culminated in a restrictive law in 1924 which ended the mass migration. Ellis Island was closed in 1954. In its newly refurbished state it is a wonderful learning experience, and an emotional one as well for anyone who descended from all those Germans, Greeks, Italians, Jews, Irish, Turks, Jamaicans and others who first came to these shores.

HOURS, ETC.: Check Statue of Liberty entry.
TELEPHONE: (Circle Line) 201-435-9499; (Ellis Island) 212-363-3204

WORLD TRADE CENTER

The *"Top of the World"* observation deck at the World Trade Center advertises that it is the closest thing to Disney World in the area. About the only similarity between the two places is the long lines set up in serpentine fashion. On a clear day, you can see forever from the 107th floor of the tallest building in New York. Unfortunately so can a few thousand other people. The renovated spot features the view, "a simulated helicopter ride" and a full cafeteria where you can buy overpriced fast food. You get your tickets on the mezzanine floor and then wait on long lines for the elevator to whisk you to the top. Your ticket also allows you to go two escalators up to the open terraces, but that venue is often closed on windy days.

When you arrive on the 107th floor, there is a 360 degree view of the metropolis, the river, New Jersey and Brooklyn, and it is terrific. There are computer stations where you can bring up information on the various landmarks. Murals on the interior walls show typical Manhattan neighborhoods. But the simulated helicopter ride turned out to be a film in a small theater that offers helicopter"shots" of Manhattan. As for the food—you can get the same stuff cheaper down in the shopping corridors of the WTC. Or you can opt for the pricey *Windows On The World*, the restaurant on the top of Tower Number One, and get the same view (the windows are not as large) without the aggravation.There's a cocktail lounge up there too. The outside plaza of the WTC can be pleasant on a warm day.

HOURS:	9:30 AM - 9:30 PM daily.
ADMISSION:	Adults: $13.00; Children: $6.00; Senior Citizens: $9.00; Under 6 free.
LOCATION:	2 World Trade Center Plaza, N.Y.C. Take PATH direct from Hoboken or Jersey City.
TELEPHONE:	212-323-2340

THE EMPIRE STATE BUILDING

It must be the movie, "Sleepless in Seattle", or the image of King Kong - this 1932 Art Deco building, once the tallest (but not the cleanest) in the world, has come back into vogue. The 86th floor observatory has both an enclosed area and an open promenade. High powered binoculars are available for a fee. Here you will also find the snack bars, vending machine and souvenir counter. The view to the west offers New Jersey and the Hudson, to the north you get Central Park and beyond, while the east gives you the UN building and Queens.

While the observation windows here may not be as wide as those in the World Trade Center, you are closer to the heart of Manhattan from this vantage point. There is an observatory on the 102nd floor included in the same ticket. This one is enclosed, although it may not always be open. Here again, during tourist season, expect long lines.

HOURS: Daily: 9:30 AM - Midnight
ADMISSION: Adults: $9.00; Seniors: 7.00; Children: $4.00. Under 5 free.
LOCATION: 34th Street & 5th Avenue, N.Y.C.
TELEPHONE: 212-736-3100

WEST POINT

West Point has a beautiful view of the Hudson, grey Collegiate Gothic buildings that rise from rocky inclines, parades of cadets on Saturday mornings and football games in the fall. Many people begin their tour at the Visitors Center, which is several blocks outside of the actual gates of the Point.

The center has displays, a movie about army life, and a busy gift shop. It is also the point of departure for bus tours which leave regularly during the warm weather for a 50 minute tour of the campus (Tel.: 914-446-4724). The narrated tour stops at the magnificent Gothic chapel where all those spiffy weddings take place, the old chapel, at various monuments and at scenic views. If you don't want to wait for a bus tour, you can park within the campus and walk around yourself. There are benches where you can picnic, and the Thayer Hotel, which is on campus, has restaurants open to the public.

But before (or after) you take the tour, check out the building behind the Visitor Center. It is **The West Point Museum,** and it boasts three floors of exhibits, models, mock-ups and memorabilia.

The decisive battles of the world are recreated here. The Dark Ages began because the Roman infantry could not hold out against the Gothic cavalry. The Modern Age began when guns replaced swords, and technology replaced prowess. An interesting place with a particular point of view. Lots of armor and costumes around. The West Point trivia is fascinating also. Did you know that James Whistler dropped out because he couldn't pass chemistry? His watercolors are great, though, and those of Ulysses S. Grant aren't bad either.

If you're visiting with your family, you may find the kids are most fascinated by the clean-cut cadets who are unerringly polite and meticulously dressed. Hikers will like the hilly terrain and outstanding view. Free. Fee for bus tour. You can also now take a cruise out on the Hudson on a reconditioned World War 1 boat. This one leaves from the South Dock at 12:15 on weekdays. Telephone 914-534-7245 for prices and particulars.

HOURS: Visitor Center. Daily 9-4:45; Museum: 10:30-4:15.
LOCATION: Palisades Pkwy to 9WN to Highland Falls, N.Y.
TELEPHONE: 914-938-2638. Museum: 914-938-2203 / www.usma.org

INDEPENDENCE NATIONAL HISTORIC PARK

This national park covers several square blocks and includes twenty-four different sites. You can drive right off I-95 into the historic area (via 676) in a wink. First stop should be the great big, brick **Visitor Center** at Chestnut and 3rd Street. Here you can pick up a clearly marked map of the historic areas. A thirty-minute film is shown here about once an hour, which will give you the necessary background for your tour. Special exhibits are also on view, and sometimes costumed characters are on hand.

Check in to see **Franklin Court** (at Market and 4th Street). This complex includes a steel outline of the original Franklin house (which was torn down) plus interesting underground museum. As you descend a winding ramp you pass many displays of Benjamin Franklin's inventions, furniture, until you come to a center where there are interactive exhibits the kids will like, and a film about Franklin. Outside in the complex there is a replica of a colonial printing shop and an authentic old time post office.

Next, it's on to the grassy mall (bounded by Chestnut, Walnut, 5th and 6th Streets) where **Independence Hall** and the **Liberty Bell** await. The bell is in its own glass pavilion, where you can take a picture. The bell is huge, of course, and looks just like you would expect it to. A Park Service person gives a talk on the strange history of this particular icon (and how it got its crack) at specified times.

Independence Hall is shown only by a Department of Interior guide, so there may be a wait but there's a separate room where you can sit down and hear a preliminary talk. The Hall is most impressive, although

124

not very large by today's standards. You can see the inkstand used by the signers of the Declaration of Independence, benches, and so forth. The guide gives a very full explanation of the events surrounding the adoption of the Declaration. Other buildings in the historical park include Carpenters Hall, the Army-Navy Museum, Old City Hall and several other sites of importance. These all have informative displays and are worth visiting. The U.S. Mint, right nearby, is also a fascinating visit both for coin collectors and history buffs.

Since it's only a few blocks away, most tourists walk over to the **Betsy Ross House** at 239 Arch Street which is open daily (except Monday). This small building with its narrow staircase is always so crowded that you only have time to glimpse the mannequins who represent Betsy and other colonials. In fact, the small house is almost overpowered by the adjacent gift shop. Here you can stock up on Liberty Bells, facsimiles of the Declaration of Independence, and of course the 13-star flag which Betsy is reputed to have sewn. (Telephone. 215-627-5343).

> **HOURS:** Some buildings may be closed in winter. Otherwise 9-5 Daily
> **ADMISSION:** Free
> **TELEPHONE:** (Visitor Center) 215-597-8974 / www.nps.org

SOUTH STREET SEAPORT

Boston has its Quincy Market; Baltimore has its Inner Harbor; and New York has its own quaint seaport area. The South Street Seaport has a holiday atmosphere about it that makes it one of the city's most popular tourist spots.

The "museum" (as it is called) is actually the entire restoration of eleven square blocks that were the nucleus of New York's earliest seaport. Schermerhorn Row, Water Street, Fulton Street and South Street boast some of the few remaining federal style townhouses to be found in the big city. These gracious rowhouses have been beautifully restored and now house shops and restaurants. At the water's edge there are several ships available for touring. Tours of the lightship *Ambrose,* and the 4-masted barque, *The Peking,* can be fascinating with the right docent. The talks really give you a feeling for the hard work, danger and close quarters of the old ships.

A more fanciful view of the sea may be obtained from a ride on the *Seaport Liberty Cruise Line,* a Circle Line that offers a one-hour, bay area version of its standard cruise, or the narrated harbor cruise run by NY

Waterways. In warm weather you can also book a two-hour sail on the schooner *Pioneer*. Other cruises may also be available.

Photo by Pam Morse

On the schooner Pioneer out of South Street Seaport.

Ship tours and rides cost extra, of course, as does entrance to the formal exhibit galleries, the Children's Center and the guided tour of the historic area. Tickets may be purchased at the Pier 16 ticket booth or the Museum Visitor Center at 12 Fulton Street.

But the main attraction is the food and shops. The tourist section of The Fulton Market now purveys ethnic fast food for the most part—sushi, empanadas, moussaka, etc. Pier 17, a large building that juts out into the water, is like a Jersey mall inside. Luckily, it has balconies which allow you to observe either the street scene or the passing boats. The Plaza next to Pier 17 attracts performers and musicians.

There are some well known seafood restaurants around, but it is the open air cafes with their wide plazas that seem to be most popular. Since car traffic is prohibited in certain areas during the day, one can actually sit here and relax without breathing auto exhaust. There are wide open walking spaces here and it makes a photogenic venue for tall ships, fireworks and other special occasions.

> **HOURS:** Daily for shops and restaurants.
> **ADMISSION:** (Museum): Adults: $6.00; Seniors: $5.00; Students: $4.00; Children $3.00. Excursion boats extra.
> **LOCATION:** Fulton & South Sts. just off FDR Drive, NYC.
> **TELEPHONE:** (Museum): 212-748-8600 / www.southstseaport.org

THEME PARKS, WATERPARKS
AMUSEMENT PARKS &
BOARDWALKS

Photo by Barbara Hudgins

In This Chapter You Will Find:

Six Flags/Great Adventure, NJ
Hurricane Harbor, NJ
Hersheypark, PA
Dorney Park- Wildwater Kingdom, PA
Sesame Place, PA
Mountain Creek, NJ
Land of Make Believe, NJ
Wild West City, NJ
Clementon Park, NJ

Boardwalk Amusements, NJ
    Keansburg
    Point Pleasant
    Seaside Heights
    Beach Haven
    Atlantic City
    Ocean City
    Wildwood

Other Amusement Parks
    Bowcraft
    Fairy Tale Forest
    Gingerbread Castle
    Storybook Land
    Camelbeach Waterpark
    Shawnee Place

SIX FLAGS GREAT ADVENTURE

After years of pussy-footing around while waterparks opened up all over the place, Six Flags Great Adventure, has taken the plunge. The largest theme park in the area has opened Hurricane Harbor, a water-park so large that it has its own hours and prices. You can buy a combination ticket however.

So what do we have at the original 1100 acre spot that shares a theme park with a drive-through safari? (See Zoo chapter for a write-up on the safari). There seems to be two trends: more children's rides and a few more family rides on the one hand—and bigger and faster roller coasters to attract the teenagers and young adults on the other. The section of the park that always had a western theme (the great Teepee for gifts, and Runaway Train), still has a frontier look. But most of the other themes are tied to Warner Brothers movies and cartoons such as Batman, Lethal Weapon and Looney Tunes.

As for thrill rides, *The Batman Ride* (an upside down roller coaster with decor from the second film) remains a big attraction. *The Chiller* based on the *Batman and Robin* movie is a double track inverted coaster. Others include *Skull Mountain* (an indoor coaster) and *The Viper, a* steel machine with snake-like coils. The classic wooden *Rolling Thunder* and *The Great American Scream Machine* are still in business too. But the big news this year is *Medusa*, a "floorless" coaster with seven loops and sharp curves that moves at 60 mph. There seems to be an unwritten law that each year there is a new and scarier thrill ride and each year the price goes up. Not much fun for non-coaster-lovers.

For young kids there is Looney Tunes Seaport with expanded kiddie rides plus some interactive play areas. Costumed characters (Bugs Bunny, Daffy Duck, etc.) put on a show at the small theater which youngsters seem to enjoy. There are also more "family rides" such as a log flume ride where parents and kids ride together.

For those who hate thrill rides (there are, after all, grandparents around) there are still variety shows, the original high diving act, a "Lethal Weapon" racing boat show over at the lake, and fireworks on weekends.The Showcase Theater has hypnotists and acrobats. Friday and Saturday nights, rock and country bands are sometimes on hand in the Northern Star arena.

As for food - don't expect gourmet fare. Veteran visitors bring picnics in their coolers and just tailgate it in the parking lot. (You are not allowed to bring food inside the park except to the designated picnic area near the Safari section). Bring along towels—there are still flume rides that drench you! Lockers available. And of course there are plenty of shops, drink vendors, and concession stands along with the carousel and other leftovers from the original Great Adventure.

HOURS: Early April-mid June: call for hours.
Late June-Labor Day: 10-10. Safari: 9 -4.
Open weekends, Sept., Oct.
ADMISSION: $48.70 (Combination Park-Safari ticket). Under 48": $24.35;
Seniors: $30.70. Under 3, free.
Parking extra. Season tickets available.
LOCATION: Jackson Twp., Ocean County, Take NJ Tpke to Exit 7A, then 195 to Exit 16.
TELEPHONE: 732-928-2000/9281 / www.sixflags.com

HURRICANE HARBOR

Since this place is so big, it is unlikely you can do both parks in one day. However, there is a combination ticket available. You can also buy an add-on ticket ($15.90) to enter the regular **Six Flags Great Adventure** theme park after 4 p.m. (which gives you the option of deciding whether you have the energy).

Hurricane Harbor consists of 45 acres of wave pools, high-flying waterslides, and roving rivers. Six Flags has spent a lot of money on the "look" of a Caribbean/Polynesian Aztec island. In fact, part of the water-park has a theme of a shipwrecked inventor on a tropical island. For families there is *Discovery Bay* a large wading pool that features a giant bucket that pours 1000 gallons of water onto the waiting crowd below. There are all sorts of climbing nets and water gadgets for kids here. Also 1400 lounge chairs are located within the park for parents who are ready to flop.

Thrill-seekers will find multi-colored, sky-high waterslides both for passenger rafts and for body-surfing. Adventure River is a meandering tube ride that has a bit more swirls and eddies than the usual ones. It also acts as transportation between one part of the park and another.

No outside food or drink are allowed, but remember to bring suntan lotion, hats, towels, and swim sneakers if you have them. Changing rooms and showers are provided—lockers are extra.

HOURS: mid-June- Labor Day. 10-8 full season.
ADMISSION: Adults: $28.61: 48 inches & under, seniors: $21.19
LOCATION: Check Six Flags entry for location & telephone

HERSHEY PARK

When the urge to get away for a two day vacation (complete with amusement park for the kiddies) combines with an urge to avoid the crowds at the seashore, one place to consider is Hershey, Pennsylvania. Set in the green and rolling hills of the Pennsylvania Dutch dairy country, the town that gave birth to the great American chocolate bar offers a theme park, a zoo and several resorts for an overnight stay. Since it is situated a bit of a drive over the New Jersey border, many travelers find it more convenient to sleep over and spend one day at Hersheypark, one day exploring the countryside. For those who have time, a visit to the town itself, the nearby rose gardens (separate listing in this book) and *The Hershey Museum* are all pleasant excursions.

As for Hersheypark, itself; it's a theme park very much like Six Flags, only smaller. There are several open theaters where parents can rest their feet and enjoy entertainment while the kids try the Fender Bender for the fourth time. The crowds here are well behaved and there is little problem of anyone ducking ahead in line.

The newest section is called Midway America and it recreates the carousels, Ferris Wheels and whip rides of a 1930s amusement park. There is also a special section for childen where costumed characters dressed as Hershey Kisses or Reese's bars walk around.

For the strong of stomach, there are several roller coasters including a looping inverted steel roller one called The Great Bear. The latest addition is a twin wooden coaster called Lightning Racer which matches two coasters in a race against each other. Then there are the usual assortment of flume rides, centrifugal rides and things that take you up and down.

An aquatheater featuring dolphin acts, an amphitheater for the song-and-dance shows and theaters for puppet shows and children's comic shows all offer alternatives to rides.

There is a good, medium-sized zoo covering eleven acres on one side of the park, which gives an alternative to families. *The Kissing Tower*, a gentle space needle, offers a nice view and is something different for mothers with young children. Monorails and skyrides make this park well suited to families with kids under ten, although there are enough thrill rides to please the teenagers and young adults. No picnicking allowed but there are plenty of places to find amusement-park-style food.

Outside the park and absolutely free, is Hershey's **"Chocolate World,"** a simulated factory tour in the Disney style. There you ride in automated cars past scenes of dairy farms, African cocoa tree plantations, and assembly belts full of kisses and chocolate bars.

In its off-season, during various weeks in the fall, Hersheypark features a Halloween special and *Candyland* . These weekend outings combine shopping in the cutsey shops and certain rides in the amusement park, along with food and more shopping in *Chocolate World*. All this set to twinkling lights and a pre-Christmas air.

HOURS:	Full season: 10:30 - 10:00.
	Weekends & shortened hours, May, June, autumn.
ADMISSION:	Adults: $32.95; Children 3-8 & Seniors: $17.95;
	2 and under, free.
LOCATION.	Route 322, Pennsylvania, approachable from either 283 off
	The PA Tpke or Route 83 off 81.
TELEPHONE:	HersheyPark: 717-534-3900/800-HERSHEY /
	www.hersheypark.com

DORNEY PARK & WILDWATER KINGDOM

This is basically a double-personality park. On one side is Dorney Park - once a standard, old-fashioned amusement park (its been around since 1884). The new owners (Cedar Faire) are souping it up with new rides and attractions. And that means a 200 ft. high inverted megacoaster called "Steel Force" and a huge Dominator that sends you down twin shafts among other thrill rides.

For those who like nostalgia *Thunderhawk* is an old-fashioned wooden coaster left over from Dorney's old days. A replica steam engine train takes passengers around the park and the Center Stage features acts and song and dance revues. Then there's Camp Snoopy a section for kids which includes costumed characters, easy rides and some interactive play elements.

On the other side of Dorney park is Wildwater Kingdom. This is a highly popular waterpark which offers water slides in all sorts of variations. You will find looping, speeding, inner tube and kiddie water slides here. The taller water rides include the Pepsi Aquablast which features a raft for four or six people that hurtles down a slide. The giant wave pool (which manufactures artificial waves every ten minutes) has two sections: one for those who ride plastic surfboards and mattresses and one for those who stand and jump. Don't expect to be able to swim in all this mass of bodies. But the park does provide plastic sun chairs and lounges so that parents can sit and sun while their offspring surf and slide. Locker rooms and showers are available, as are surfboard rentals.

There is a special section for young children in each park. Wildwater Kingdom has Lollipop Lagoon, a large wading pool interspersed with water-umbrellas and a "submarine" with play elements and other The park is located just beyond Allentown and is no further away than other major parks for many New Jerseyans. Food no longer allowed inside the gates (they do cater picnics for groups). Parking is extra.

HOURS:	Daily 10-10, full Season. Shorter hours April-mid-June & Sept
ADMISSION:	Combo ticket: Adults: $31.00;
	Children Age 4 to 48" & Seniors: $7.00. Under 3 free.
LOCATION:	3830 Dorney Park Road, Allentown, PA.
	Take Route 78 past Allentown, to Exit 16B.
TELEPHONE:	610-395-3724; 800-551-5656 / www.dorneypark.com

SESAME PLACE PLAYPARK

When Sesame Place first opened it was the first activity park devoted directly to the younger set. Children from three to thirteen were supposed to stretch their minds and muscles in a series of innovative "play concepts" like swimming in thousands of plastic balls and climbing up cargo netting. While these activities still exist, the park is now more commercially oriented with enough grownup rides to interest Dad, Mom and older siblings. A mild roller coaster called "Vapor Trail" is now on tap.

As for the water rides—they come in large and small sizes. For those who like it slow, there is Big Bird's Rambling River, a level waterway for rubber tubing. The Rubber Duckey ride is for small fry who want to take a tube ride with a little roll to it. The larger water rides are exactly like the ones at the Jersey shore- - metal structures where you chute down on a cushion of water. Some twist and turn, some are partially enclosed and some are straight down - you end up in a small pool of water all the same. The lines are long but they move in an orderly fashion and the park personnel make sure you don't bump into your neighbor. For those who are scared of water rides, there is a simple fountain in the center of the park where everybody can just jump around and get wet. In another section, a tropical island allows kids to squirt water guns and play steel drums.

There are lockers available for a fee (you have to get on line immediately if you want to grab one) and changing rooms (which can get pretty messy, so wear your bathing suit when you come).

What if you hate water? Well, there are shows: one features bird or animal acts; another is a song-and dance revue starring Bert, Ernie, Elmo and others. Every afternoon a musical parade by costumed characters rocks down Sesame Street and affords plenty of picture taking opportunities. There are two eateries, but since plenty of picnic tables are available, why bother standing in line for food?

When is the best time to visit Sesame Place? Because season tickets are bought by nearby families, and daycare buses come in droves on weekdays, this place is often overcrowded. Early morning and late afternoon are suggested. Bring food, towels, and suntan lotion.

HOURS: 9:00— June-August; Shorter hours off season. Weekends only Sept.-Oct.: 10-5
ADMISSION: $31.95; 2 and under, free. Parking fee
DIRECTIONS: Route 1 South through Trenton to Oxford Valley Mall, Langhorne, PA. Turn right at New Oxford Valley Road just before Mall.
TELEPHONE: 215-757-1100 / www.sesameplace.com

MOUNTAIN CREEK

In the old days *Action Park* was a thrill-seeking park that appealed to teenagers and young adults. It was transformed into Mountain Creek a few years ago and the new owners tried for a family-oriented park. Now they're back to action again. The "dry" side of the park emphasizes extreme sports. You have mountain biking and trails that wind down the steep and craggy terrain. There are thirty trails (this place is a ski area in winter) and bikers can ride the eight-person gondola up the mountain to get to the top. You can also play extreme golf from up there also. A 12,000 square-foot skate park for rollerbladers and lots of ramps and demi-ramps for skateboards makes this a popular place for followers of those sports.

As for *Water World*, here again, the more adventurous rides are emphasized, although there are moderate rides such as a lazy river jaunt and a special kids area. A 99-foot-high waterslide (with a new name) beckons the adventurous. Some water slides are built up against the mountain. There are rubber tube rides that twist and turn, straight slides that jackknife you into the water, closed chute rides, and a Tarzan water hole where you just jump in from a swinging rope. The tidal wave pool is comparatively tame except when it gets overcrowded, and there's a new beach club above it for sunset drinks.

Courtesy Six Flags Hurricane Harbor

Waterparks, waterparks, everywhere. Above, a scene from the new Hurricane Harbor. Below, the curliqued waterslides at Runaway Rapids in Keansburg.

Photo By Barbara Hudgins

HOURS: Varies for waterpark and extreme sports. Call
ADMISSION: Water World: 48″ & above: $24.99;
Kids 36- 48″ & seniors: $14.99
DIRECTIONS: Route 80 to Route 23N to 94E for 4 miles
TELEPHONE: 973-827-2000 / www.mountaincreek.com

LAND OF MAKE BELIEVE

For years this was a simple, down home amusement park, set in rural Warren County, next to Jenny Jump State Park. It catered to children from 3 to 9 at a time when most parks were geared to teenagers. There were a few mechanical rides and a miniature train ride. Also such simple attractions as a talking Scarecrow, a haunted house with a few scary exhibits, and an old fashioned hayride

The park now is in its 47th year and the space encompasses thirty acres. Every year, Chris Maier, who took over from his father, adds new attractions. He has also expanded the age range to kids up to twelve. There are two sections: the waterpark side and the amusement ride side, but the place is small enough that you can easily do both sides within one day. And many of the dry rides are definitely for the younger kids.

The **Pirate's Cove** waterpark includes a lazy river ride and several mid-sized water-slides (including one that is partially covered). There is a giant wading pool for youngsters with a life-sized pirate ship in the middle. This one squirts water and has a simple slide. Parents can sit on lounge chairs around the pool. The river ride can be used by children and parents alike and it fairly mild. A new covered waterslide called The Black Hole is geared to older kids (you must be at least eight years old to use it). Lockers and changing rooms are available, but bathrooms can get crowded.

On the amusement park side there is a carousel, Frog-Hopper, Tilt-A-Whirl and a number of small kiddie rides. You will also find a petting zoo, picnic tables, hamburger and ice cream stands, concession stands, a small theater for play-acting and still a few simple attractions like the maze. Free parking.

HOURS:. Mid-June - Labor Day. 10-5; Sun.: 10-6.
Call for May, Sept. hours
ADMISSION: Adults: $12.50; Children 2-12: $15.50.
LOCATION: Route 80 to Exit 12. Two mi. south to Hope, Warren County.
Follow signs.
TELEPHONE: 908-459-5100 / www.lomb.com

WILD WEST CITY

This northern New Jersey version of a western "Dodge City" comes complete with marshal, cowboys, shootouts and a posse of kids. Run by the Stabile family for many years, it is still going strong. On a dusty street flanked by stores and a blacksmith shop, you can watch cowboys who twirl ropes and go through a series of trick lassoing. But the big deal of the day is when the bad guys are caught and the "deputized" kids get to help round them up.

For the last few years, the management has added more educational shows, such as frontier cooking, Native American dances, mountain men get-togethers and so forth. The Golden Nugget saloon offers food but there are also some simple shows inside. There are two other eateries, and the stores along the street sell real western goods plus plenty of tin guns.

You can take stagecoach ride down the main street and a miniature train ride (these cost extra). And don't be surprised if there's a hold-up on the way. You can also "pan" for gold and take a pony ride. Picnicking allowed.

> **HOURS:** mid-June – Labor Day-Daily: 10:30-6.
> Weekends, spring & fall
> **ADMISSION:** Adults: 7.50 ; Kids: 6.75
> **LOCATION:** I-80 to Route 206N,(Exit 25) Netcong, Sussex County.
> **TELEPHONE:** 973-347-8900 / www.wildwestcity.com

CLEMENTON PARK

Set on 40 acres about eight miles east of Camden, this amusement park has been operating for years now. Rides include an old-fashioned carousel and a large log flume for families. Several new rides such as the up-and-down Frog Hopper have been added. There is an interactive playport for kids, plus the traditional kiddie rides one finds in amusement parks such as the Kite Flyer. Larger rides, and ferris wheel available for older kids.

Splashworld, is a 13-acre waterpark alongside the amusement park, with separate entry or you can buy combination tickets. Splashworld includes a Pirate Ship set in a 10,000 square foot kiddie pool for the little ones, and a 700- foot enclosed chute waterslide called the Black Viper that appeals to older kids and the usual host of curling and straight slides. Changing rooms, showers and lockers available. Free parking.

HOURS;:   Mid-May -Late June: Weekends only, 12-8.
                July - Labor Day: Daily, except Monday, 12-10 PM.
ADMISSION: $22.65 combo or $15.95 each park.
LOCATION: 144 Berlin Road (Route 534) off Routes 30 or 42, Clementon,
                Camden County.
TELEPHONE: 856-783-0263 / www.clementonpark.com

BOARDWALK AMUSEMENTS

There are small arcades, video game rooms and miniature golf places at any number of Jersey shore resorts. However, you can find the larger amusement centers at the following towns. They are located on the beach. Don't always expect cleanliness or the best restroom facilities at these places. However, the larger amusement piers have become more sophisticated over the years. They have increased the size of their rides so there are now huge rollercoasters, full pirate ships and taller rides than ever. And on certain days they offer a set price for all rides if you buy for six hours.

Many boardwalks now offer waterparks that are as big as anything you'd find at a theme park (although they may be more compacted to save space.) What's more, they have plenty of lifeguards around. You'll find the lazy river ride for kids (and timid adults), slides that are partially enclosed (to give you a scarier feeling), slides with mats and slides where the only cushion on the water is your backside.

Boardwalk amusements differ from theme parks in another way. You pay per ride by buying tickets (or group or tickets). With the waterpark you usually buy a bracelet that allows you a certain number of hours of use.

KEANSBURG: An older area that is slowly being resurrected with new rides. The boardwalk runs about 4 or 5 blocks long and includes plenty of kiddie rides, plus adult rides, concessions and arcade. Keansburg doesn't have a real beach but it does have a fishing pier.

Across from the amusement area is the block-long waterpark called **Runaway Rapids.** Definitely gives class to the place with its large water chutes and slides. A high speed mat slide, and double wide slides for tubes make the 12-year-olds happy. A Lazy River ride, kiddie pool with giant bucket and lounge chairs for parents offer the less adventurous something to do. You buy bracelets for two or three hour sessions. Grandmas can buy a "dry" spectator bracelet at half price. Directions. G.S.P. to Exit 117, then Route 36. Open seasonally. *Telephone*: 800-805-4FUN / www.keansburgamusementpark.com

POINT PLEASANT: *Jenkinson's Amusements* at 300 Ocean Ave. dominates the boardwalk at the beach here. There are several blocks of rides, mostly mid-size, for both for kids and adults. A large cafeteria and fishing pier, *Jenkinson's Aquarium* (q.v.) plus an indoor arcade and miniature golf rounds out the picture. Less spectacular than some of the larger amusement areas, but the atmosphere is not as honkytonk. Special events such as fireworks and concerts. Directions. G.S.P. Exit 98S or 90N. *Telephone*: 732-892-0600 / www.Jenkinsons.com

SEASIDE HEIGHTS: New Jersey's version of Coney Island. One of the largest of the boardwalk amusement centers, with solid amusements and concessions along the boardwalk and at both the Fun & Casino piers. Many larger rides are here such as a big Ferris Wheel and the Pirate Ship besides the usual assortment of Trabants and Red Barons. **Water Works** is a complete condensed version of a waterpark on the square block opposite **Casino Pier** (800 Ocean Terr. *Telephone*: 732-793-6495). Everything from easy tube rides to the "adult" twisting waterslides. The indoor arcades, such as **Coin Castle** include a carousel, air hockey games and food- stands along with the usual Skeeball and machine games. Rides active even during the day. A popular teenage hangout. Weekly fireworks. Directions. G.S.P. Exit 82 to highway 37E. Go through Toms River to bridge, follow signs.

BEACH HAVEN: Catering to families vacationing on Long Beach Island is a small cluster of amusements. **Thundering Surf** - a combination of curliqued water slides and fancy miniature golf takes up one square block at 8th and Bay. At **Fantasy Island** a block away at 7th you can find a small carousel, kiddie rides, arcades, more golf, and an old-fashioned ice-cream parlor. *Telephone*: 609-492-4000.

ATLANTIC CITY: As mentioned in another chapter, **The Steel Pier,** directly across from Trump's Taj Mahal is open during the warm weather season. Coasters and Himalaya style rides, cotton candy and hot dogs and sporadic thrill shows (such as high wire walking) are available. However, since legislation now allows casinos to extend their operations onto the piers, there's no telling how long this will last Arcades can be found in most hotels and at a few spots on the boardwalk. *Telephone*: 609-345-4893.

OCEAN CITY: A giant Ferris Wheel dominates the skyline at **Gillian's Wonderland Pier** (Boardwalk & 6th). This amusement park has other adult rides such as a log flume, as well as an indoor area with monorail and kiddie rides for inclement weather. **Playland** (Boardwalk & 10th) offers arcade games and about 18 rides. And **Gillian's Island**

Water Park (Boardwalk at Plymouth Place; *Telephone*: 609-399-0483) offers a full waterpark (in condensed version) and lush miniature golf next door. The two-mile boardwalk here also includes a movie theater, karoake parlor, several restaurants and the usual beach stores and ice cream stands. The more sedate Music Pier provides popular concerts and shows for the family crowd here. There are a record number of miniature golf courses in this town.

WILDWOOD: The boardwalk stretches from North Wildwood through Wildwood itself and is several miles long. It includes games of chance, food stands, T-shirt and souvenir shops. A tram ride goes up and down the boardwalk for those who get tired. Start with Morey's Pier - (Boardwalk & 25th St, North Wildwood) at the northern end. It's the most visible because of the really high Condor Ride. The pier offers all sorts of other rides and amusements plus a complete water park **(Raging Waters)** tacked onto the end of the pier. This one includes a kid's area with dumping water bucket, a lazy river ride and all those turning, twisting slides. Parents can watch from an overview area. **Nickels Midway Pier** doesn't jut out into the ocean - it goes inward -just at the midway point of the boardwal. Castle Dracula and the roller coaster are standbys here.

Morey owns two other piers besides his namesake. There's the **Wild Wheels Pier** (Boardwalk & Spencer) with drive-your own rides like the dune buggy. **Mariner's Landing** (Boardwalk & Schellenger) includes a water park very similar to the one at Morey's Pier, with both teenage and kid's area slides and slopes. The awesome coiling Sea Serpent coaster, other thrill rides and kiddie rides are all packed onto the site here. *Telephone*: 609-522-3900. www.moreyspiers.com

OTHER AMUSEMENT PARKS

BOWCRAFT AMUSEMENT PARK : A small park set down plunk amidst the hurly-burly of Route 22 in urban Union County, now under new management. Includes a swing carousel, a miniature train ride, and several other kiddie rides. A mini-coaster and a frog-hopper are recent additions. An arcade keeps older kids busy and the 18-hole miniature golf engages the whole family. Fast food available. Free parking and it's pay per ride. Convenient for area people and you don't have to battle beach traffic to get there. Open warm weather. Call for hours. *Location*: Route 22, Scotch Plains, Union County. *Telephone*: 908-233-0675 / www.bowcraft.com

FAIRY TALE FOREST: Actually it's now called *Hot Diggity's Fairy Tale Forest* but it still looks like an old-fashioned style kiddie park set in a wooded area in northern Jersey reminiscent of the Black Forest. Molded Storybook characters, such as Goldilocks and the Three Bears, inhabit twenty little decorated houses where you can peek in. Carousel and fire engine ride ($1.00 extra). Picnicking allowed but *Hot Diggity's* indoor grill features food. Magician and other acts on weekend. Available for parties and special events. Gift store. Moderate admission fee. *Hours*: Tues.-Sun.: 11-5, summer season. Call for fall hours. *Location*: Route 23, Oak Ridge, Passaic County. *Telephone*: 973-697-5656 / www.fairytaleforest.com

THE GINGERBREAD CASTLE: This fanciful castle with its stone turret stone spiders, sculpture witches and Humpty-Dumpty was created in 1928 by a stage designer. Nowadays, guides costumed as Hansel and Gretel take kids through and put on small shows. It's for young kids. There is also a petting zoo. A small dinosaur park is for older siblings. *Hours*: late June—Labor Day: 10:30-5. Last cars let in at 3 p.m. *Admission*: $8.00/$7.00; under 2 free. *Location*: Route 80 to Route 23N to Hamburg, Sussex County. *Telephone*: 973-827-1617.

STORYBOOK LAND: A well-known children's park with small structures in the shape of The Gingerbread House, The Old Woman's Shoe, Noah's Ark, etc. The petting zoo, miniature train ride, antique car ride, and other attractions are included in the price. Some special events. Christmas light display in December. Picnic area, snack bar. Ten miles west of Atlantic City. *Hours*. Mid-May-early Sept.: 11-5:30. Shorter hours, spring & fall. Special Christmas hours. *Admission*: $12.25 + tax (under 1, free). *Location:* Routes 40 & 322, Black Horse Pike, Cardiff, Atlantic County. *Telephone:* 609-641-7847 / www.storybookland.com

CAMELBEACH WATERPARK: The Camelback Ski area in the Poconos becomes transformed in the summer into a good-sized waterpark. Their waterslide down the mountain called The Titan is eight stories tall and 819 feet long, a world's record, according to them. There are also lazy river tube rides, water slides, and even a swimming pool for grownups. Bumper boats, too. Picnicking allowed. Open during summer season. *Admission*: Adults: $21.95; Children & seniors: $17.95. *Location*: Tannersville, PA (off I-80). *Telephone*: 570-629-1661 / www.camelbeach.com

SHAWNEE PLACE: Children's "active play"park in style of Sesame Place, only much smaller. Convenient to Poconos area vacationers (it's at the Shawnee Ski Area). Includes simple water slides, playport, wading pool, plastic ball "swim", magic show. Pony rides and video games extra. Snack bar and evening restaurant. *Hours*: Mid-June—Labor Day: Daily, 10-5. Sept: weekends only. *Admission*: Participant & non-participant fees. *Location*: Off Rte. 209, Shawnee, Poconos, PA. *Telephone*: 570-421-7231.

ZOOS, AQUARIUMS, NATURE CENTERS, WILDLIFE REFUGES

Photo: Courtesy Six Flags/Wild Safari

143

In This Chapter You Will Find:

THE BRONX ZOO

While the smaller zoos of New Jersey are fine for younger children, once the kids have reached third grade it's time to take them to the largest urban zoo in America.There are still some of the old zoo houses here, but for the most part open sections allow the animals to roam free while visitors watch them from across moats. And *Jungle World*, an indoor home for tropical Asian wildlife, combines a natural habitat with controlled climate for the best of both worlds.

Since there are over 5 miles of terrain to cover and over 4,500 animals to see, it's a lot easier to take either the skyride or the monorail (or both) when they are in season. These may cost extra. The open sections are divided geographically as follows: *Wild Asia*: Open only in warm weather, it's a 40 -acre habitat where elephants, rhinos, deer and antelope roam free. Visitors view them from the glassed-in monorail, "The Bengali Express." *Africa*: Lions, gazelles, antelopes, zebras and gnus roam the grassy slopes. You can view them from surrounding walkways and bridges or from the slow moving Safari ride. There is also the Congo Gorilla Forest just for lowland gorillas and another compound for baboons. *South America*: a smaller section devoted to anteaters and such. There is a wildfowl pond nearby where you can enjoy the aquatic birds at their colorful best. *North America*: an extensive section that includes a walk-in Wolf Wood, polar bears, and lots of bison, bull elk and grizzly bears.

Special houses offer interesting treats. At *The World of Darkness*, there's a top-notch display of bats, owls, and other nocturnal animals. Special lights allow you to watch the racoons, porcupines and bush babies cavort on the forest floor. They think it's night because the zoo has reversed the light cycles. It's a world of strange creatures with glittering eyes. To top it all, there are special bat-flying demonstrations.

The World of Birds is housed in an ultra-modern concrete cylindrical building. Here you will find three floors of birds in a unique setting. Trees vault up the three stories while a variety of birds perch on the first second and third story branches. Other special houses include the Penguin, Aquatic Bird, the extensive Reptile House and the Zoo Center.

The Children's Zoo offers a host of fun things especially for kids under ten. Giant rope "spider webs" to climb, snail "shells" to ride in, and prairie dog burrows to explore turns this into an educational amusement park. Extra fee, but well worth it—you could spend almost an hour here alone.

If you don't bring a sandwich (and there are plenty of tables if you

145

do), there is a cafeteria open all year round. Warm weather opens the snack stands. Children under 17 must be accompanied by adult. Remember, many of the special sections require an extra fee.

HOURS: Daily: 10-5, Weekends: 10-5:30 PM. (Winter 10 AM - 4:30 PM.)
ADMISSION: Adults: $9.00; Children 2-12 and Seniors: $5.00. Wed. free. Parking fee.
LOCATION: Take George Washington Bridge to Cross Bronx Expressway East to Bronx River Parkway North. Take exit marked "Bronx Zoo".
TELEPHONE: 718-367-1010 / www.bronxzoo.org

THE SAFARI AT SIX FLAGS

The largest safari outside of Africa takes about an hour to drive through and covers six miles and six continents. Some animals, such as camels, elk in heat, jealous giraffes and short-tempered rhinos can get almost too close for comfort. The brochure warns that you should keep car windows closed at all times so take an air-conditioned car if you're visiting on a 90-degree day.

The road through the Safari is three lanes wide and you may travel at your own speed. Each area is separated from the other by wire fences so you must wait for the guards to open the gates between one habitat and another. Surprisingly, the warning signs to keep windows closed are apparent only in the dangerous cat sections. I noticed a number of cars with open windows and people who nuzzled deer and fed popcorn to camels. Camels, in fact, seem like the beggars here - they sidle up to the cars looking for handouts.

In the African Plains section you can watch herds of elephants eat and socialize. And nothing can make you feel smaller than to sit knee-high to a giraffe as he nudges up against your car. The animals have right-of-way here, so if you get in real trouble, honk for a Safari guard.

The Australian section is unique. Kangaroos, wallabies, wallaroos and the flightless emu strut, waddle and bound on the hilly terrain. The kangaroos are much smaller than I had imagined. They move about on all fours and since their front legs are so much shorter than those powerful hind-quarters, they look for all the world like lopsided dogs with giant tails. In another section, the Bengal tiger has its own Indian pavillion.

For those with metal-topped cars the ride through monkey territory is always of interest. These curious simians will scamper all over your car, check on the occupants, pull on the hood ornament, knock your grille-work and then pass on to the next car.

An air-conditioned bus ride through the whole park is an alternative to driving your own car, but it costs extra for each rider.

HOURS: Daily: 9-4 late June - mid-Sept.; weekends April, May
ADMISSION: Safari: $15.50. Combo: See Six Flags/Great Adventure entry.

THE PHILADELPHIA ZOO

This is America's oldest zoo and like the Bronx Zoo, it still has some old fashioned zoo houses alongside the many modern landscaped animal "habitats". The zoo has finally recovered from the devastating 1996 fire that destroyed many of its primates. The new **Primate Reserve** features lowland gorillas, orangutans, gibbons, lemurs and others in a lush habitat of 2.5 acres. There is also the **Carnivore Kingdom** which is a big draw with the rare white lion as one of its stars. And elephants and rhinos, giraffes and zebras are always on hand.

The zoo is well-known for its **Treehouse** - a special exhibit for children which allows kids to climb into a ficus tree, ride on a caterpillar and explore a river, a marsh, a meadow and other environmental features. One can smell the rainforest, hear the birds chirping, feel the skin of various animals and generally have a good time at this popular hands-on exhibit housed in a separate building.

Besides the lions, tigers, bears and hooved animals one would expect at a major zoo, you can also find Australia's gift to the world -kangaroos and wallabies, plus a *Rare Animal House* filled with some unusual varieties of monkeys and other species.

During summer a *"Birds of Prey"* show on an open stage has hawks, eagles and such demonstrate their prowess during free flight. Other features are a monorail ride around the premises, (extra fee), and a baby animal nursery where you can watch the newborns frolic. The zoo covers 42 acres, which makes it large, but not impossible to cover in one day. There are several nice picnic areas, plus two major eateries. It is inside the huge Fairmount Park which also includes many of Philadelphia's museums and historic houses.

HOURS: Weekdays: 9:30-5; Weekends: 9:30-6; Dec.-Feb.: 10-4.
ADMISSION: 12 & up: $10.00; Seniors, children 2-11: $8.00
LOCATION: 34th & Girard (Use Girard Ave. Exit of Route 76).
TELEPHONE: 215-243-1100 / www.phillyzoo.com

CAPE MAY COUNTY ZOO

Cape May County has poured a lot of money into this park and the landscape artists have been out in force to make this an attractive place. Various animal enclosures are arranged along meandering paths with pleasant foliage all about. Some of the enclosures simulate the natural terrain of the animals. Others, particularly those for the big cats, are the traditional cement floor cages. But the zoo is within a park filled with the tall scrub pine and sandy soil of the region, so the general effect is of seeing animals within a natural environment

Among the many species of animals here, you will find zebras, llamas tigers, jaguars, alligators, bears, spider monkeys and a lion. The white-maned tamarin was the most unusual specie I saw there. Quite a variety of birds are on hand , including cockatoos, toucans, a myna bird, peacocks, eagles and barnyard fowl.

This is one of the best looking zoos in New Jersey, with colorful plantings and bridges over ponds. It offers a complete African savannah where giraffes and oryx roam and visitors can watch from a shaded gazebo. Outside the zoo, a children's playground, a picnic area and a number of concession carts can be found. All in all, a very pleasant outing. Still free, but during tourist season, there's a man at the park entrance taking "donations". A few dollars should do it, and it's well worth it. Note: the parking lot gets really crowded on summer weekends!

> **HOURS:** Daily, 9-4:30 weather permitting
> **LOCATION:** Route 9 & Crest Haven Road, Cape May Court House.
> **TELEPHONE:** 609-465-5271 or 465-9210

TURTLE BACK ZOO

Twenty years ago, Turtle Back was probably the best zoo in northern New Jersey. There were seven hundred animals, and fanciful settings such as a large wedge of cheese to house rodents and a large piggy bank for the pigs. Well, a loss of funds plus a change in direction left this zoo in limbo. The cute settings were gone, the number of animals down, and the place needed a turn-around. In fact, the county was ready to close it down at one point

Now there are new walls and walkways and construction for some areas, but not too much in the animal department. The zoo has a new sea otter building and there's a prairie dog area in the plans. The Wolf Woods, which is a naturalistic exhibit for a lair is still popular. Penguins have taken over the old seal pond. The only reminder of its former glory is the peacock that struts freely around.

The miniature train that travels through the South Mountain Reservation is still around. The petting zoo, which is always popular with kids, returns each summer with goats, pigs and lambs. A few large cats such as cougars and bobcats can be found in cages. And of course there are always birds, turtles and deer.. But will this be enough to entice families to pay "New York" prices for a local zoo? Food and gift concessions, picnic area available.

HOURS: Mon. Sat: 10-4:30; Sunday: 10:30-5. Call for winter hours.
ADMISSION: Adults: $7.00; Children (2-12), seniors: $3.00. Under 2 free.
LOCATION: 560 Northfield Ave., West Orange (behind South Mountain Arena), Essex County.
TELEPHONE: 973-731-5800

STATEN ISLAND ZOO

This square-block, city zoo is of interest for three reasons: 1) it is convenient to those within easy driving distance of the Goethals Bridge, 2) it is primarily an indoor zoo, so it is available during the winter, 3) it is reasonable priced.

The big collection here is the snakes. Since snakes take up little room (experts assure us that snakes like those little glass cubicles where zoo-keepers put them), it is possible to crowd an amazing variety of them into one large zoo-house. The biggest rattlesnake collection in the world resides here, along with cobras, pythons, cottonmouths, a krait, and asps. Since reptiles are not very active you may find two - or is it three, or one? - pythons curled around one another with head and tail indistinguishable. At the end of the room a family of alligators remind you there's more to the reptile class than just snakes.

The zoo is unusual in that it also sports a small aquarium. Coral fish, sea anemones, and piranhas are among the colorful and dangerous fish floating behind glass. There are even a few small sharks. The biggest exhibit is the African Savannah with its leopards, baboons, lizards and rock hydrax - an ambitious undertaking. And a separate Tropical Forest includes roomy homes for monkeys and tamarins.

A pleasant children's center includes a farm and petting zoo with lambs, pigs, oxen, geese and other animals who nibble rye krisp through the fencing. Altogether, a pretty place with trees, benches, picnic tables and snack bar.

HOURS: 10-4:45 Daily. Closed major holidays.
ADMISSION: Adults: $3.00; Children & Seniors: $2.00;
Wednesday afternoon: Donation.
LOCATION: 614 Broadway, Staten Island, Take 278 E to Slossen Ave.,
Exit. left on Slossen then right on Martling.
TELEPHONE: 718-442-3100

SPACE FARMS ZOO

A private zoo, (in itself an endangered species) in a rural area that closely approximates the natural surroundings of many of the animals housed there. The trip takes you well into the mountains of northern Sussex County, past farms and horses grazing peacefully among the green hills. The family name here is Space and yes, it was a farm before it became a zoo. The granddaughter of the original owner has a degree in animal biology

The zoo is set up for family outings with many picnic tables, swing sets and slides for the youngsters. One hundred acres are devoted to rather simple cages of bears, lions, tigers, hyenas, monkeys, etc. plus several buildings filled with antique cars, sleighs and other collections. A large pond at the center of the acreage allows ducks and geese to paddle about while pens of yak, llamas, buffalo and goats dot the surrounding hills—altogether 500 animals. There is a separate den for snakes and plenty walking around the acreage

The entrance building to the property includes a *Museum of Americana* (everything from Indian arrowheads to old clocks), a snack shop and a gift shop. And on the hills to the left of the zoo there are more museums with collections of old buggies, cars, sleighs, tractors, dolls, and everything but the kitchen sink. Between the animals, the museums, the swings and the slides you can make a day of it. Picnic lunches allowed.

HOURS: Daily 9-5, May 1 - Oct 31.
ADMISSION: Adults: $8.95; Children 3-12: $4.50 plus tax.
LOCATION: 218 Rte. 519, Beemerville, Sussex County.
TELEPHONE: 973-875-5800 / www.spacefarms.com

Photo by Laszlo Vasko

Goliath is still a star at Space Farms Zoo.

OTHER SMALL ZOOS (NJ)

There are a number of other zoos tucked away in local city and county parks that are pleasant to visit when you are in the vicinity. Among them are:

BERGEN COUNTY ZOO: A popular zoo in Van Saun Park which features a 1890's Farm with domestic animals, a miniature train ride, some large cats including a mountain lion in a "landscaped" setting and a large aviary. Many hooved animals such as elk and bison and exotic species such as the golden tamarind are on display. There are 200 animals here—and all set in a park with lots of picnic tables and a duck pond. Admission fee ($2.00) on summer weekends only. *Location:* Forest Ave. (off Route 4) River Edge. *Telephone:* 201-262-3771.

COHANSIC PARK: Good sized city zoo set inside an 1100 acre park that borders the river in Bridgeton. Over 200 animals including lion, bears, wolves and zebras. You can find leopards, a tiger, alligators and some unusual species—many in a new setting. The park also includes picnic areas, nature trails, lots more.Free. *Location:* City Park, Bridgeton (routes 49 and 77) Cumberland County. *Telephone.* 609-455-3230.

POPCORN PARK A 7-acre licensed zoo that caters strictly to injured, abandoned and unwanted wildlife. One section houses rescued animals such as lions, tigers and llamas, another includes the kennels of abandoned pets waiting for adoption. The facility is run by the Associated Humane Society. Small admission fee. *Hours:* Daily 11-5. *Location:* Humane Way and Lacey Road, Forked River, Ocean County. *Telephone:* 609-693-1900.

THE RAPTOR TRUST: Okay, it's not a zoo, it's a wildlife shelter for wounded birds, primarily birds of prey such as owls, hawks and falcons, but the unreleasable ones are kept in aviaries so you can look. Run by a non-profit organization which also gives talks to school groups. Brochures available at parking lot. *Hours.* Reasonable daytime (call first). *Admission:* By donation. *Location:* 1452 White Bridge Road, Long Hill Twp. (a mile beyond Somerset Environmental Education Center,in the Great Swamp). *Telephone.* 908-647-2353.

LAKOTA WOLF PRESERVE: At Camp Taylor in Columbia Township way out in Warren County. Home to two dozen wolves, wolf pups, bobcats and foxes. Photographers and other interested persons are invited to spend a few hours at the preserve. Call for information and prices. *Location:* 85 Mt. Pleasant Rd., Columbia. *Telephone:* 908-496-4533

NEW JERSEY STATE AQUARIUM

What do you do when you want to jazz up an aquarium with lagging sales? How about adding a gaggle of penguins? How about teaching your harbor seals some learning behaviors? How about sprucing up the place by adding a children's garden right in front of the building. They've done all that, and really freshened up the place.(For the *Camden Children's Garden* check the listing in the Gardens chapter).

Although there's more to see and do outside now, inside the huge Aquarium building there's a concentration on sharks as a point of interest. When you enter there is now a set of Megalodon Jaws featuring 275 fossilized teeth from some earlier monster-size shark facing you. Smaller varieties such as the tiger and hammerhead are popular denizens of the huge 760,000 gallon Open Ocean tank that dominates the building.

Upstairs a new exhibit replaces the long-running Weird and Wonderful fish. This one is called COOL and concentrates on South American fish and even tropical birds. Plenty of colorful and peculiar species here.And there are permanent exhibits of coral reefs and submarine paraphenalia and of course a touch tank.

If you get hungry and don't plan to picnic in the Children's Garden, the cafeteria on the first floor offers fast food. The outdoor deck here has a nice view of Philadelphia across the river. There is also a little coffee stand, and of course, a large gift shop filled with stuffed animal versions of whales and penguins.

Outside, the are several permanent exhibits. A cutaway of a rushing trout stream offers a view of the native fish. At the "Seal Shores" section, bleacher seats allow the audience to watch harbor and grey seals go through "learning behaviors" Since there are no whales or performing dolphins here, these short-flippered seals have to take on such audience-pleasing chores as catching frisbees and rings.

Meanwhile the penguin area, *Inguiza Island,* feature the small-sized African birds known as "Blackfooted Penguins". Their exhibit pool has a beach, rocks, and both an underwater and above-water viewing area where you can watch the birds torpedo through the water.

HOURS:	Apr.-Sept.: 9:30-5:30. Shorter winter hours
ADMISSION:	Adults: $12.95; Seniors and students: 11.45; children 3-11: $9.95; 2 and under free.
LOCATION:	3 Riverside Drive, Camden, near the Entertainment Centre. Parking Garage across street ($5.00 for 3 hours)
TELEPHONE:	856-365-3300 / www.njaquarium.org

AQUARIUM FOR WILDLIFE CONSERVATION

It used to be called *The New York Aquarium* and it's in Brooklyn, so now, with the new name you should be thoroughly confused. But you can get there by taking the Verranzano Bridge and it's within easy driving distance for those near Staten Island. Since the aquarium is right smack in the middle of Coney Island, many people prefer visiting in the spring or fall to avoid getting caught up in the hurly burly of boardwalk amusements.

This concrete aquarium is home to whales, sharks, seals, penguins and a variety of tropical fish. The whales swim around lazily in the big tank - what you see is mostly their underbellies, and the sharks, most of which are rather small, have a building all to themselves. For many, its the yellow tangs and other strange and beautiful denizens of the deep in a fancy new environment that make a trip to the aquarium worthwhile.

In warm weather a training show takes place in an outside arena. A dolphin jumps up and learns to take a fish from the trainer. In this age of sensibilities to dolphin rights, it's rare to see such a show. There are sea lions in summer also.

For northern New Jerseyans this is the only decent-sized aquarium within easy driving distance. Although it's on the small side, it does have real whales and real sharks and an area where children can handle starfish and other creatures of the sea.

The Sea Cliffs exhibition which include both indoor and outdoor sections have lavish displays for penguins, walruses and other aquatic creatures. There is a souvenir stand , a cafeteria, and a nice view of the beach and ocean. No children under 16 unless accompanied by an adult

HOURS: 10-4:45 daily. 10-6 weekends. Shorter winter hours.
ADMISSION: Adults: $9.75; Children & Seniors: $6.00. Under 2 free.
LOCATION: W. 8th Street & Surf Ave., Brooklyn. take the Verranzano Bridge to the Belt Parkway (direction of JFK Airport) and stay on until 8th Street exit. There is a sign for the Aquarium. Parking fee.
TELEPHONE: 718-265-3474

PEQUEST TROUT HATCHERY

This sparkling modern concrete building complex has three purposes. One is to raise the trout that are later thrown into the state park lakes to become some lucky fisherman's catch. The second is to introduce youngsters to proper fishing techniques and to educate them in wildlife conservation. The third is to manage this huge acreage and the wildlife that lives therein (including the birds whose chirping is amplified in the main building).

The Visitor Center includes a large room with many hands-on exhibits. There are also charts, displays, and a tankful of adult trout so that even those who do not fish can get a look at these ugly fellows. In another room a continuous movie shows how the fish are bred, fed and finally transported by truck to be dumped in fresh water streams. Finally you can go outside to see the ponds where the young fish are. A look into a glass sided building will allow you to see the tiny fingerlings.

This is a popular place for school and scout groups, because during a group tour the kids often get to wield a fishing rod. There are also special Saturday classes on fishing techniques. You can buy fishing and hunting permits here plus the special trout stamps which help to fund this state center. Free.

HOURS: Daily 10-4.
LOCATION: 605 Pequest Road, Oxford, Warren County (off Rte 46).
TELEPHONE: 908-637-4125

SHORE AQUARIUMS

There are a number good-size aquariums along the Jersey shore. A popular one at Point Pleasant Beach is **Jenkinson's Aquarium,** on the boardwalk near Ocean Avenue about a block north of the amusement rides. It is roomier than you would expect inside, and it includes tanks of small sharks and rays, a penguin area, an alligator pit and some hard working seals. Centerpiece is the sunken ship, *The Bounty*, with freshwater tropicals around it. Coral reef fish and colorful parrots are here also and you can walk around the center to get a view from all sides. Open summer and winter. Admission fee. *Telephone: 732-899-1212.*

Atlantic City once had an aquarium on the boardwalk—now it has one again over at Historic Gardner's Basin. Only this one is much larger and environmentally friendly than the old dinky tanks at Central Pier.

Ocean Life Center is a new multi-million aquarium that is meant to anchor the maritime park (which also sports two restaurants and excursion boats). The aquarium has some large tanks of fish, both tropical and local. It also shows a diving suit, the wheel of a boat and lots of explanations about barrier reefs, and life along the sea along with 17 computer stations. There is a nice open deck on the upper floor where you can walk out and watch the boats. The jitney now stops at Historic Gardener's Basin (at least in warm weather) so you can visit from the boardwalk. Admission fee. *Location*: 800 N. New Hampshire Ave. Atlantic City. *Telephone*: 609-348-4002.

Just north of Atlantic City you can visit the **Marine Mammal Stranding Center** in the beach town of Brigantine. This center is devised mainly as a rescue outfit but don't expect to find any dolphins or whales here. The garage-sized pool isn't large enough to hold them. You may find harbor seals or turtles. However the visitor center contains a really large fish tank where you can peer through a magnifying glass, exhibits on conservation and a gift shop filled with T-shirts and educational stuff. *Location*: 3625 Brigantine Blvd. (on the curve of the circle), Brigantine. *Telephone*: 609-266-0538

Wildlife Refuges / Nature Centers

HACKENSACK MEADOWLANDS DCEC

That title is short for *The Hackensack Meadowlands Development Commission Environment Center,* which boasts a modern circular building which sits out in the center of the urban salt marsh it overlooks. It is part of the larger Richard W. de Korte Park. In the distance trucks and cars whiz by on the Turnpike. The place has plenty of pontoon walkways into the marshlands, where you can spot ducks, egrets and the omnipresent Canada goose. They even have canoe trips out here.

But the Center is best known for the **Trash Museum** which occupies several rooms inside the building. Did you know that 23,000 tons of newspapers are discarded each day? That enough aluminum cans are jettisoned to build 30 jet planes? These are some of the facts you learn in this interesting museum which is set up to appeal to children. Colorful

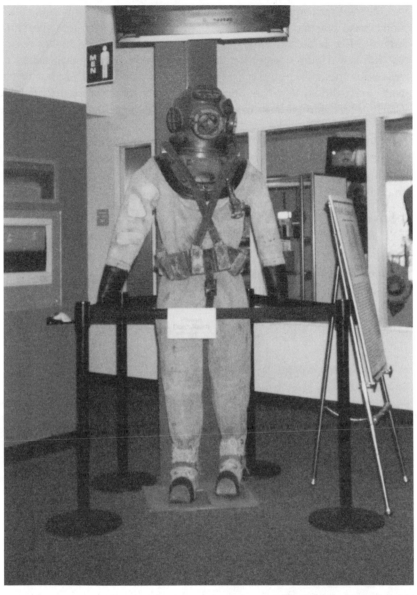

Photo by Barbara Hudgins

The new Ocean Life Center in Atlantic City features marine lore as well as fish tanks.

cartoon characters guide visitors through a maze of exhibits which include real garbage-everything from Burger King throwaways, glass bottles, and plastic containers to rubber tires. There are interactive buttons, life-size games and overhead audios and videos to make things fun. If this museum doesn't shame you into recycling, nothing will!

Besides the museum, the Center offers a wide circular room (often used for birthday parties) with views of the surrounding open marshland and the Manhattan skyline beyond. An outside deck allows closer inspection. The main lobby showcases a 30 x 7 foot diorama of a salt marsh and its inhabitants. A gift shop offers stuffed animal toys and environmentally correct merchandise. May be under reconstruction. Many school programs.

> **HOURS:** Weekdays: 9-5. Weekends: 10-3.
> **ADMISSION:** Adults: $2.00. Under 12, free.
> **LOCATION:** 2 De Korte Park Plaza, Lyndhurst Bergen County.
> From NJ Tpke, take Route 17S, left on Polito Ave., left on Valley Brook Ave., then 2 miles.
> **TELEPHONE:** 201-460-8300

THE GREAT SWAMP

The remains of a glacial pocket, the Swamp serves as both a refuge for animals and a 5,800-acre barrier to suburban development. It was saved some years ago from the fate of airport development by a group of conservationists and donated to the Federal Government which now administers it. The area is a combination of marshes, grassland, swamp woodland and hardwood ridges. There are some stands of mountain laurel and rhododendron but a botanical wonderland it's not.

Actually, there are sections that look like a great locale for a movie called "The Creature From the Black Lagoon." Tall, leafless trees, crackling twigs, swampy underbrush - well, it's a swamp after all. Not smelly like the Okefenokee, and not deep, but still a swamp. Wooden boardwalks have been built in several observation areas so that families can traverse the wetlands and observe whatever wildlife is around. Mostly it's small - woodchucks, muskrats, frogs - and there are deer and fox, too, though they tend to stay in the interior. There are blinds for picture taking. Swamp officials recommend visits in the early morning or late afternoon.

The Swamp consists of two-thirds wilderness and one-third management area. There are several hiking trails in dry areas but picnicking is verboten. Observation centers in Basking Ridge and Chatham Twp. Old sneakers or waterproof shoes are recommended. Insect repellent in the evening. Free.

> **HOURS:** Dawn until dusk.
> **LOCATION:** Headquarters at Point Pleasant Road, Basking Ridge.
> **TELEPHONE:** 973-635-6629; 973-425-1222

EDWIN B. FORSYTHE REFUGE

Well, actually it's **The Brigantine Division** of the **Edwin B. Forsythe National Wildlife Refuge** and believe it or not, Mr. Forsythe has several other wildlife areas named after him (which confuses mapmakers enormously). However, this is the place that attracts the bird watchers, the photographers and the naturalists. Only eleven miles from Atlantic City but it's a world of immense quiet and peace. There are over 20,000 acres of grassy tidal marsh interspersed with tidal bays and channels with some brush upland area that support deer, fox and other small animals here. But the main area of the refuge is for the protection of waterfowl that use the Atlantic Flyway in their travels from Canada to Florida. Many birds (up to 150,000) winter completely in New Jersey now.

The snow goose, Canada goose, brant and black duck are among the many birds who stop here. The refuge offers a calendar of wildlife events - eg., November 1-10: 100,000 ducks, geese and brant; June 20th: Canada goose round-up.

A self-guided tour of eight miles by car or foot circuits the waterfowl impoundments. Hundreds of birds are here no matter what time of year you visit The vistas are flat and beyond the muddy marshes where the birds feed you can see the towers of Atlantic City. There are places where you can stop your car to take pictures (and even eat lunch, they say) but the insect population is heavy here also. The Noyes Museum (q.v.) is just before the entrance. There is a fee for cars during summer months.

> **HOURS:** Daylight except during hazardous conditions.
> **LOCATION:** U.S. 9, one mile east of Oceanville, Atlantic County.
> **TELEPHONE:** 609-652-1665

WETLANDS INSTITUTE

Set in the middle of 6000 acres of publicly owned salt marsh, not far from the beach at Stone harbor, this attractive cedar shake building includes classrooms, an exhibit hall and six research laboratories. There is a large separate room which houses a touch museum for children and other exhibits. A salt-water aquarium and a large book and gift ship are also on hand. There is also an observation tower which provides a view of the surrounding wetlands (and an osprey nest). Periodic guided tours of the marsh, plus a number of lectures and ecology classes are available. Of course, individuals can use the boardwalk trail anytime during visiting hours.

Once a year the institute operates the *"Wings 'N Water Festival"* a popular weekend fest in September that includes special events in all the local towns. Wooden duck carving, seafood dinners, and open houses are included.

> **HOURS:** Tues.-Sat.: 9:30-4:30.
> **ADMISSION:** Adults: $5.00; Children: $2.00.
> **LOCATION:** 1075 Stone Harbor Blvd., Stone Harbor, Cape May County.
> **TELEPHONE:** 609-368-1211

Note: The nearby **Stone Harbor Bird Sanctuary** (a 21-acre tract dedicated to nesting herons and egrets) is located on 3rd Ave. between 111th and 116th streets in Stone Harbor. However, very few birds have appeared in the last few years and the pay binoculars have disappeared.

OTHER NATURE CENTERS

FLAT ROCK BROOK NATURE CENTER: 443 Van Nostrand Ave., Englewood, Bergen County. *Telephone:* 201-567-1265. Solar-heated building, 150 acres of forest with trails, brook. Various weekend activities, tree identification, classes for schoolchildren, local artists' show. Run by self-supporting environmental organization. Open daily.

JAMES A. McFAUL ENVIRONMENTAL CENTER: Crescent *Ave.* Wyckoff. *Telephone:* 201-891-5571. Run by Bergen County, this well stocked center includes snakes, turtles and other small animals, a waterfowl pond, nature trail and garden. Films and slide shows plus museum programs inside. Open daily except for legal holidays.

TRAILSIDE NATURE CENTER: Coles Ave. & New Providence Road, Mountainside, Union County. *Telephone:* 908-789-3670. Part of Watchung Reservation. Modern building includes auditorium and a whole museum display of stuffed animals, beehives, eggshells, arrowheads, etc. Weekend programs, nature walks. Separate planetarium also.

GREAT SWAMP OUTDOOR EDUCATION CENTER: 247 Southern Blvd., Chatham Twp., Morris County. *Telephone:* 973-635-6629. On one edge of the swamp and run by the county. Wooden building contains exhibits, library, classrooms. Nature trails, guided walks, wooden walkways into the swamp, special programs such as maple-sugaring.

SOMERSET COUNTY PARK ENVIRONMENTAL EDUCATION CENTER: 190 Lord Stirling Park, Basking Ridge. *Telephone:* 908-766-2489. At the other edge of the Great Swamp. Modern solar building with classrooms, displays, separate solar-heated house, 8 _ miles of trails and wooden walkways. Bird-watching, guided hikes, cross country skiing, nature programs.

STONY BROOK NATURE CENTER: 31 Titus Mill Road, Pennington. *Telephone.* 609-737-3735. A Discovery Room with nature exhibits make this Mercer County site popular with families.

MERRILL CREEK RESERVOIR ENVIRONMENTAL PRESERVE: 116G Montana Rd., Washington Twp., Warren County. *Telephone:* 908-454-1213. Hiking, wildlife observation and photography of 290 acre preserve. Visitor center with hands-on exhibits. Timber trail, stocked reservoir. Hours: Daily.

PORICY PARK NATURE CENTER: Oak Hill Road, Middletown Twp., Monmouth County. *Telephone:* 732-842-5966. 250 acres of land with trails. Fossil bed in park, fossil walks. Museum has art and nature displays, art programs, school programs. Run by the township, this center boasts a modem building with nature displays and art programs and a separate colonial farmhouse that is open by appointment All this, plus clay fossil beds which can be found in a stream just a short drive away.

SPERMACETI COVE VISITORS CENTER: Sandy Hook. Gateway National Recreation Area, Highlands, Monmouth County, off Route 36. *Telephone:* 732-872-0092. Summer activities include canoe trips and dune walk. Center has slide show, exhibits, bookstore. Year round weekend activities: holly forest walks and passes for lighthouse tours and Fort Hancock. Classes by reservation.

NEW JERSEY AUDUBON SOCIETY

The Society operates a number of centers, wildlife sanctuaries and bird observatories throughout the state. Here you might find art shows, gift shops chock full of books and binoculars, libraries, sample backyards with lots of birdhouses and trail maps for the surrounding fields or forests.

Scherman-Hoffman Sanctuaries at 11 Hardscrabble Road, Bernardsville (off Childs Road-take Exit 30B from Route 287). Currently the headquarters for the Society, the site is a combination of two former estates on the Bernardsville mountain. The Sanctuary runs programs such as nighttime or morning rambles, van trips and art shows, school programs, etc. Lots of mountain trails for the individual. There is also a nice nature center inside plus a well-stocked gift shop. (Tel. 908-766-5787). Other centers are:

Lorrimer Sanctuary, 790 Ewing Ave. Franklin Lakes, has a living museum and demonstration farm, besides nature programs and field trips. Lots of bird-watching. (Tel. 201-891-1211)

Weis Ecology Center, Snake Den Road, Ringwood is a small center at the edge of Norvin Green State Park. Trail guides available for hikers. (Tel. 201-835-2160).

Owl Haven lies within Monmouth Battlefield State Park and bird watchers use it as their headquarters. It's on Englishtown-Freehold Road in Tennent. (Tel. 732-780-7007).

Rancocas Nature Center, 794 Rancocas Road, Mt Holly in Burlington County is a favorite for bird watchers. It covers about 120 acres at the edge of the state park and has nature displays inside. (Tel. 609-261-2495)

The Cape May Bird Observatory 707 East Lake Drive Cape May Point (Tel. 609-884-2736) is famous for its early May Cape May Weekend when millions of birds can be tracked. **The Nature Center of Cape May** at 1600 Delaware Ave. is right in the town of Cape May (Tel. 609-884-9590). The newer **Cape May Research Center** is at 600 Route 47 near Goshen in the middle of the county. This is a 6000 square foot building which boasts lecture rooms, a large gift shop, a model backyard habitat and much educational activity. (Tel. 609-861-0700)

Note: Many other nature centers are to be found inside of state parks. Check the state and county parks listing at the end of *The Outdoor Life* chapter.

THE OUTDOOR LIFE

Photo - Courtesy NJ Travel & Tourism

In This Chapter You Will Find:

Ski Areas
    New Jersey Ski Areas
    The Poconos Ski Area
    New York State Ski Areas

The Jersey Shore
    The Upper Shore
    Long Beach Island
    The Cape

Hiking, NJ
Fishing, NJ
Camping, NJ
Pick-Your-Own Orchards, NJ
Adventurous Outings, NJ
State Parks and Forests, NJ
County Parks, NJ

SKI AREAS

Since there have been warm winters for the last few years, many ski areas have closed and others have limited operations. Not all trails or facilities may be available. Please call first.

New Jersey Ski Areas

MOUNTAIN CREEK: The new name for the old Vernon Valley ski center which incorporated Great Gorge. By far the largest ski area in New Jersey. Ski instruction is available at all levels. Night-skiing and half-day tickets available.Gondola and chairlifts. Two mountains, 46 trails, ski rentals. Cafeteria and bar at base lodges. Vertical drop of 1033 feet. Two half-pipes for snowboarding. Snowtubing. *Location*: Rte. 23 to Rte. 94E near McAfee, Sussex County. *Telephone:* 973-827-2000 - for general information. 973-827-3900 827-3900 ski report. www.mountaincreek.com

HIDDEN VALLEY: Once partially private, now a public ski area with day, twilight and night time skiing. 6 slopes, variety of trails, 620 foot vertical drop. Ski lessons plus separate racing program. Cafeteria, bar, lodge entertainment. *Location*: Breakneck Road, Vernon Twp., Sussex County, *Telephone*: 973-764-4200

BELLE MOUNTAIN (Mercer County): One chairlift, three rope tows, four ski trails including one intermediate 190 ft. vertical drop. Open evenings during the week and weekends (when it snows). Lighted for nighttime skiing. Lessons, snack bar, beginner packages. Snowboarding. *Location:* Valley Road (off Route 29), Hopewell. *Telephone*: 609-397-0043

CAMPGAW MOUNTAIN (Bergen County): For beginners and intermediates. 100% snowmaking equipment. Main slope and two learning slopes, 5 lifts/tows, vertical drop of 300 feet Lighted for night skiing, cafeteria in lodge. Lessons Snowtubing. *Location:* Campgaw Road, Mahwah. *Telephone*: 201-327-7800.

Note: Cross-country skiing is available at most state parks in New Jersey and many county parks.

The Poconos Ski Areas

SHAWNEE MOUNTAIN: Close by— Shawnee offers, nine lifts, 23 trails, snowmakers, ski school, accessory rental, cafeteria, bar and nursery. Trails include cross-country. Day, night and twilight skiing. Snowboarding, snowtubing. Family packages. *Location:* Take Route 80 to exit 52, then north on 209 for six miles. *Telephone*: 570-421-7231.www.shawneemt.com

JACK FROST/BIG BOULDER: You buy a combination ticket for these two popular mountains. Each mountain has seven lifts, two J-bars and many trails that run the gamut from "Powderpuff' to Thunderbolt." Rentals, ski school, restaurant cafeteria, nursery. There are 11 slopes at Big Boulder, 19 at Jack Frost. Snowtubing, half-pipe.Location:Lake Harmony and White Haven, Pennsylvania. Rte. 80 Exit 42 or 43.*Telephone* :570-443-8425; 800-468-2442. www.big2resorts.com

CAMELBACK: About a half-hour further on and part of the Big Pocono State Park, Camelback offers a variety of trails and attracts a pleasant crowd. 33 trails, 13 lifts. This 2,100 ft. mountain is the largest in the area. Two base lodges. Snowboarding, snowtubing. *Location*: Tannersville, Pa. I- 80 Exit 45. *Telephone*: 570-629-1661. www.skicamelback.com

New York State Ski Areas

HUNTER MOUNTAIN: For ski groups and more advanced skiers, Hunter is very popular. A goodly drive away, but the mountain here offers a 1,600 foot vertical drop and a large variety of trails on three different mountains for beginners, intermediates and those who really want to hone their skills. Ten chairlifts, one tow, 53 trails, all services available. Variety of eateries. Snowboard park and instruction. *Location*: Garden State Parkway to New York Thruway, then Exit 20 to Route 32 for 19 miles. *Telephone*: 518-263-4223/ 800-FOR-SNOW. www.huntermtn.com

SKI WINDHAM: 7 miles west of Hunter. Two peaks, 33 trails, 7 lifts. Includes restaurant, cafeteria, ski school, nursery. Snowboard park, snowtubing. Weekend nighttime hours (til 10 p.m.) *Location*: Windham, NY (take NYS Thruway to Exit 21). *Telephone*: 518-734-4300. www.skiwindham.com

STERLING FOREST SKI AREA: Really close at hand, in fact it is right over the border in Tuxedo. Once the site of a popular garden, this ski area now services families and is pleasant for beginners and intermediates. Four double chairlifts, seven trails, 400 ft. vertical drop. Cafeteria, warming hut, lessons, rentals and snowmakers. Snowboarding. *Location*: Route 17 north to 17A north, just above Tuxedo, New York .*Telephone*: 914-351-2163.

Note: Unless otherwise noted, snowmaking is available at all ski areas. Number of trails (and trails available) change all the time. The number of chairlifts may be upgraded from one season to the next. It is always best to call first. Typical price for adult day ticket is $45.00.

THE JERSEY SHORE

There are 127 miles of beach along the coast of New Jersey which offer swimming, boating and fishing. But for most people going to the shore means visiting one particular portion of that lengthy coastline. Here's a roundup of the various types of shore resorts that await the newcomer or oldtimer.

First of all, the beaches. Some are narrow, some are wide but few are free. Sandy Hook (run by U.S. Park Service) charges a parking fee during season, but can become crowded nevertheless. Atlantic City and the beaches of the Wildwoods are free. Island Beach State Park (State run) charges a per-car admission. Most other beaches require beach badges (which you buy from a man sitting there selling them), or admission through a private bathhouse. The price of badges varies depending on whether you buy per day, week or season. If you stay at a hotel which owns its own beachfront, you don't have to bother with all this. Guest houses and motels usually provide beach tags to clients. And then there are a few select beaches which are accessible to residents only.

Cottage and beach house rentals vary according to size, closeness to beach and the social status of the town. Guest houses remain the cheapest accommodation especially if you don't mind walking a few blocks to the beach. Bed and Breakfasts, their rich cousins, actually charge more than motels. Most motels offer efficiency apartments for those who want to cook in. Motel rates compare well to other beach areas along the

Atlantic Coast. Major amusement areas are found at Point Pleasant, Ocean City, Seaside Heights, and Wildwood. (See chapter on Amusement Parks.) Otherwise, there are arcades and minature golf in close proximity to beachgoers, even in towns where boardwalks are non-commercial.

The Upper Shore:

Sandy Hook to Island Beach State Park

The closest and most accessible to the crowded urban and suburban areas of northern New Jersey, the upper shore is naturally very popular for daytime and weekend trips as well as the two-week vacation. **Sandy Hook** beach is part of the Gateway National Park and is run by the Department of the Interior. The beach is free but there are parking fees mid-June to Labor Day (up to $8 a car for weekends). Besides the several beaches, Sandy Hook offers the oldest lighthouse in the U.S., a nature center, a visitor's center, tours of Fort Hancock and surf fishing.

Below Sandy Hook there begins a string of beachfront communities, each with a slightly different personality. Some, like **Belmar** and **Manasquan,** cater to a young, singles crowd who share cottages and guest houses. (Although Belmar has cracked down on "groupers"). Others, like Deal, are quiet and rich and interested primarily in full-time residents and full-summer rentals. (It does have one admission-fee beach though.) **Avon,** with its lovely hotels looks like a "beach painting," and has a pleasant non-tacky boardwalk. **Long Branch** has a Spa-hotel and a public beach called Seven Presidents Park (there's an admission fee, here also). Otherwise it's rather unprepossessing. You can find **Spring Lake** with its turreted late-Victorian homes and little old lady customers plus a good smattering of singles. The late-night scene is often more important at some of the singles beach resorts, than is the beach.

Asbury Park is an older resort with a rundown look. It is best known for its rock clubs, including the Stone Pony, where Bruce Springsteen began. The boardwalk is practically deserted although there is always talk of a renaissance. Separated from Asbury by a canal, **Ocean Grove** is quiet, reserved and primly Victorian, with a well-known auditorium. The stick style houses here remain from the early camp meeting days and are popular now with yuppies (or whatever yuppies are called nowadays).

Further on, are **Brielle** and **Point Pleasant,** towns with a large fishing fleet and large residential areas including an increasing number of condos. Summer rentals, popular amusements and several marinas keep this area bustling. Lots of seafood restaurants here, also. Point Pleasant has a classical concert on summer Wednesday nights and fireworks on certain nights too.

A bit down the strip, comes more reasonable rentals. At **Seaside Heights** and **Seaside Park** there are over 1200 cottages, many of them minimal comfort types with just two rooms and a couple of screened windows. Hundreds of guest houses and almost 100 motels service the many vacationers who come to this popular area, with its large amusement center. Neighboring *Island Beach State Park* with its beach and nature area gets the daytime visitors. Parking at this popular public beach runs $7 on weekends, $6 on weekdays.

Long Beach Island

For many middle executive families the place to go is Long Beach Island only an hour and a half away from North Jersey's affluent suburbs. A long, narrow strip of beach that extends from Barnegat light to Holgate, the island is actually a series of little towns connected to the mainland by a bridge. Here you will find closely quartered beach houses and a few motels leading up to the dunes. The spanking clean air reminds one of Cape Cod. Since most people rent beach homes or apartments for at least two weeks, there is an air of leisure and permanence about Long Beach Island. Also some very fancy digs near Loveladies and Harvey Cedars.

Courses in art photography, Yoga and such are offered at both the *Foundation of Arts and Sciences* and at *St. Francis Center*. A dinner theater assures visitors there's more to summer life than basking on the beach. An amusement area and boutique shopping center attracts both teenagers and families with kids to Bay Ave. between 7th and 9th Streets in Beach Haven.

Of course a trip to Long Beach Island would not be complete without a visit to "Old Barney" which is the main attraction at **Barnegat Lighthouse State Park.** The park allows picnicking, surf fishing and a view of the panorama from the red and white 19th century lighthouse —it only takes 217 steps to climb. The only access to Long Beach Island is the one road, Route 72 from the mainland to the center of the island. For the **Atlantic City** area (see separate chapter) you must return to Route 9 or the Garden State Parkway.

The Cape:

Ocean City to Cape May

Like Atlantic City, this last strip of coastline is considered Philadelphia's shore as well as New Jersey's. However, people from all over come to these beaches, especially Canadians. Ocean City, the first down the line, bills itself as America's oldest family resort. It has never allowed liquor to be sold in its environs, the beach is wide and clean and the long boardwalk is filled with stores, arcades, major amusement centers,a waterpark and a movie house. **Stone Harbor** has rental houses and apartments plus a bustling main boulevard filled with boutiques, bistros and yuppies. Good restaurants are a major attraction here. Vacationers from neighboring **Avalon,** which has its own beautiful beach, often come down here too.

Among the Wildwoods, Wildwood Crest may have the advantage of getting the biggest family crowd but the beaches all along this area are very wide and kept quite clean despite the huge crowds that come on weekends. The surf is definitely milder down here and shallow enough for a toddler to wade a little. And the beach is free—no badges required. Both Wildwood and the Crest are solid motels from start to finish with guest houses and rental houses a block behind. **Wildwood** has the nightclubs, the boardwalk amusements and the swinging nightclub crowd, while the Crest is more family centered.

Twenty minutes down the coast and at the very tip of New Jersey lies **Cape May City.** Here is a beautiful Victorian town with colorful gingerbread houses and green lawns set against a placid shore.

Young couples and older folks seem to love the environment here. The beach has received new sand, but automobile congestion is a real problem in town—or trying to get into the town!

As mentioned earlier in this book, one center of attraction here is the "Victorian Town," a series of renovated houses, quaint boutique shops, gaslight lamps and brick walkways. The shops lining Washington Mall offer an evening's entertainment in themselves with their art & crafts.

Beyond the town, **Cape May Point Beach** offers a wide beach, a refurbished lighthouse (you can climb all those steps for a fee), and those little pieces of quartz known as Cape May Diamonds. And at the very tip of the county, the line begins for the *Cape May-Lewes Ferry,* a ride that takes you to Delaware for outlet shopping or the beach at Reheboth.

HIKING

There are any number of County Parks which offer both easy and more difficult hiking trails. Popular among these are the trails in the Watchung Reservation in Union County, the South Mountain Reservation in Essex County, the Lenape Trail in Nutley, the Mahlon Dickerson Reservation in Morris County. Almost all State Parks include hiking trails and you will find the complete list of State Parks at the end of the chapter. There are, furthermore, two areas of extreme interest to outdoor enthusiasts in New Jersey - the **Pine Barrens** and the **Delaware Water Gap National Recreation Area.** Both of these include or neighbor state parks.

Information on hiking trails and other events at Delaware Water Gap is available at the *Kittatinny Point Station* right off of Interstate -80 as you travel toward the Pennsylvania border. Among the many activities sponsored by the Recreation Area are: the Peters Valley Craftsmen - a summer place where you may watch master potters, weavers, jewelry makers, at work, the Walpack Art Center (basically an art gallery); and Slateford Farm, an 1800's farmhouse over on the Pennsylvania side. Millbrook Village, a restored 19th Century town is mentioned separately in this book. The Kittatinny Point Center is also a staging area for canoeists (who bring their own) and includes a picnic area, restrooms and lots of leaflets, including hiking trail guides. Whether you hike or take the car to an outlook point, a view of the Delaware Water Gap (which is a deep gorge cut by the river between two sets of mountains) is probably the most spectacular view in New Jersey. It should not be missed.

Stokes State Forest which is right nearby in the northern section of the State includes 17 named and marked trails plus a nine-mile stretch of the Appalachian Trail that transects the area. Here you will find Tillman Ravine. The 10,000-year-old ravine offers a host of natural wildflowers and trees. The trails here are for the more experienced hiker.

High Point State Park, also in the northwestern portion of the state offers many hiking and nature trails, including a portion of the Appalachian trail.The highest point in the park is marked with the 220 foot High Point Monument which one can climb for a view of three states (although it's usually closed). However there's camping, biking, cross-country skiing and lots of activities available here.

The Pine Barrens in southern Jersey offers a completely different experience. The terrain is flat but the flora and fauna of the region are unusual. Trails and old sand roads wind through the pines and swamps.

171

The Batona Trail is the longest, extending from Carpenter Spring in Lebanon State Forest to Batsto in Wharton Forest Another, shorter trail in the Pine Barrens is called the Absegami. Since trails in the Pine Barrens can be confusing and people have gotten lost it is best to start your hike at Batsto where you can talk with the Rangers at the visitor's center and obtain hiking guides.The Barrens covers several counties in New Jersey. Check Bass River and Wharton State Forest listings.

Those interested in hiking can obtain further information by writing to the *New Jersey Division of Travel and Tourism, P.O.* Box 400, Trenton, NJ 08625. Another good place to contact, especially if you are interested in joining group hikes is: *The Sierra Club*, 360 Nassau Street, Princeton, NJ. Telephone 609-924-3141. Although this club is primarily devoted to environmental protection, their hikes and canoe trips are graded according to difficulty and led by a responsible hiker. They are very knowledgeable in the area of New Jersey trails. Another hiking group is the Appalachian Mountain Club- the local chapter can be reached at 973-890-9280.

FISHING

Most people think of fishing in New Jersey as off-shore fishing. Indeed, there are fleets of boats from Atlantic Highlands to Cape May, just waiting to take customers out. Party boats go out seven days a week during the summer either for half or full day excursions. They come complete with tackle, bait, food and drink although you pay for the extras, of course. These boats can handle over a hundred people and are sturdy enough to go well out into the ocean in their quest for bluefish, weakfish, tuna, fluke, and striped bass.

Charter boats are hired by groups for the day and in the busy season must be reserved weeks in advance. **Brielle,** on the Manasquan Inlet is one of the largest centers of party and charter boats in the state. Check the Sports Section of your daily newspaper (the Friday edition, especially) for the names and rates of party and charter boats. You can also write or call The NJ Division of Fish, Game and Wildlife, CN 400, Trenton, NJ 08625 (609-292-2695) for a NJ Party & Charter Boat Directory.

Fresh-water fishermen have several favorite spots in New Jersey, two of them in State Parks. **Round Valley** is deemed to have the best sport fishing with 22 species of fish, including rainbow and lake trout and largemouth and smallmouth bass. The Round Valley Reservoir is part of the State Park about one mile south of Lebanon in Hunterdon County. It was created by two dams and is stocked by the State. In **Swartswood**

State Park both Big and Little Swartswood Lakes are known for their fishing quality. This is a beautiful area high in the mountains of Sussex County. **Greenwood Lake** in northern Passaic County is a huge lake that lies partially in New York State. There are several private marinas along the shore and one or two public beaches maintained by local municipalities. **Lake Tomahawk** is a private lake with swimming, picnicking, and some kids water rides, located near Sparta in Sussex County (Tel. 973-478-7490)

The Pine Barrens is a magnet not only for hikers but for campers and fishermen as well. **The Bass River** in the State Forest of that name, the Batsto, River and many lakes and inlets are dotted with fishing camps, both public and private.

While boating ramps are available at most of these state parks you must bring your own boat along, although canoes may be rented. Anyone over 14 years of age must have a license for fresh water fishing. You can buy your Fishing License at any sporting goods store.

CAMPING

New Jersey has many state parks that offer beautiful, clean and well equipped campgrounds. All you have to do to enjoy them is to bring your own camping equipment, a minimum cash entrance fee, and tote your own garbage out (state policy - they provide the bags). Best to call the campgrounds for details (a listing of state parks can be found at the end of this chapter.)

Bass River and **Swartswood State Parks** are excellent for family outings. Camp sites are adequately sized. Facilities include flush toilets and showers, and they are kept fairly clean. Swimming, boating and picnic areas are close to the sites. At Bass River, the shallow lake allows for canoeing and paddle boating. Swartswood lake is good for sailing as well. Canoes, rowboats and paddle boats can be rented.

The problem with these two attractive grounds (and many other state parks) is their popularity. For good weather weekend camping, reservations are recommended. At most state parks, half of the available sites can be reserved ahead so long as you stay a minimum of two days. So if there are 70 sites, 35 can be reserved. The rest are given out on a first come-first served basis. Sites are usually $10.00 a night plus $7.00 reservation charge. Group sites can always be reserved in advance. If you try for a site during midweek, your chances are better of just driving up and finding one.

Waywayanda and **Worthington Parks** are definitely primitive. Waywayanda is especially suitable for group camping and day trips to the beach or for fishing. The group camp sites are served by outhouses. However, toilets, changing rooms and food concessions are found at the beach area. No flush toilets are to be found at Worthington on the Delaware. Outhouses or bring your own potty have to suffice. Using the port-a-potty turned out to be the best amusement of the weekend for the six-year-old son of friends who tried this spot. Located a few hundred feet from the Delaware, this large open site will appeal to those who choose to fish, raft, or canoe on the river. There is no bathing beach.

For the truly hardy, scenic **Round Valley Reservoir** offers real wilderness camping. Campers must hike or boat to the sites. The key interest here is sailing, boating and fishing. (Round Valley's popular bathing beach with its excellent facilities is in a separate part of the reservoir.) **Spruce Run,** with facilities for boating, fishing and swimming, takes camping out of the woods and puts it in the sunshine, where, in the heat of summer, it doesn't belong. Sites are on a hill and there is no shade. Again, there is a beach for swimming with the usual facilities. During summers with low rainfalls, these sites may sometimes be closed.

At all parks, (remember, Worthington has no formal facilities), swimming, boating and fishing are open daily in season for noncampers. Check the parks to learn boat limits.

Aside from the camping facilities in the State parks, you can also find hundreds of sites in the many private campgrounds around the State. The Pine Barrens and the southern portion of New Jersey abound with these camps which usually offer more sophisticated facilities than the State-run sites (higher rates too, of course). A limited number of county parks offer camping also (check park listings at end of chapter). For a full listing of private RV and camping sites call 800-CAMP-NJ for a brochure.

PICK-YOUR-OWN ORCHARDS

Who would have guessed that stooping over in the hot sun and picking strawberries, blueberries, etc. would become a "bonding" experience for young families. It's also attractive to people who want to save a little money and people who want to be sure their fruits and vegetables are fresh.

Usually you buy the empty basket and then fill it up, but arrangements vary. Also weather conditions can throw off standard picking times. Most orchards are open from June until Halloween when hayrides and contests often accompany the picking. Those places that specialize in one fruit (such as blueberries) are open only during that season.

The best source for a list of picking farms is the Rutgers Cooperative Extension which puts out a leaflet listing them by county and giving their farm specialties.

In Burlington County, there are seven farms specializing in blueberries in Pemberton alone. The extension suggests calling first to see what is pickable at the moment getting directions (most farms are out-a-ways) and learning prices. Most farms also have already picked stuff for those who get tired.

Some better known farms include **Terhune's** (330 Cold Soil Road, Princeton) which offers farm animals for petting and a busy cider mill also. **Matarazzo Farms** (Route 519, Belvidere) runs a strawberry festival and a winery next door. In Monmouth County you'll find **Casola Farms** with a variety of produce and the **Berry Farm** which specializes in raspberries. Both are on Route 34 in Colts Neck very close to **Delicious Orchards** which is a gorgeous indoors market with fruits, vegetables, baked goods and candies—definitely made for the gourmet who doesn't want the thrill of picking his own. Even in crowded Bergen County, there is the **Demarest Farm** at 244 Werimus Road, Hillsdale. And Mullica Hill in southern Jersey, known for its antique shops, has several pick-your-own places.

You can get the list from Rutgers Publication Distribution Service, Cook College, Rutgers University, Dudley Road, P.O. Box 231, New Brunswick, NJ 08903-0231. Also try your local county extension agent, and newspaper and magazine listings during picking season.

ADVENTUROUS OUTINGS

For those who like to add the element of adventure to their summer activities, there are a number of options available. You don't have to live in California to surf, skydive, parachute or raft down a river. Here are a few of the places where you can jump into action:

1. Skydiving/Parachuting: If you want to learn how to skydive and parachute (well, if you expect to land safely, you had better learn both) there is an outfit in New Jersey where they teach you both in one day. You get jump training on the ground, then they take you up and out. **Contact Skydive East,** Sky Manor Airport, Pittstown, NJ 08867. Call for hours (they are generally active during warm weather).. *Telephone*: 908-735-5119.

Another outfit specializing in freefall and tandem jumping is called **Skydive Sussex,** affiliated with the U.S. Parachute Association. They are located at the Sussex Airport, scene of a popular summer air show, on Route 639, Sussex and operate from April to November. *Telephone:* 973-702-7000

2. Windsurfing: All you need for this one is wind, water and a surfboard with a sail attached. Popular areas are the lakes at such state parks as Round Valley and Spruce Run. The bay side of the Jersey shore also affords windsurfing territory for experienced practitioners. Sandy Hook is popular and you can find windsurfing rentals (along with rowboats & motorboats) on Long Beach island and other shore resorts.

3. White Water Rafting: rafting can run the gamut from lazy tubing down the Delaware to the more exciting white water stuff on the Lehigh River in Pennsylvania. New Jerseyans who want to try the Lehigh River can use either **Whitewater Challengers** which operates out of Whitehaven, PA (Tel.800-443-8554) or **Pocono Whitewater** in JimThorpe, PA. (Tel. 800-WHITEWATER). These outfits offer guided trips (the guides accompany the rafts on kayaks) and have graded outings ranging from easy to more challenging. Call for reservations and information on what to bring and what can be rented (wet suits, etc.).

Kittatiny Canoes in Dingman's Ferry, PA, (Tel: 800-FLOAT-KC) is not only one of the biggest of the canoe renters along the Delaware River, they also offer rafting and tubing trips. Further south you can find **Point Pleasant Canoes** which offers canoeing, leisure rafting, and river tubing. They operate out of three places: Point Pleasant in Bucks County, PA (Tel 215-297-TUBE); Upper Black Eddy, PA (Tel. 215-982-9282); and Martins Creek Base (215-252-TUBE). Picnic facilities are available at the bases, since the amount for food and drink allowed on trips is limited.

4. Hot Air Ballooning: For those of you who want to go back in time, hot air ballooning offers fancy flights (often with champagne included) over Hunterdon, Mercer and Somerset counties. Fancy prices, too. Flights are usually at sunrise and just before sunset. Some of the outfits currently operating are: *In Flight Balloon Adventures* (908-479-4674) which leaves from a restaurant in Clinton and *Tewksbury Balloon Adventures* in Oldwick (908-439-3320).

5. Plane Gliding: You soar in a glider (which is pulled by an airplane) over the Delaware Water Gap, the Kittatinny Ridge and other scenic areas Good picture taking possibilities. Contact *Yards Creek Soaring Glides*, 36 Lambert Road, Blairstown Airport, Blairstown, Warren County. *Telephone:* 908-362-1239..

6. Open Cockpit Bi-Plane Ride: A professional pilot takes you up in an antique (but completely restored) bi-plane for rides over the country-side. There is also a World War 11 fighter plane on hand. Located at old Bridge Airport; Englishtown. Contact *Del Rossos's Blue Baron BiPlanes*. *Telephone:* 732-446-1300.

STATE PARKS AND FORESTS

Following is a listing of the State Parks and Forests of New Jersey. Most charge a parking fee: $7.00 for weekends, $6.00 weekdays for parks with swimming facilities, $4.00 weekends, $3.00 weekdays for others. A few are actually free. This charge is only operational from Memorial Day to Labor Day. Some of the parks with historic sites or beaches, have been mentioned in greater detail elsewhere in this book. For information about how to reserve campsites, call the office of the state park.

State Parks

ALLAIRE STATE PARK, Route 524, Allaire, Monmouth County. 2,260 acres includes restored Allaire Village, narrow gauge railroad, picnicking, hiking and horse trails, camping, fishing, golf course, nature center, lively calendar of events. 732-938-2371.

ALLAMUCHY MOUNTAIN STATE PARK, Allamuchy, Warren County. Undeveloped section with fishing, hunting, and trails. Developed section is Stephens State Park (q.v.). 908-852-3790.

BARNEGAT LIGHTHOUSE STATE PARK Long Beach Island, Ocean County. 172-foot lighthouse with 217 step spiral staircase. Picnicking, fishing from restored jetties, no swimming. Nearby museum. 609-494-2016.

CAPE MAY POINT STATE PARK, Cape May County. Picnicking, tours of restored lighthouse, bird watching, nature center, surf fishing. 609-884-2159.

CHEESEQUAKE STATE PARK, off GSP Exit 20, Matawan, Middlesex County. Camping, swimming beach, fishing, hiking, picnicking. 732-566-2161

CORSON'S INLET STATE PARK, Route 619 south of Ocean City, Cape May County. Small boat launch, fishing, hiking. 609-861-2402.

DELAWARE & RARITAN CANAL STATE PARK, Somerset County. There are two separate sections to this park- one in Bull's Island and one following the path of the old canal. Canoeing, fishing, hiking. 732-873-3050.

DOUBLE TROUBLE STATE PARK, Double Trouble Road, Berkeley Twp., Ocean County. Includes historic village, cranberry harvesting, hiking, boating. 732-341-6662.

FORT MOTT STATE PARK, Fort Mott Rd., Salem, Salem County. 104 acre park. Picnicking, playgrounds. Next to Finn Point National cemetery, site of confederate and union soldiers graves. 856-935-3218.

HACKLEBARNEY STATE PARK, 119 Hacklebarney Rd.,Long Valley, Morris County. A river runs through it-fishing, hiking, picnicking. 908-879-5677.

HIGH POINT STATE PARK, Route 23, Sussex County. 220 ft. monument lookout, swimming, fishing, hiking, camping, nature tours, skiing, bike riding. 973-875-4800.

HOPATCONG STATE PARK, Landing, Morris County. Public beach on Lake Hopatcong, New Jersey's largest Picnicking, swimming, boating, fishing. 973-398-7010.

ISLAND BEACH STATE PARK, Central Ave. south of Seaside Park Ocean County. Popular beach with ocean bathing, bathhouse, surfing area, fishing, picnicking and separate nature area and wildlife sanctuary. Year round parking fee. 732-793-0506.

LIBERTY STATE PARK, Jersey City, Hudson County. Pool, marina,

Liberty Science Center, ferry to Statue of liberty & Ellis Island, restored RR Terminal, nature center. Picnicking, special events. 201-435-8509.

MONMOUTH BATTLEFIELD STATE PARK, 347 Freehold-Englishtown Rd., Manalapan, Monmouth County. Visitor Center, picnicking, yearly reenactment. 732-462-9616.

PARVIN STATE PARK, Rt. 540, Pittsgrove Twp., Salem County. Campsites and cabins, bathing, boating, fishing, hiking, over 1100 acres. 856-358-8616.

PRINCETON BATTLEFIELD STATE PARK, 500 Mercer St, Princeton. Small park with historic house on grounds. Open fields for walking, hiking. 609-921-0074.

RINGWOOD STATE PARK, Ringwood, Passaic County. Historic Mansions, Longpond Ironworks, botanic gardens, picnicking, swimming, boating, fishing, hiking. 973-962-7031.

ROUND VALLEY, Rte. 629, Lebanon Twp. Hunterdon County. Wilderness camping, boating, fishing, hiking, swimming beach, picnicking. Second largest lake in NJ. 908-236-6355.

SPRUCE RUN, Clinton, Hunterdon County. Lake with fishing, boating, sailing, swimming beach, picnicking. 908-638-8572.

STEPHENS STATE PARK, Now a section of Allamuchy Mountain State Park. Hackettstown, Warren County. Camping, fishing, picnicking, playground. 732-852-3790.

SWARTSWOOD STATE PARK, Route 619, Swartswood, Sussex County, excellent fishing, boating, hiking, camping. Swimming beach. 973-383-5230.

VOORHEES STATE PARK, Rte. 513, Glen Gardner, Hunterdon County. Hiking, picnicking, camping, nature study, astronomical outlook. 908-638-6969.

WASHINGTON CROSSING STATE PARK, Route 29, Titusville, Mercer County. Nature center, outdoor theater, picnicking, playing fields, historical museums. 609-737-0616.

WASHINGTON ROCK STATE PARK , 16 Rock Rd., Greenbrook, Somerset County. Picnicking, overlook views.

WAWAYANDA STATE PARK , 885 Warwick Tpke., Hewitt. Passaic/ Sussex County. Camping, fishing, boating, swimming beach, hunting, horseback riding. 973-853-4462.

State Forests

ABRAM S. HEWITT STATE FOREST, West Milford, Passaic County - hiking and hunting cross-country skiing. *Telephone.* 973-853-4462.

BASS RIVER STATE FOREST, Burlington/Ocean Counties bathing, picnicking, hiking, nature study, hunting, fishing, boating, canoeing, Lake Absegami. Cabins and campsites. *Telephone:* 609-296-1114.

BELLEPLAIN STATE FOREST, Route 550, Woodbine. Cape May/Cumberland Counties- bathing, picnicking, boating, camping, hunting, fishing. 609-861-2404.

JENNY JUMP STATE FOREST. Hope, Warren County - picnicking, camping, nature study, hunting. 908-459-4366.

LEBANON STATE FOREST, New Lisbon, Burlington County - bathing, picnicking, hiking, hunting, camping. 609-726-1191.

NORVIN GREEN STATE FOREST. Ringwood, Passaic County— hiking, hunting.973-962-7031.

PENN STATE FOREST. Burlington County- bathing, picnicking, hiking, hunting, fishing.609-726-1114.

STOKES STATE FOREST,1 Coursen Rd. Branchville, Sussex County. Cross-county skiing, bathing, picnicking, hiking, camping, fishing, hunting. 973-948-3820.

WHARTON STATE FOREST - Huge area in pinelands. Includes *Atsion* Section with a swimming beach and bathhouse (route 206, Atsion) and Batsto (qv.) in Hammonton, which includes historic village and campsite headquarters. Camping, canoeing, hiking, picnicking, nature center. 609-268-0444, 609-561-3262.

WORTHINGTON STATE FOREST, Sussex County - hunting, fishing, hiking, picnicking, camping. . 973-841-9575.

COUNTY PARKS

New Jersey has many outstanding county parks, and unlike the state parks they do not charge entrance admission (although there may be a fee for programs). Here are some of the better known ones. Call for directions since many large parks have several entrances. Also check *The Garden Variety* chapter for gardens that are run by county parks. Nature centers and zoos within county parks are described in more detail in the Zoos chapter.

Atlantic County Park in Estell Manor consists of 1742 acres and includes nature center, biking, cross-country ski and hiking trails, fishing and picnic areas. Historic sites. Route 50 south of Mays Landing. 609-625-1897, 645-5960.

Berlin Park, Park Drive, Berlin. Almost 150 acres with fishing, hiking, picnic area and playground. Site of Camden County Environmental Studies Center. 609-795-7275 (Camden County)

Campgaw Mountain Reservation, Mahwah. Site of winter ski area, plus acres of hiking trails, camping. 201-327-7800. (Bergen County)

Cape May County Park: Route 9 & Crest Haven Blvd., Cape May Court House. Includes zoo, botanical area, picnic area, playground, hiking trails. 609-465-9210.

Colonial Park, Metlars Road, Franklin Twp. Rose garden, fragrance garden and arboretum, tennis courts, boating, fishing, hiking, picnic areas. 908-722-1200. (Somerset County)

Duke Island Park, Old York Road, Bridgewater. Fishing, picnicking, concerts, hiking along Raritan River. 908-722-1200. (Somerset County)

Eagle Rock Reservation: Eagle Rock Ave., West Orange. Mountainous formation allows for hiking. Private restaurant in park (Highlawn Pavilion) offers great views. 973-857-8530. (Essex County)

Garret Mountain Reservation, Valley Road, Paterson. Includes Lambert Castle, scenic overlook, hiking, fishing, stables, riding trails. 973-881-4832. (Passaic County)

Holmdel Park: Longstreet Rd., Holmdel. Reconstructed farm, large arboretum, picnic pavilion, fishing lake, hiking. 732-946-2669, 946-3758. (Monmouth County)

Hunterdon County Park: 1020 Highway 31, Lebanon. Includes a full arboretum, picnicking, hiking, trail map areas for canoeing and horseback riding. 908-782-1158.

Johnson Park, River Road, Piscataway. Large picnic area, small horse track, small animal zoo, ballfields, hiking trails, restored village. 732-745-3900. (Middlesex County)

Lewis Morris Park, Route 124, Morristown. Adjoins Jockey Hollow. Swimming lake, fishing, hiking, picnic area, ice skating. 973-326-7600. (Morris County).

Mahlon Dickerson Reservation: Weldon Road, Jefferson Twp. Large park offers hiking, mountain biking, equestrian trails, fishing, canoe rentals, group picnic area. Small camping area for trailers and some tents. 973-326-7600 or 973-326-7631. (Morris County)

Manasquan Reservoir: Windler Rd., Howell Twp. Newly upgraded. Over 1200 acres for rowboats, fishing, hiking trails. 732-919-0996. (Monmouth County).

Mercer County Park, Route 535, West Windsor Twp. Includes large lake with marina, fishing, ice-skating, picnic facilities, hiking trials. 609-989-6530.

Ocean County Park: Route 88, Lakewood. Once a vacation site for John D. Rockefeller; includes swimming lake, fishing lake, playgrounds, mature trees. Cross-country skiing in winter. 732-506-9090.

Roosevelt Park, Oakwood Ave., Edison. A compact park known for its summer theater series in outdoor amphitheater. Lake fishing, trails. 732-745-3900. (Middlesex County)

Schooley Mountain Park. Camp Washington Road, Long Valley. Swimming beach and lake, boating, hiking, bridle trails, summer environmental center. 973-326-7600 (Morris County)

Scotland Run Park, Clayton-Williamson Road, Clayton. Nature center, boating, swimming, fishing, picnicking, hiking on almost 1000 acres. 609-468-0100. (Gloucester County).

South Mountain Reservation, Northfield Rd., West Orange: Includes ice skating rink, Turtle Back Zoo, fishing, hiking, scenic views, cross-county skiing, picnicking. 973-857-8530. (Essex County)

Stony Brook, 31 Titus Mill Road, Pennington. Nature center, fishing, hiking on 585 acres. 609-737-3735. (Mercer County)

Thompson Park: 520 Newman Springs Rd., Lincroft. Beautiful mansion holds art shows. Grounds include a display rose garden, fitness trails, picnic area. Many activities with summer theater in barn. 732-842-4000. (Monmouth County)

'Tip" Seaman County Park: baseball, tennis and bocce fields for the locals. Site of yearly Decoy and Gunning show. Lakeside Drive, Tuckerton. 609-296-5606. (Ocean County)

Turkey Swamp Park: Georgia Road, Freehold. One of the few county facilities to include camping (with a restroom and showers). There are 64 campsites plus a lake for boating. Trails, playgrounds, ball fields. 908-462-7286. (Monmouth County)

Van Saun Park. Forest Ave. off Route 4, Paramus. Includes Bergen County Zoo, lake, fishing, ice-skating, large picnic area, playground, walking paths. 201-646-2680. (Bergen County)

Warinoco Park, St. Georges Ave., Roselle. Lake for rowing, fishing, ice-skating in winter. Picnic area. 908-298-7850. (Union County)

Watchung Reservation. Mountainside. Part of the Watchung Mountains, includes trails, picnic areas, planetarium, nature center, horseback riding stables, fishing and plenty of deer. Telephone: 908-527-4900. (Union County)

Wells Mills County Park & Nature Center: 905 Wells Mills Rd., Waretown. Inside the pinelands, this 810 acre park includes a nature center, hiking trails, lake fishing, canoe rentals in season. 609-971-3085. (Ocean County)

FEDERAL AND INTERSTATE

SANDY HOOK: (Officially the *Gateway National Recreation Area - Sandy Hook Division*)—encompasses the Spermaceti Cove Visitor's Center with nature displays, pamphlets and maps; several guarded beaches with bathhouses, changing rooms, and concession stands. Picnicking allowed. Although most people come for the beach there is also Fort Hancock which allows some tours, the Sandy Hook lighthouse which is good for picture taking, and hiking in the nature area. Fishing allowed at several points. Windsurfing and snorkeling on the bay side. Located across bridge from Highlands, Monmouth County (Take Route 36E from the GSP Exit 117) 732-872-5970..

KITTATINNY POINT CENTER: Visitor's center for Delaware Water Gap National Recreation Area. Hiking, canoeing, historic sites, picknicking, nature trails, etc. on both sides of Delaware. Telephone: 908-496-4458; 717-588-2435.

PALISADES INTERSTATE PARKWAY. Exit 2 off Parkway (Alpine). Multi-acre park parallels the Hudson River for much of its area. Shared by New York and New Jersey. Hiking trails, picnic areas,boat launch, scenic outlooks. Historic area at Fort Lee (q.v.), historic house at Alpine. Boating and fishing available. Parking fees in summer. 201-768-1360.

THE GARDEN VARIETY

Photo by Barbara Hudgins

In This Chapter You will Find:

LONGWOOD GARDENS

Without a doubt the most extensive formal gardens in the area (and considered among the best in the United States), this impressive display by the Dupont family offers an amazing variety. The gardens are open all year round and there is always something of interest whatever the weather. Over 1000 acres are open to the public, including some beautifully laid out conservatories, so bring good walking shoes.

You enter through the main Visitors Center which looks like a standard institutional building from the front but like an underground house from the back - its cleverly concealed under a hillock of green. At the Center you purchase your tickets and watch a four-minute film which introduces you to the highlights of the gardens. There's a gift shop chock full of books and plants where you'll want to stop on your way out. But first, get a guide map at the information desk - you'll need it. Here are some of the highlights:

The Conservatories are huge glass-enclosed rooms that surround a patio. Inside there are hanging basket mobiles sprouting flowers; stone herons in a pond surrounded by seasonal flowers; a ballroom featuring organ concerts; and the hot and humid Palm House with its banana and breadfruit trees. There is one room for insect-eating plants, another just for orchids.The main conservatory displays change four times a year. (The Christmas display alone attracts more than 100,000 people a year.) An indoor Children's Garden nearby allows a hands-on experience for kids with mazes and stepping stones.

Outside, directly in front of the conservatories is the main water fountain area. The fountain display, with its many spouting water jets, is framed by trimmed boxwood. Certain nights during the summer, colored lights and music from the Carillion make a spectacular *"Son et Lumiere.* There are even fireworks added to the fountain displays on special Saturday nights - these must be reserved in advance. The carillion in its own little romantic nook with a cascading waterfall and a rock garden looks like something out of a 19th century painting. Further on, are the *Idea Garden, Heaths of Heather,* the *"Eye of God"* (a low, circular water sculpture), a topiary and a rose garden.

The right side of Longwood boasts the long walk - bordered by seasonal flowers, and the open air theater with display fountains. *The Peirce-DuPont House* is open to visitors (extra fee). This 1730 home had only two owners - the original Mr. Peirce, who owned the park from which Longwood Garden was born, and the DuPonts, who saved the property from becoming a sawmill in 1906.

Further on there are wisteria and rose gardens, forest walks and meadows, a lake with gazebo and ducks, and last of all, a complete Italian Water Garden in the manner of the Villa D'Este. Luckily there are many benches and shaded spots at which to rest along the way.

The Terrace Restaurant, located near the conservatories, offers both regular dining and cafeteria-style buffet and a nice view. No smoking is allowed at the gardens, and no food can be brought in, but there is no prohibition on strollers and children are welcome.

> **HOURS:** Daily. April - Oct., 9-6; Nov. - Mar. 10-5, Extended hours for special events.
> **ADMISSION:** Adults: $12.00, Children: $2.00, Under 6, free.
> **LOCATION:** Route 1, Kennett Square, Pa.
> **TELEPHONE:** 610-388-1000. www.longwoodgardens.org

THE DUKE GARDENS

Open from October to May, and one of New Jersey's foremost attractions, the Duke Gardens feature a series of interconnecting hothouses with an amazing variety of plants. They are part of the Duke Estate in Somerville. Indeed, from the moment you board the little van in the parking lot that takes you through a winding road you are aware that this was once Rich Man's country. The administration building where you get your tickets and wait for the tour is a Tudor style gardener's cottage replete with rich woods and carpets. From here the guide takes you across to the hothouses where you enter a different world.

Each hothouse contains a shortened version of an international garden. The layout of the flowers and the walkways are all planned to reflect the atmosphere of that particular garden. The first one you enter is the Italian Romantic garden. Here you find statuary amid overgrown plants, birds-of-paradise, and the type of Mediterranean setting that threw nineteenth century poets into ecstasy.

Each garden is controlled for climate and humidity. Enter the Edwardian Conservatory and it's warm. Here, in a hothouse with tropical plants such as sego palms and elephant ears, the English gentleman would propose to his lady love (or at least he did in all those old movies on late night television). He would probably clip an orchid and hand it to her. For there are enough big, fat orchids in here to send an entire graduating class to the Senior Prom.

The long *English garden*, on the other hand, is temperate. A brick walkway takes you through sedate rows of hollyhocks, primroses and mani-cured boxwoods. A small herb garden is here also. The *French garden* is formal, with flowers set out in greenery shaped in a fleur-de-lis pattern. Lattice work covers all, and a far statue of a goddess reminds you that this is a small version of what you might find at Versailles.

The *Chinese garden*, with its overhanging willows, stone walkway and arched bridge over a goldfish pond is for serene meditation. The scent of the fragrant tea olive permeates the air. Among the other gardens you will find an Arizona desert with succulents and tall cacti; a Japanese rus-tic style meditation garden; and a Persian with decorated tiles and foun-tains.

Many gardeners attend the plantings, so the Duke Gardens changes the flowers on display often, but the overall scheme remains intact. It is a favorite destination of garden clubs, but individuals enjoy the gardens as well. Advance reservations are required however. High heels are not permitted (you'll understand why when you walk on those arched stone bridges).

HOURS: Oct - May, 12-4 Daily, by reservation.
ADMISSION: Adults: $5.00, Children, Seniors: $2.50, Under 6 free.
LOCATION: Route 206, south of Somerville.
TELEPHONE: 908-722-3700

THE CAMDEN CHILDREN'S GARDEN

What's the latest thing in interactive education for moppets? Answer: a children's garden. They're popping up all over the place, mostly in already established gardens. However, The Camden Children's Garden has helped to spruce up the boring façade of the New Jersey State Aquarium. Although a separate entity, it adds much needed color and variety to the Camden waterfront. It is placed in front and to the left of the large aquatic building-and you can visit it alone or buy a combina-tion ticket. One of the best things about the Garden is that it offers picnic benches for groups and families alike. Considering that there is no food allowed in the aquarium itself and that the offerings at the cafeteria are of the hot dog and fast food variety, a picnic area is a welcome sight.

The Children's Garden opened 1999 and is a pleasant spot for adults also. There are lots of colorful play areas—many of which are not whol-ly dependent on flowers or plants. The Dinosaur Garden for instance, offers a prehistoric environment of rock walls , waterfalls and huge trees.

Here you can find a 35 foot long Apatosaurus (he's actually made out of recycled automobile parts and created by sculptor Jim Gary). Hand-painted benches and a painted wooden violet add color to the nearby Violet Plaza which also features an interactive water fountain.

Over at the Storybook Gardens there are three little houses made of straw, wood and brick, fanciful topiaries and a chair made out yew where children can hide and play in the Three Little Pigs area. A ten- foot aluminum beanstalk leads the way to The Giant's Garden where there are plenty of oversize plants and foliage. A slide sends children down the rabbit hole to the Alice in Wonderland Garden. Many other interactive sites beckon for play areas. As a focal point, a statue of Walt Whitman (in a token nod to the poet who lived his last years in this once bustling city) stands in front of the Butterfly Garden. The Ginkgo Tree gift shop specializes in garden gifts. Since this is primarily an outdoor garden it may not be available off-season.

HOURS:	Daily: 9:30-5:30. Shorter hours mid-Sept.-mid Mar.
ADMISSION:	(combo w/aquarium)Adults: $12.95; Children: $9.95. Gardens alone: Adults: $5.00; children: $3.00.
LOCATION:	3 Riverside Drive, Camden, near the Blockbuster-SONY Entertainment Centre. Parking Garage across street ($5.00 for 3 hours)
TELEPHONE:	856-365-8733

BROOKLYN BOTANIC GARDENS

New Jerseyans often combine a trip to these gardens with one to the Brooklyn Museum (which is right next door) since parking in the museum lot can serve for both places.

The Brooklyn Gardens are known for the cherry blossom walk - a wide swath of lawn with Japanese double blossoms, white and pink, that come out in mid-April. Another famous display is the *Japanese Hill and Pond Garden* which were originally designed in 1914, and recently reconstructed.

Here a vermilion Torii rises from the calm waters. The quiet meditation walks, the willow trees and the stone turtles create a duplication of a Kyoto scene set down incongruously in the midst of urban high-rises.

The Brooklyn gardens follow the natural cycles: daffodils in March, then the lilacs, then the cherry blossoms, then the wisteria and rhododendrons in May. The rose garden is spectacular but is open certain months. The butterfly and hummingbird trail is a summer attraction.

Walt Whitman points the way to the Butterfly Bush and other flowers at The Camden Children's Garden.

However, other features are seasonless - the formal prospect from Eastern Parkway, the rock garden and brooks, and of course the *Conservatories* which feature bonzai plants, cacti and tropical plants.

There are 50 acres to the gardens and lots of hills and dales.. A Terrace Cafe offers sandwiches and drinks and the gift shop has a wide assortment of items. They are fairly strict about behavior here: no picnicking, no bicycles, no dogs, no sitting on the grass (except in the Cherry Esplanade) and no children under 16 unless accompanied by adults. And they enforce these rules. Perhaps that is why the Brooklyn Botanic Gardens have remained a verdant oasis throughout the years.

HOURS: Apr.-Sept: Tues.-Fri. 8-6; Weekends and Holidays: 10-6; Sept-Apr.: Tues.-Fri. 10-4:30; Weekends and Holidays: 10-4:30.
ADMISSION: Adults- $3.00; Seniors & students: $1.50
LOCATION: Eastern Parkway and Washington Ave., Brooklyn, N.Y.
TELEPHONE: 718-623-7200. www.bbg.org

NEW YORK BOTANICAL GARDENS

Recently refurbished and much ballyhooed, these 250 acres of grassland, trees and formal gardens are the pride of The Bronx. Everything has been upgraded and prettified. Not only have the conservatory been re-opened, but there's an extensive new Children's Garden as well.

A tram ride circles the park interior - best take it early before the crowds come. But check your map first. The ride has four major stops, takes twenty minutes and features live narration. You can visit the ornate Main Building, a Beaux Arts structure that is fronted by a landmark fountain statue. Inside are orchids, a herbarium, a library and a Gift Shop. The beautiful Rock Garden with its pond, alpine meadow and splashing waterfalls is another stop you should not miss. Of course, if you have kids with you, you'll want to stop at the new, interactive garden created just for them.

Check out the Enid A Haupt Conservatories which had a $25,000,000 facelift. This 1903 "Glass Palace" with its Victorian-style rotunda and structural iron framework is most impressive. Inside, the tropical rain forests of the Americas (both North and South) are emphasized. Banana trees, native huts and pineapple plants in one section; the tall cacti of the Arizona and Mexican desert in another.

Outside the conservatory, there are nicely stylized perennial and herb gardens with brick walkways, shaded lattices, colorful flowers and plenty of benches. In June, the formal Rose Garden is lush with a variety of blooms. As for eating--there is a pleasant cafeteria, or you can bring your own lunch and eat at designated picnic spots. Tram rides, the conservatory and children's garden are extra unless you buy a "Passport" ticket.

HOURS:	Tues.-Sun. & Monday holidays, 10-6.
ADMISSION:	Adults: $3.00; Children & seniors $2.00. Wed. free.
LOCATION:	200th St & Southern Boulevard, The Bronx
TELEPHONE:	718-817-8700. www.nybg.org

WAVE HILL

A public garden located in the upper reaches of the Bronx in a quiet section called Riverdale, Wave Hill still gives the sense of a private estate filled with beauty and serenity. There are lovely vistas of the palisades and the Hudson from the many stone benches and Adirondack chairs on the "hill". There are greenhouses filled with tropical plants and desert cacti and outdoor gardens devoted to herbs and seasonal flowers. An aquatic garden, several pergolas and many flowering trees dot the landscape.

Two houses stand on the estate. The one called Wave Hill, was once rented to such notables as Mark Twain, Theodore Roosevelt and Arturo Toscaninni. The building currently houses a gift shop and a small lunchroom. French doors lead out to a stone terrace with yet another view. The other building features art shows.

While Wave Hill was build by William Morris in 1840 it later became home to several millionaires. The gardens and conservatories, under constant restoration by horticulturists, allow the plebian tourist a feel for the ambience of a private home landscaped for leisure and gracious living. Groups, families, mothers with children and adult hikers all come to enjoy these pleasant grounds.

HOURS:	Tues.-Sun. 9:30-4:30. Apr.-Oct.: 9:30-5:30.
ADMISSION:	Adults: $4.00; Seniors, students $2.00, Under 6 free. Tues. & Sat morn. free.
LOCATION:	675 W. 252 St., Riverdale. Take G.W. Bridge to Henry Hudson Parkway to Exit 21.
TELEPHONE:	718-549-3200. www.wavehill.org

HERSHEY ROSE GARDENS

Not far from the Hershey Hotel, the Rose Garden and Arboretum began as a small 3 - acre plot devoted to roses and now covers over 23 acres with other flowers, trees, lakes and shrubs.. Individuals take a self-guided tour through ten-acres of roses and past a man-made lake filled with goldfish, ducks and swans and the statue of a *Boy with a Leaking Boot*. A holly collection, a rock garden and a large variety of herbs, rhododendrons, and evergreens are part of the display all season long.

A butterfly house in an outdoor mesh enclosure is a popular attraction during the summer. Other major flowerings are: mid-April to mid-May daffodils, tulips, magnolias and early azaleas; May 15 - June 1 - azaleas, rhododendrons, peonies. Then, from June 1 to September 15, rose plants bearing 1200 varieties of roses are in bloom. From September 15 to November 1 -chrysanthemums. Tapes available. Picnic area and sale shop.

> **HOURS:** Mid-Apr. – Sept.: 9-6. Oct.: 9-5
> **ADMISSION:** Adults: $6.00; Seniors: $5.50; Children: $3.00.
> **LOCATION:** Hershey, Pa. on Route 322.
> **TELEPHONE:** 717-534-3492

REEVES-REED ARBORETUM

A small estate is the setting for this arboretum, hidden by tall trees on one of Summit's stately old streets. You follow a winding path down to the parking lot which has room for about fifty cars. The stone and shingle manor house on the rise above the lot was built in 1889 and is surrounded by trees, shrubs and flowering plants.The house has recently been expanded. But the major part of the gardens are out back behind the house. It is rather like visiting the house of a rich old aunt and being allowed to wander through the backyard yourself.

You can follow the nature trails through oaks, maples, walnuts and beeches. The open area of this hilly site is devoted to both flower and herb gardens. A deep depression (called a kettle hole in geological terms) is the setting for a spectacular flowering of daffodils in April, followed by summer field flowers. Azaleas, rhododendrons and a small rose garden are also to be found along the walks.

The main house offers a variety of classes and Sunday lectures. You

Photo by Anne Ross

A tranquil spot in the Reeves Reed Arboretum in Summit.

can pick up literature there. Among the brochures is a garden guide to help identify the species in the arboretum. You will also find an attached greenhouse and a small gift shop on the premises. Free

HOURS:	Grounds: Daily, daylight hours.
	Office: Mon., Tues., Thurs., Fri.: 9-3.
LOCATION:	165 Hobart Ave. Summit, Union County. Take Route 24 to Hobart Ave.Exit.
TELEPHONE:	908-273-8787

LEAMING'S RUN GARDENS

Leaming's Run Gardens was created as a bulwark of quiet woods and colorful plantings against the encroachments of motels and gasoline exhaust fumes. It can transport you back to your childhood. Everyone has probably explored a forest at least once, felt the crackling of pine needles underfoot and heard the whipoorwill above. That's the kind of woods that covers thirty acres of sandy soil here, all interspersed with colorful gardens. You come across the gardens at a bend in the road. Many are assemblages of color. The yellow garden mixes gourds, gladiola, banana peppers and taller plants. Another garden is a medley of oranges. The English garden and reflecting pool typify a particular form. There are twenty-six gardens here, each planted to provide color and texture during the entire season from late spring to early fall. The most recent is a sweetheart garden in the shape of a heart that attracts romantic picture-takers.

Three acres are set aside for a colonial farm. Here you will find a traditional log cabin and a fenced-in kitchen and herb garden—and even goats and chickens! Beyond the farm there are nooks and crannies in the road— with snapdragons, pinks and a cinnamon walk. There are benches where you can enjoy the view and even spy a hummingbird in August!

At the end of the one mile walk, you come to *The Cooperage*, a shop where you can buy a variety of dried flower arrangements and other gifts. There are a few rules for the gardens, by the way: no smoking, no pets, no drinks and no radios.

HOURS:	Mid-May to mid-Oct: 9:30-5.
ADMISSION:	Adults: $7.00; Children 6-12: $4.00.
LOCATION:	Route 9, Swainton, Cape May County. Take Exit 17 GSP to Route 9, then south.
TELEPHONE:	609-465-5871

WELL SWEEP HERB FARM

A commercial herb-growing farm, Well Sweep is located way out in the hinterlands. It has now expanded to 120 acres with display gardens and perennials open to the public. Visitors may browse the rectangular beds of rosemary and sage at any time, but special tours are reserved for groups. However, owner Cyrus Hyde does give lecture tours to the general public at specific times. There are also other lecturers on hand on to give particulars on herbs and flowers. Fees vary for particular lectures.

Mr. Hyde's lectures grew out of his once-a-year Open House. He would take groups around and distill information. Did you know that horsetail grass can be used for fine sanding? Or that tansy, planted next to the door, will keep ants away? Want the recipe for rose geranium sugar? No wonder this tour is popular with garden clubs. Of course the principal activity here is growing and selling herbs so there is always a wide selection at reasonable prices (plus pottery and books). Tours and lectures must be reserved beforehand.

> **HOURS:** Mon. 1-5; Tues.-Sat, 9:30-5.
> **LOCATION:** 205 Mt. Bethel Rd., Port Murray, Warren County.
> **TELEPHONE:** 908-852-5390

PRESBY IRIS GARDEN

From the last week in May to the second week in June, an outstanding display of irises can be found in this lovely suburban park in Upper Montclair. Hilly terrain and gracious homes are the setting for this local park where a Mr. Presby began his iris beds many years ago. Every color in the rainbow is reflected in irises. There are thousands of varieties of these bearded and straightstalked flowers, planted in long linear beds that parallel the street and 40,000 plants. Peonies can be found at the adjoining headquarters. Free.

> **HOURS:** Daily. Display runs approximately 3 weeks, beginning May 24.
> **LOCATION:** Mountainside Park, 474 Upper Mountain Ave.,
> Upper Montclair, Essex County
> **TELEPHONE:** 973-783-5974

SKYLANDS

A popular springtime attraction is the preserve flowering around the Skylands Mansion in one section of **Ringwood State Park**. A half-mile alley of crabapple trees, 400 varieties of lilacs, azaleas and peonies and a small formal garden surround the Tudor-style 44-room home(q.v.). In the back of the house there are interesting terraced gardens with greenery and statues. Because the mansion's owner was an avid horticulturist, there is a great variety of trees and bushes as well as flowering plants.

You'll find plenty to see here, summer and autumn also. A winter garden, an octagonal garden, a lily pond, formal terraces with stone balustrades, and a number of vistas make this a beautiful place all year round. Since there are only a few gardeners on hand, where there once were eighty (back in the days of the millionaire owner), it is difficult to keep all the formal gardens up to par. Designated as New Jersey's state botanical gardens—now if only the state would put more money into them! A volunteer group,*The Skylands Association* does tours of the house and garden the first Sunday of the month (afternoons only). They also do garden tours for groups and handle a Christmas Open House.

> **HOURS:** Daily
> **ADMISSION:** Car entrance :$3 summer weekends
> **LOCATION:** Ringwood State Park. Rte. 17 to Sloatsburg Rd. (NYS)
> **TELEPHONE:** 973-962-7031; Association: 973-962-7522

COLONIAL PARK GARDENS

There are several attractive gardens in this county park. The original rose garden, once part of the Mettler Estate, was developed and expanded by a horticulturist so that it now covers an acre. *The Rudolf van der Goot Rose Garden* displays over 200 species, with 3,000 bushes which form a formal display garden to exhibit the A.A.R.S. Award Winning Roses each year. Included here are the original York and Lancaster roses, tearoses, floribunda, and more. They are all labeled to show type and date of introduction into the horticultural world. A flagstone walk makes for easy ambling.

Behind the rose garden is the *Fragrance and Sensory Garden* which provides braille plaques for the blind and a handrail for the handicapped. Set inside of Colonial Park (one of those beautiful county parks that one comes upon so often in New Jersey)there is also an arboretum and meandering stream. Beyond that there are tennis courts, paddle boats and picnic tables for family get togethers. A gazebo inside a perennial garden is a popular picture-taking spot (formal pictures are by permit only).

Garden clubs, school classes and other groups can arrange for guided tours for a fee. Otherwise the gardens are free. Major bloomings are the first week of June and the first week of September.

HOURS: Daily,10-8 Mem. Day - Labor Day; 10-4:30 to Oct. 31.
LOCATION: Franklin Twp., Somerset County. Take Rte 206 to 514 (Amwell Rd) then left to Mettlers Rd.
TELEPHONE: 732-873-2459. www.park.co.somerset.nj.us

OTHER COUNTY AND CITY GARDENS

Leonard J. Buck Gardens: (Somerset County). The former estate of a Far Hills millionaire, the treed and grassy acreage is filled with rock gardens and interesting ferns. The Buck mansion stands atop a winding hilly path but is not open for viewing. Plenty of walking here, with stops at various benches for the vistas. The terrain varies from low lying swamp to steep hillsides. The gardens are best seen in the spring when thousands of tiny flowers peek out from designed rock formations, (plenty of irises and rhododendrons too). Unusual trees plus a pleasant lake that is home to several ducks make for good picture-taking. Pick up a walking map at the visitor's center. Free. *Hours.* Mon-Sat 10-4; Sun.: 12-5. *Location:* 11 Layton Rd. (off Rte. 512), Far Hills. Tele*phone:* 908-234-2677.

Branch Brook Park. (Essex County) More than 3,000 cherry trees that bloom in the middle of April beautify this large park which stretches from Newark to neighboring Belleville. The cherry blossom area covers two miles in length but is only $1/4^{th}$ mile in width. Originally donated by Caroline Bamberger Fuld, these pink and white, single and double flowering trees now outnumber those in Washington D.C. A cherry blossom festival with many special events (including a foot race) coincides with the spring blossoming. *Telephone:* 973-482-7649; 973-857-8530.

Deep Cut Gardens: (Monmouth County). Once the home of a Mafioso chief in the 1930s, these well-kept gardens still have a slight Mediterranean flavor. The ranch style house is now the Horticultural Center where you can find a good library and some plant specimens in

199

the enclosed porch.There are 52 acres of gardens and greenhouses that are planned as a living catalog of cultivated and native plants.

Two ponds (one sporting lily pads) are home to brightly colored Koi. An azalea and rhododendron walk are springtime favorites, while the butterfly and hummingbird garden attracts in the summer. Greenhouses, shade gardens, cascading pools and a long meadow walk make this a pleasant place to meander. Free. *Location*: 352 Red Hill Road, Middletown, 1 $1/2$ miles east of GSP Exit 114. *Telephone*: 732-671-6050.

Frelinghuysen Arboretum: (Morris County) Tulips, azaleas, rhododendrons, a rose garden and a wealth of flowering trees are part of the display at this 127 acre tract that was once the home of the Frelinghuysens. Cherry trees, crabapple and magnolia blossoms along with a lilac garden and a dogwood copse bring color and contrast to the many evergreens in the collection. Headquarters of the Morris County Park System which uses the mansion for offices and library. Separate building for lectures, a nice lawn for concerts and a gift shop which specializes in garden items can all be found here. Hours: Daily 9 a.m.-dusk. *Location:* 53 East Hanover Ave. (Route 511), Morristown. *Telephone*: 973-326-7600.

Willowwood/Bamboo Brook: (Morris County) The Willowwood Arboretum offers extensive walking paths and a conservatory. Flowering gardens, wildflowers, extensive trees. Adjoins the Bamboo Brook Outdoor Education Center which includes some formal gardens originally created by a well-known landscape artist, and a white cedar allee. *Location:* Longview Road, Chester Twp. *Telephone*: 973-326-7600.

Cora Hartshorn Arboretum and Bird Sanctuary: In the Short Hills section of Millburn Township, this 16-acre refuge includes a small stone building used as a nature center. Once the estate of a millionaire's daughter, it is now a pleasant, hilly spot where you can walk among the trees and listen to birdsongs. Rhododendron dell, ferns and wildflowers. No parking lot, so you must use the street. Nature center offers many programs. *Location:* 324 Forest Drive South, Short Hills. *Telephone*: 973-376-3587.

See Also: Formal gardens and landscaped lawns are often attached to the historic houses treated elsewhere in this book. For outstanding examples, see in particular, *Winterthur, Nemours, Lyndhurst,* and *The Vanderbilt Mansion* (Homes of the Rich and Famous) and *Buccleuch Mansion* (Where Washington Fought).

FLEA MARKETS
AND OUTLETS

Photo by Linda Kimler

In This Chapter You Will Find:

OUTLETS
    Reading, PA
    Flemington, NJ
    Secaucus, NJ
    Woodbury Common, NY
    Franklin Mills Mall, PA
    Other Outlets

FLEA MARKETS
    Englishtown Auction Sales, NJ
    Rice's Flea Market, PA
    Columbus Flea Market, NJ
    Dover Flea Market, NJ
    Other Flea Markets

ANTIQUES, NJ

READING, PENNSYLVANIA.

Reading is the grandaddy of outlet towns. It was here that someone decided to take old factory buildings and turn them into stores that would sell direct to the customer. For years people would drive from all over to get these manufacturer's goods at 50% off.

Nowadays, with outlets all over the place, Reading has lost some of its draw. Still the busses and cars come and some real bargains can be found. Things have changed over the years - most outlets now take charge cards (take your checkbook along, just in case) and there are several decent eating places around, and many of the shops are discount rather than outlet.

The original **Reading Outlet Center** is now a series of buildings, some of them the old factory, red brick variety,where you have to walk up stairs, and some new, white and low-slung. Building No.1, the biggest is on Windsor St. between N. 9th and Moss. Building #2 is across the street while Building #3 is catty-cornered to #1. If you walk down N. 9th Street past Douglass and Oley you will pass Buildings Nos. 5 & 6 and later, Nos. 4 & 7 plus the Rawlings Building. There are a variety of discount shops stuffed into these buildings. In one or the other of these buildings (they keep moving around all the time) you'll find the Kleins (Calvin and Anne) the NY Joneses, Liz Claiborne, and lots of other "names". Check www.readingoutlets.com

There are a number of other "pocket outlets" but the most popular of all is the VF Outlet at 801 Hill Ave., in next door Wyomissing. This is a series of huge buildings which store racks and racks of Vanity Fair robes and nightgowns at half-price, plus a whole lot of other goods.The complex is surrounded by gates and parking lots (with preferred parking going to the tour buses). Those companies owned by VF (e.g.Lee jeans, Jantzen sportswear, Healthtex) go for the straight 50% off. Other sections in the complex include American Tourister and Black & Decker with prices anywhere from 10% to 40% off.

The various buildings have colored flags and are designated as the Blue Building, the Red, the Purple, etc. That's so you don't get lost in the shopping canyons forever, and can find a landmark for your bus or car. It's worth checking out the nooks and crannies of these buildings, for shoes, silver,or whatever. On heavy shopping days at the VF Outlet you may have to park blocks away and take a shuttle to the buildings.

HOURS: Most stores open Mon. - Sat, 9:30-5:30 or 9:30 and Sun. 12-5
(except Jan. & Feb.)
LOCATION: Rte. 78 to US 222 to 422W to Reading, Pa. VF Outlet is on
Park & Hall Roads, Wyomissing.
TELEPHONE: 610-772-8336; VF: 800-772-8336 / www.readingoutlets.com

FLEMINGTON OUTLETS

Flemington is a pretty Victorian town in the middle of Hunterdon County, an area that is still partially farmland. Over the years Flemington has grown from a town that offered a few discount shops to a name that has become synonymous for outlet shopping.

If you're driving down Route 202 from the north, the first outlet you see is **Dansk,** which is on the Flemington Circle itself. This building includes Dansk modern design items, Gorham Silver and other stores. If you proceed onto Route 12 and then to Main Street you will find several shops including *Mikasa* (#95) and *Flemington Glass* (#156) and a number of nice lunchtime restaurants. Flemington Glass has sprouted annexes like crazy so you can find not only glass but pewterware and dinnerware also.

Next stop is **Liberty Village** (follow signs - it has a huge parking lot behind the railroad tracks). Liberty Village started out in the 1970s as a restored colonial village, but converted into an outlet center years ago. The white clapboard buildings and brick walkways lend a pleasant air to the job of bargain hunting.

If the ambience is pleasant, the prices are higher these days. And although there are now 60 stores, the size of some seem to have shrunk. At the Van Heusen outlet, for instance, men's jackets were once available at good discounts. Now, the jackets have gone and it's down to shirts and ties. Which is not to say you can't find bargains anymore. Just that they won't be much different from department store sale prices. *Coat World* (a discount house for jackets and coats) has moved out of Liberty Village and to its own little world called **Heritage Place** at Route 31 and Church St. But Ann Klein, Hanes, Corning and all the usual suspects are still around.

South of the Flemington Circle on Route 202/31 you pass yet another discount mall - this one called **Circle Outlet Center.** It contains another 16 stores, including discount chains like Bed, Bath and Beyond, Shoe-Town and Dress Barn.

Much of Flemington's unique attraction has gone by the wayside, as discount stores open up everywhere and outlets prices edge upward. But when it comes to pleasant surroundings and good, reasonably priced restaurants, Flemington, particularly around the Main Street and Liberty Village areas, certainly takes the prize. However, don't be surprised if some of your old favorites have closed or moved elsewhere.

LOCATION: Route 78 to 31 south, or Route 202. From Flemington Circle follow signs for "business district"
TELEPHONE: 908-806-8165; Liberty Village: 908-782-8550
www.premiumoutlets.com

SECAUCUS OUTLETS

Set in one of the busiest areas of New Jersey, just the other side of the Meadowlands Complex, the outlets here are dispersed over a huge area in between warehouses, office buildings, streets and flat open spaces. You will definitely need a map. Fortunately, you can pick one up at the first outlet mall you hit **(Outlets at the Cove)** which is conveniently placed on Meadowlands Parkway. This small enclosed mall features air-conditioning, clean restrooms, and designer outlets. At one of the stores here you can pick up a Secaucus booklet which not only includes a map but often offers discount coupons as well.

As you drive further to streets with names like Enterprise Avenue and Hartz Way, you will find the large outlet stores devoted to a single name. Mikasa China and Glassware and Liz Claiborne have their own building, chock full of merchandise at 20% to 30% discount. Of course if you hit a sale you will get even further reductions, and many people put themselves on the mailing list to take advantage of sales. You will also find a number of discount chains (such as Linens'NThings) in the complex. Syms Clothing takes up a full square block.

The **Harmon Cove Outlet Center** (20 Enterprise North) is a large enclosed mall with a variety of shops of varying value. But it also contains a food court ringed by food counters where you can rest your feet and partake of pizza, chicken, ice cream and other examples of fast food. And there's another small enclosed mall, the **Designer Outlet Gallery** at 55 Hartz Way, which includes designers with "names" like Anne Klein, Adolfo, Jonathan Martin, etc. If you check your map and drive back onto the Meadowlands Parkway above the Route 3 entrance, you'll find the **Swan Plaza,** a small strip mall that includes a delicatessen, and a rather good Corningware outlet. There are other little enclaves to be found within the outlet "territory" on the map.

Although the drive to Secaucus and the hunting for bargains can be exhausting, once you have found the store that fits your needs, or carries the name brand you usually buy, the trip is certainly worth it. And if you wait for the special warehouse sales (Mikasa has one, twice a year) you can stock up like crazy on all your presents.

HOURS: 7 days a week. Individual stores vary.
LOCATION: Secaucus. Take NJ Tpke to Exit 16W to Route 3 East to Meadowlands Parkway.
TELEPHONE: 201-348-4780 / www.secaucusoutlets.com

WOODBURY COMMON

For people who live in the northeastern section of New Jersey, this is a popular shopping stop. It's in New York State so you don't get the advantage of "no sales tax on clothes" that you do in New Jersey and Pennsylvania.

What it does have, is lots of stores—220 at the moment, and 25 of them are shoe stores! Scads of clothing stores and a little of everything else (Judith Leiber, Harry & David, Godiva). The place is divided into color quadrants with a Red Apple Court, a Green, Blue etc. There are directional maps placed around. A trolley tram makes the rounds of the parking lot to take you to the different sections, because once you've managed to find a parking space there's no way you're going to give it up—not during the heavy pre-Christmas season anyway! Special events in summer. A fast food place and a Applebee's are often crowded but in warm weather they have lots of hot dog and ice cream vendors outdoors.

LOCATION: Route 32, Central Valley, NY. Take GSP to 1-87 to Harriman, Exit 16.
TELEPHONE: 914-928-4000 / www.premiumoutlets.com

FRANKLIN MILLS MALL

While many outlet centers evolved from nearby factories or the conversion of unused buildings, Franklin Mills is a huge, superplanned, hi-tech mall designed as a magnet for shoppers from Philadelphia and New Jersey. It combines the convenience of an indoor mall with the bargain prices of discount stores and outlets.

Inside the 1.8 million square foot complex, you will find hundreds of stores, food courts (a square of tables ringed by numerous fast food eateries) plus entertainment and resting courts. Each corner of the huge complex is anchored by large store. Each section of the mall is color coded and everything is on one level. The planners seem to have thought of everything, except (since they undoubtedly were men) enough ladies rooms!

You can also find a Levi Strauss outlet, plus chain discount shops such as Linens'N Things and Flemington Fashion among the many stores. There have at various times been arcades and other diversions for kids who are dragged along. They do have banks of TV screens at some courts.

HOURS: Mon.-Sat: 10-9:30; Sun.: 11-6.
LOCATION: Northeast Philadelphia. Take 1-95 to Woodhaven Road Exit, turn right onto Franklin Mills Blvd.
TELEPHONE: 215-632-1500; 800-336-MALL.

OTHER OUTLETS

Close to the Jersey shore, the **Circle Factory Outlet Center** in Manasquan (just off Route 35) offers a smattering of outlets including Corning Ware, Mikasa, and Chaus. And in the northern part of the state, in Sussex County, you can find **Olde Lafayette Village** where Routes 15 and 94 meet just below the town of Lafayette. This "village" is half-and-half with colonial-style attached buildings featuring bridal shops and fudge emporiums rubbing elbows with such outlet regulars as Corning Ware, Cape Isle Knitters and Van Heusen. *Telephone*: 973-383-8323.

Princeton Forrestal Village, at the juncture of Route 1 and College Road West is another addition to the outlet scene. This started out in the '80s as a yuppie mall with all sorts of boutiques and gourmets shops. Well, now there are over 35 outlets here, including many regulars, plus WestPoint Pepperell, Lady Leslie and some designer fashions. Still some nice eating places, too. *Telephone:* 609-799-7400.

A newcomer to the outlet scene is **Six Flags Factory Outlets** on Route 537 off Route 195 in Jackson, Ocean County, just a few miles beyond *Six Flags Great Adventure*. It's not that big but you can find Brooks Brothers, Big Dog Sportswear (they seem to be everywhere) and Samsonite, for example. *Telephone*: 732-833-0680. And **Penn's Purchase** another mid-size outlet complex lies across from Peddler's Village in Lahaska (q.v.) Pennsylvania.

The Crossings: A favorite for those who live in northwest Jersey, *The Crossings* is right off I-80 (Exit 45) as you drive west to Tannersville, PA. People come here for Coach handbags or Stone Mountain bags, The Petite Sophisticate, Carter's childrenswear and several women's plus-size places. Also, there's Timberland, Hanes, etc. The place is growing, so parking will soon be a problem, but it's pleasant for now. *Telephone:* www.thecrossings.com

FLEA MARKETS

The term supposedly originated in the Middle Ages when peddlers gathered at the marketplace to sell old clothing and assorted junk which came already infested with fleas. Nowadays, the term covers a wide variety, including:

1. **New merchandise** from manufacturers overruns or seconds.

2. **Antique** and collectibles dealers.

3. **Garage sale items.** Since many outdoor flea markets rent their tables for the day (for as little as 10 dollars) it is not unusual for local people to simply hold their garage sales here.

4. **Craft dealers.** Generally craft people do better at craft cairs then at flea markets, since bargain hunters balk at the prices for new, hand-made items. However, at certain flea markets you might find someone selling seashell decorations or duck decoys, especially if the dealer has staked out this territory for himself.

5. **Farmer's markets.** Especially in Monmouth and Ocean Counties, summer markets include a food section where fresh corn, watermelons, beans and squash are on hand.

ENGLISHTOWN AUCTION SALES

It is one of the world's largest flea markets—this vast dusty field set in the midst of Monmouth County's farm country. What you find is something like 300 garage sales going on side by side with 700 New York street hawkers all set up on tables covering a huge field. Add to that a farmer's market with tables of fresh corn, tomatoes, melons, apples and pumpkins. And then add several buildings filled with discount clothing booths, kielbasa stands, knish stands, hamburgers and oriental food and a complete bar and grill. Then add a cast of thousands worthy of a Cecil B. DeMille movie and you have some idea of the immensity of the place. In fact Englishtown Auction Sales has everything but an auction - that term refers to the old days when cows were sold off too.

The Flea Market is open weekends only, and it opens early. What you will find is a mass of memorabilia, knick-knacks, new shoes and old tires - practically anything in the world can be discovered here. A new bell for your bicycle, a collection of porcelain doorknobs, or garage sale "junque" all mixed in with bargain basement clothing and cosmetics.

Those who search for collectibles can certainly find something of interest. Depression glass, comic books, paper-weights and German World War I helmets and medals were some that I noticed. More collectibles (along with food stands) can be found in the buildings called Red, Green, Blue, and Brown.

Englishtown Auction Sales offers you a chance to buy that elusive whatnot you could never find anywhere else. But of course, the mainstay is new merchandise sold at discount. Outdoor tables in seasonable weather. Lots of dust and dirt so dress appropriately. Small parking fee.

> **HOURS:** Sat.; 7 AM - 5 PM. Sun.: 9 AM - 5 PM all year.
> **LOCATION:** Garden State Parkway to Exit 123. Route 9 South to Texas Road. Right on Texas Road to Route 527 for 3 miles to 90 Wilson Ave., Englishtown, Monmouth County.
> **TELEPHONE:** 732-446-9644

RICE'S FLEA MARKET

If it's Tuesday, it must be Rice's. That's the day this 30-acre flea market comes to life on a flat field set on a back road near New Hope. They're open on Saturdays too. Officially named Rice's Country Market and Auction, it has a reputation for quality. To the neophyte it doesn't look much different than any other flea market. In fact, many of the vendors who set up tables here can be found at other flea markets other days of the week.

The main virtue of Rice's seems to be its size. Although the dirt field where it is held is huge, getting past all the tables is not unmanageable. You can actually walk the whole market in a morning and get a chance to peruse all the bargains. Get there early, because by one p.m. most vendors are packing up.

You can find specialty items here - one vendor sells only Guatamalan handmade goods; another specializes in ribbons and laces. There may be several booths of patterned sweaters. But the most common items tend to be college sweatshirts at reduced prices, tube socks, Chanel scarves at ten or twelve dollars, and some brand name toiletries.

Indoor stands sell coffee, bagels, doughnuts and Funnel Cakes (giant intricately designed crullers with powdered sugar on top). There are also a few merchandise vendors inside the small buildings, but this is primarily an outdoor flea market. No real place for lunch - there are some hot dog vendors, plus locals with fresh bread and fresh produce.

> **HOURS:** Every Tues. & Sat plus some holidays
> **LOCATION:** Route 202 to Aquetong, right to Green Hill Road, then another right, New Hope, PA
> **TELEPHONE:** 215-297-5993

DOVER FLEA MARKET

A flea market that ran for many years in Chester, then relocated to Dover has now transformed itself into its own unique style. While the usual venue for such endeavors in New Jersey is some dusty country field or the asphalt parking lot of a stadium, this flea market takes place on the sidewalks of a small urban town. Automobile traffic is roped off for several blocks where the vendors place their stands. One advantage is that you can take the train to Dover—the flea market is only a few blocks from the station (although trains run infrequently on Sunday). Another is that cafes and restaurants are open on the main street.

Vendors sell a variety of clothes, jewelry, unique items, crafts, collectibles, souvenir items, baseball cards and such. And you can always find a hot dog or funnel cake stand. Dover, by the way, has it's own antique stores on West Blackwell Street, including *Berman's Auction Gallery* and *The Iron Carriage Antique Center*.

> **HOURS:** Sundays, May-Dec.
> **LOCATION:** Route 80 to Route 10 (Dover) Exit
> **TELEPHONE:** 800-555-6263

COLUMBUS FLEA MARKET

This started out as a farmer's market and just grew and grew. Thursdays, Saturdays and Sundays are the days - from dawn until 2 ' p.m. with rows and rows of tables filled with pocketbooks, sweatshirts, sweaters, scarves, crazy items, knockoff perfumes, etc. It's also a traditional farmers market with fresh produce brought in from the neighboring countryside. There is also the traditional big yard sale, with people selling used "garage sale" style items next to hawkers of new merchandise.

The indoor buildings include many permanent "niche" stores plus a number of eating spots (hamburgers, bagels, etc.) In one of the buildings you can also find several Pennsylvania Dutch delicatessen counters where you can buy Amish style cold cuts and breads and fresh grown produce. Don't be surprised to find furniture and other large items in the indoor sections, which are open Thursday through Sunday.

LOCATION: Route 206, just below Columbus, Burlington County.
TELEPHONE: 609-267-0400

OTHER FLEA MARKETS

NEW EGYPT MARKET: A flea market village with fifty small buildings and many outside tables. Individual shops may feature furniture, clothing, or whatever, Outdoor tables can have everything from foundry type to garage sale items. Hours are 7 a.m. to 1 p.m., Sun. & Wed. New Egypt is located six miles west of Six Flags in Ocean County (Route 537). *Telephone:* 609-758-7440.

GARDEN STATE PARK: Highly popular market with about 500 vendors, located on the parking lot of the Garden State Park Race Track. Includes produce, flowers, discount merchandise, some old, mostly new-golf clubs, sweaters, bangles, etc. Covers 3 acres. Small parking fee. Runs from mid-March to mid-Dec. on Wed. & Sun., 8 AM to 3 PM. Route 70 and Haddonfield Rd., Cherry Hill, Camden County. *Telephone.* 856-488-8400.

BERLIN FARMERS MARKET AND SHOPPING CENTER: Traditional Jersey truck farm produce plus flea market mix. Indoor market houses over 85 stores, while the outdoor 70 spaces include new merchandise, flowers, shrubs, tools, garage sale stuff, etc. Services Camden

County area. Located at 41 Clementon Road, Berlin, (on Route 30 between Atco and Voorhees). *Telephone:* 856-767-1284.

MEYERSVILLE GRANGE FLEA MARKET: A change of pace since this market is indoors and runs only in the cold weather. The building is tiny, but there are almost 30 tables inside. Glassware, china, urns, posters and one or two craft tables that feature duck decoys or handmade quilts. On Meyersville Road, Long Hill Twp., Morris County. Sundays only, Oct. - March. *Telephone:* 908-654-3089.

POCONO BAZAAR FLEA MARKET: One of the largest in the area, this one runs all year round and has a smattering of everything. Lots of people stop by on their way to Pocono vacation spots, so when someone tells she bought her bag at that "flea market—you know-the one 209" this is the place. Take Exit 52 off I-80 to 209 north for 5 miles. Place is one mile north of Marshall's Creek. *Hours*: Sat., Sun.: 9-5.*Telephone*: 570-223-8640

Note: Flea market hours constantly change. Always telephone first

ANTIQUES

For those who do not relish the trudge through the dusty fields, there are plenty of antique stores and centers where you may browse in comfort - even air-conditioned comfort. There are over two thousand antique stores in New Jersey alone. Here is a short run-down on some of the better known centers.

The Antique Center at **Red Bank** hosts about 100 dealers in four large buildings within walking distance of one another. The shops are open from 11-5 and are located on Front Street and the 200s block. Take Garden State Parkway to Route 109, Monmouth County.

Lambertville (Routes *179 & 29*, Hunterdon County) is now one of the best antiquing towns in the state. Once a poor relation to New Hope across the river, this refurbished canal town now offers art stores, restaurants, country stores and a whole bunch of antique shops. Most are centered around Bridge Street (the main thoroughfare through town) and Union Street. *The People's Store* a large conglomerate of dealers is on Union.But don't expect cheap prices here. On weekends you can find

The Lambertville Flea market going strong on Route 29 about a mile south of the bridge.

Chester was once the home of a well-known flea market which has since moved to Dover. However, so many quaint stores and antique places have opened up in this colonial style town, that is has created its own ambience. On East Main Street, stores with cutesy names offer a mix of antiques, quilts, coverlets and cookware. An English tea shoppe and a few lunch places are nestled between antique stores with names like *Aunt Pittypat's Parlour,* and country style stores with lavender and lace. Lots of weekend special promotions here—everything from Cabin Fever in late winter to a large craft shows. (Routes 124 & 206, Morris County)

A small enclave in north Jersey is *The Mill Market* in the quaint town of **Lafayette,** Sussex County. Forty dealers run a cooperative effort in a reconverted 1842 mill. The mill is on Route 15 in the center of town next to an old-fashioned General Store and is open Friday to Monday only. There are other interesting antique shops in Lafayette also. A Sussex County town with a growing reputation is **Andover.** *Scranberry Coop* at 42 Main St., has 150 dealers under one roof here, and plenty of action. There are other stores scattered along Main Street.

An old colonial town which is known for both antiques and a pleasant atmosphere is **Hopewell** a few miles outside of Princeton in Mercer County. A few small stores plus *The Tomato Factory* (a group enterprise) makes this a nice destination for a country outing.

In south Jersey, the village of **Mullica Hill** has long attracted buyers to its country-style antique stores. Antique dolls, books and ephemera, toys, furniture, together with collectibles and arts-and-crafts items can be found in a passel of stores here. Two collectives are *Kings Row Antiques* at 46 N. Main St., and *The Yellow Garage Antique Marketplace* (yes, it's a reconverted garage). To get there, take Exit 2 from the NJ Turnpike to Route 322E for four miles, turn right at the "T" in front of the diner. Or try www.mullicahill.com

Visitors to the shore can always find antique shops open during the season, from gingerbread houses in **Cape May** to several shops on **Long Beach Island** that specialize in nautical antiques. One of the largest enclaves in the state is at the *Point Pleasant Antique Emporium* at Bay and Trenton Aves. at that shore resort. One hundred dealers, under one roof, offer furniture, quilts, dolls and collectibles, all in a beautiful air-conditioned building in the center of town.

Then there are the big fairs and conventions that bring in antique dealers from all over the east coast. Best known is the Atlantique Fair at the Convention Center in Atlantic City, with 7000 dealers. It takes place twice a year. Other large fairs can be found at Waterloo Village and the Meadowlands. Autumn is the heaviest season for such fairs. And remember, most antique stores are not open Mondays or Tuesdays and often not even on Wednesdays.

OTHER OUTINGS

Photo: NY Renaissance Faire

In This Chapter You Will Find:

THE CRAYOLA FACTORY

A popular outing for school groups, The Crayola Factory is also a place where parents can take their children for a few hours of entertainment and enlightenment. It's a combination of factory tour and children's interactive museum. The "Factory" takes up the second floor of a building called Two Rivers Landing, which also includes a Canal Museum on the upper floors. When you pay the admission price you are handed two Crayola "coins".

Upon entering the Factory floor you first see a docent who explains the crayon- making process and offers a little history. The hot wax mixture is poured into pre-made molds and allowed to cool. Then the paper wrapper is applied. Afterwards, you use your "coins" to buy a small four-crayon box. This is all for demonstration— the actual Crayola factory is thirteen miles away.

As for history— Binney & Smith (the Crayola makers) started out as a paint company selling its distinctive red paint to Pennsylvania farmers for their barns. In 1903 they added paraffin to the color, creating their first crayons. They now sell Magic Markers and Silly Putty as well as all sizes and colors of crayons.

After the demonstrations, it's on to the interactive sections. These include arts and crafts plus interesting diversions. Really young kids will enjoy the Color Garden where giant plastic vegetables can be planted, watered, gathered and put in bins. One toddler picked up every onion, carrot and apple in sight and piled them into her wheelbarrow. Other kids took produce out of bins and sold them at the sales register.

Other sites include the theater, where you can put on a puppet show, the Crayola Carrousel and several computers (the ten-year-olds have a lock on these). Then there are huge rooms where kids sit down and work with paper or clay to create anything they want. There are plenty of volunteers to help them.

A visit to the Canal Museum upstairs is of interest if your children are not too young. The canals of the early 19th century were the main means of transportation in America and you can see a mock-up of a typical flatboat and plenty of interactive maps.

The Crayola Store, which carries an incredible variety of crayons, craft works and balloons, is around the corner. The parking garage across the street charges $2.00/hour. The Factory can get crowded during the summer, so get there early, since it's first come, first served. Children under 16 must be accompanied by an adult.

HOURS: Tues.-Sat.: 9:30-5:30. Sun.: 12-5. Summer: Mon.-Sat.: 9-6;
           Sun.: 11-6.
ADMISSION: Adults & children: $7.00; Seniors: $6.50. Under 2 free
LOCATION: 30 Centre Square, Easton PA.
TELEPHONE: 610-515-8000 / www.crayola.com

NORTHLANDZ

"Northlandz" is a combination of **The Great American Railway** (the world's largest miniature railway), a dollhouse, a doll museum, and an old fashioned, frontier style music hall. All are housed in a Greek temple of a building just north of the Flemington Circle. It's a popular destination for grandparents, families and railroad buffs. The huge model railroad is a 52,000 square feet display that uses enough wood to build 42 houses— and plenty of plaster to create small towns and great gorges. There are 135 individual trains and eight miles of track that cut through looming mountains, deep quarries and unique cityscapes. They go over bridges and rivers and past Alpine scenes. Visitors walk about a mile as they trudge up and around a ramp that covers three and-a-half stories, so they can view the scenery from different angles.

You see Pennsylvania coal mining towns, horses grazing on sloping hills, and marching bands as you walk along. Some scenes are built with humor in mind. A hotel "With a view" perches precariously over a deep gorge. For drama there is a deep canyon with a complete mining town set beneath the looming railroad bridge. Some towns are peopled with miniature citizens while farms may have horses and cows set out to pasture.

The "La Peep" Dollhouse is not free-standing. It is a series of miniature rooms set into the wall, featuring typical home scenes. A doll museum of large collectible dolls in fancy costume can be seen towards the end of the tour. The separate American Music Hall, in the style of a western saloon, features a 2000-pipe organ which is played several times a day. Northlandz also includes a café and a gift shop filled with railroad caps and memorabilia. Allow at least two hours for a visit. In good weather, there is a outdoor $3/4$ scale scenic railway that takes on passengers for an extra fee.

HOURS: Daily, 10-6.
ADMISSION: Adults: $13.75; Seniors: $12.50; Children: $9.75; under 2 free.
LOCATION: 495 Route 202 S, Flemington (north of the Flemington Circle).
TELEPHONE: 908-782-4022

STERLING HILL MINE

The last operating zinc mine in New Jersey went out of business in 1986. You might wonder why anyone would want to keep and restore an old mine, but local people have put all their money and energy into it and for good reason. Besides the primary zinc deposits there are over 300 minerals in this area, half of which are found nowhere else. Dedicated townsfolk decided to keep the mine open for tours and use the buildings as a mining museum.

Tours of the mine are given at specific times (1 p.m. during off-season, 3 times a day during summer) One thing you learn right away - wear a jacket. It is 56 degrees all the time, inside the mine, and it is often damp too. Wear good, heavy shoes. Because the area of Ogdensburg and near-by Franklin has the world's largest deposits of fluorescent stones, the most effective stop on the tour is the "Rainbow Room." This is a wall that looks like ordinary rock when you first see it. The tour guide switches on an ultra-violet light and the red-fluorescent calcite and green-fluorescent willemite begin to glow in the halfdark. It is like something from a science-fiction movie.

There's lots of walking on this tour not only along the tracks of the mine itself, but in the other buildings as well. The museum—where one usually starts includes one huge exhibit hall where miners used to change clothing. You can see the high metal baskets where they once dumped their wet outer garments. Displays include dinosaur prints, zinc products and a whole range of paraphenalia.

In the mine-office building you can buy hot dogs from the grill or peruse the gift shop which includes plenty of mineral specimens. There is also an outdoor picnic area. An interesting tour, both for scout troops or for grown-ups. It can easily be combined with a visit to the Franklin Mineral Museum, three miles away.

> **HOURS:** Daily, 10-5 Apr. 1-Nov. 30.
> **ADMISSION:** Adults: $9.00; Under 17:$6.00; Seniors: $8.00.
> **LOCATION:** 30 Plant St, Ogdensburg, Sussex County. Take Rte. 517 to Brooks Flat Road to Plant.
> **TELEPHONE:** 973-209-7212 / www.sterlinghill.org

THE U.S.S. LING SUBMARINE

The U.S.S. Ling (official name: *New Jersey Naval Museum*) is only 312 feet long and 27 feet wide, and when you consider that ninety-five men and twenty-four torpedoes were aboard during its career as an active sub in 1945, you realize that this is no place for someone with claustrophobia. Nowadays, most of the torpedoes and many of the berths have been removed to allow tour groups to move about. Indeed the inside seems surprisingly spacious compared with the outside. Tickets are bought at the museum building which also houses lots of war pictures and paraphernalia - including the periscope of a Japanese sub.

Tours last about 45 minutes, depending on your guide. You begin in the torpedo room where there are still two of these sleek weapons left. (No, they are not active). I learned that torpedoes do not go off by accident since they are activated only after they leave the tube. They also had to be aimed right, since a miss would give away the sub's position to an enemy ship.

I also learned that much of the time on the sub was devoted to eating and cooking. Besides three meals a day and night for all shifts, sailors could raid the refrigerator at any time. When the Ling first left port, space was so dear that fresh fruit and vegetables were stacked in one of the showerheads. Since it was hot and cramped in the sub, showers were popular, as was Lifebuoy soap.

Tours include the Control Room, Maneuvering Room, Main Engine Room, sleeping quarters and more; but the Conning Tower with its periscope is off limits. You are allowed to handle certain equipment, including the wheels and gauges, and the guide does sound the diving signal (memorable from a host of old war movies starring Cary Grant and John Garfield).

While modern submarines are larger and sleeker, this black, fleet-type vessel is a memorial to the World War II submariners who must have been a hardy lot. An interesting place, both for older children and ex-servicemen. Birthday parties, too.

HOURS:	Wed.-Sun.: 10-5
ADMISSION:	Adults: $4.00; Children: $2.50
LOCATION:	150 River Street, Hackensack
TELEPHONE:	201-342-3268.www.njnm.com

THE STATE HOUSE

You don't have to be on a political mission to visit Trenton. The Legislative Section of the State House is open to public tours after years of refurbishing. One can see the architectural richness of this building which predates the 1930s "institutional" style of many government structures.

Inside, the main hall is lit by Victorian style chandeliers, once fueled by gas. There are arches of faux marble and pilasters of dark wood. One eye-catching piece in the center of the hall is a porcelain Boehm sculpture which features the state tree (the red oak) the state bird (the goldfinch) and even the state insect (the honeybee). The rotunda features paintings of the governers. If it's not in session, you can visit the handsome Senate Chamber with its stained glass skylight or the General Assembly Room. Sometimes the Governor's Reception Room is open.

One also discovers some interesting Jersey facts on the tour. For instance - we don't have a Lieutenant Governor and the legislature only works part time. Tours run hourly. Groups of more than ten should reserve in advance. Free.

HOURS: Tours are Tues., Wed. & Fri.: 10-3 & Sat 12-3.
LOCATION: 125 W. State St. (Take Rte. 29 to Calhoun St Exit)
TELEPHONE: 609-633-2709

TWIN LIGHTS LIGHTHOUSE

An unusual brownstone building that looks more like a castle than the lighthouse it once was, Twin Lights is perched on a mountainous bluff in Highlands and affords a sweeping view of Sandy Hook and the ocean beyond. The "twin" lights, (one is square and one octagonal) are towers on either side of the main building. The first Fresnel lights were used here in 1841. The present fortress-like structure was built in 1862 and was the scene of many "firsts". The museum inside includes exhibits on early life-saving equipment and Marconi's demonstration of the wireless from this site.

Naturally part of the enjoyment of visiting a decomissioned lighthouse is making the climb up the stairs. The ascent up the spiral staircase involves only 65 steps and leads to an excellent view. Downstairs, there is a small gift shop and outside you will find a picnic area and several historical markers. Free.

HOURS: Daily,9-5 in summer. Closed Mon. & Tues. rest of year
LOCATION: Highlands, Monmouth County, Take Route 36S make right
turn just before Highlands Bridge, then right onto Miller Rd.
Follow signs.
TELEPHONE: 732-872-1814

BUSHKILL FALLS

For families who wish to avoid the hurly-burly of amusement parks, there are scenic attractions which offer a day in the country with the simpler amusements of an earlier time. One of these is Bushkill Falls, set in a primeval forest in the foothills of the Poconos. The area is cool in the summer and colorful in the fall, and while the main waterfall is nowhere near Niagara in width or grandeur, it does present both photographers and hikers with a pleasant outing.

You enter through a "nature" museum to a pathway through the forest. Although you get a good view of the cascading water from up top, it is more impressive to see it from below by way of a "natural" log stairway.The Main Falls drop over the edge of a 100-foot cliff to a deep pool below. From that point the water drops another 70 feet through a large gorge strewn with gigantic boulders. The falls are fairly narrow, but the drop is spectacular.

There are three routes to follow to the falls. The short route, with a green trail marker, takes only 15 minutes to walk. It is the "chicken" trail to a lookout where you can take a picture, then sit down. The second or "popular" route takes 45 minutes and is for those who want their money's worth. This takes you down and around the bottom of the main falls. The third route takes 1 1/2 hours. Here you pass a series of mist-laden falls to a lookout where you can enjoy a panoramic view of the Delaware Valley. It is absolutely necessary for one to wear good walking shoes.

When visiting the Falls, check the map in the brochure you receive with your ticket. It clearly marks the trails to follow. Food service, concessions, paddle boats and beer are available for those who need rest and relaxation after their exertions. Picnic tables also.

HOURS: April - Nov.: Daily, 9-5.
ADMISSION: Adults: $8.00; Seniors: $7.00; Children 4-10: $2.00; Under 4, free.
LOCATION: Bushkill, Pa. Take 1-80 to Exit 52, then 209 N. Follow signs.
TELEPHONE: 570-588-6682. www.bushkillfalls.com

NEW YORK RENAISSANCE FAIRE

This festival has been running for many years now and has become quite popular. For ten weekends - from early August to mid-September - the greenery at Sterling Forest in New York is taken over by knights in shining armor, ladies, peddlers dressed in motley, jugglers and mimes. A joust on horseback is the big attraction here (one at 2 p.m., the other at 6). Otherwise a series of "shows" depicting outlaws, queens and jesters are part of the festival. However, the mud wrestling, juggling, and other attractions are operated by free lancers who expect the customers to come up with some coin of the realm so bring extra money along. Rides (some simple ones) and games are extra too. The main attractions - such as the living Chess Game, and the joust, take place at particular locations at specific times - so you must buy a program to enjoy everything.

Shortened versions of Shakespeare's plays are put on in the Festival's rustic Globe Theater. Vendors in tents offer such unusual items as brass rubbings and flower circlets for milady's hair. **Note:** no outside food or drink allowed.

HOURS:	Weekends, 10:30-7; Aug.-mid-Sept
ADMISSION:	Adults: $16.50; Children 5 -12: $7.00; Under 5 free.
LOCATION:	Sterling Forest Tuxedo, N.Y. Take Route 17A West; look for signs.
TELEPHONIE:	856-351-5171 / www.renfair.com

NEW JERSEY RENAISSANCE FESTIVAL

This is a local effort and runs along the same lines as the major fests, only you will not find a joust on horseback. However this has been running a continuous storyline about kings and queens, knights and ladies for several years. You can watch costumed actors follow storyline and engage in swordplay. In the afternoon there is a "living chess game". There is story telling and puppeteers for children. Grownups can join in a Maypole dance, run around the "forest" in costume, watch pirates, weddings and whatever. Food court and vendors in a Tudor Village. The whole thing takes place in a large park in Somerset (Franklin Twp.) re-named the Kingdom of Somerset for the occasion.

The same park is host to a Haunted Village on Halloween weekend in October that includes a tour guide through some scary places and runs from 6 to 10 p.m. in the evening.

HOURS: Late May-Late June: 11-6.
ADMISSION: Adults: $12.00; Seniors: $8.00; Kids: $6.00.
LOCATION: Somerset Park, Franklin Twp. Take Exit 6 off 287.
TELEPHONE: 732-271-1119 / www.NJKingdom.com

MEDIEVAL TIMES

Combine a horse show, a night club, a dinner theater and a Renaissance Festival, put it all in a circus-like arena inside of a huge stucco castle and plunk it down near one of New Jersey's busiest intersections (right near the Meadowlands) and you have the northern version of Medieval Times. Here you get not one, but six jousts, a steady narrative by a Master of Ceremonies and a chance to eat dinner without any utensils!

When you enter the cavernous castle to buy your tickets you are handed a paper hat with a special color. This color will determine which section you sit in, and which knight you root for. These colored hats are a great gimmick, for it is in cheering on a particular champion that the audience becomes part of the show.

After a chance to look at medieval artifacts and inspect a torture dungeon (and buy such stuff as shields and banners at the gift shop) you are ushered into the arena where chairs are set against long banquet tables. These are set in tiers so that everybody in the huge oval arena can see the show.

And now, the menu. As the serving wench tells you, there is soup (served in a porringer), chicken, potato and barbecued ribs plus dessert, coffee or punch. You also get a huge napkin which is best tucked into your collar in standard Henry the Eighth style. (Bring a wetnap along— some people even sneak in a plastic spoon for the soup).

As for the show— first some fancy dressage and a magician. Then it's on to the jousts. The knights not only fight on horseback, but engage in swordplay after being unhorsed. This goes on for all six knights until the final victor is announced. All this while, the wenches are either serving supper or selling you pictures, banners or wines.

After the jousts, many couples stay on to dance at a small nightclub set up in the anteroom. Families often hang around until their knight shows up to autograph the picture or shield their kids have bought. An interesting evening.

EXCURSION RAILROADS

New Jersey's best known excursion railroad is the **Black River and Western** which leaves from Mine Street and Turntable Junction in Flemington. In fact, the tracks are right next to the outlet shops of Liberty Village. Trains run in season, (usually mid-April until December) on weekends and weekdays in summer. It's a real old-fashioned steam engine that pulls the train (with real soot and ashes) and you travel through well-wooded Hunterdon County. However, due to the popularity of the ride, diesels are also used for some trips. The train goes to Ringoes for a short stop, then back again. Call for schedule. Telephone: 908-782-6622 / www.brwrr.com.

A popular attraction at Allaire State Park in Monmouth County is the **Pine Creek Railroad** which runs a ten-minute trip. The narrow gauge steam train ride is part of several attractions at this large park. The ride operates mostly during the summer season. Check the Allaire Village listing for further information.

Another train ride, this one well into Pennsylvania Dutch territory (and therefore, technically, beyond the periphery of this book) is the **Strasburg Railroad.** Located on Route 741, Strasburg, in Lancaster County, Pennsylvania, the ride is so well known that it attracts tourists from across the border. The 45-minute ride offers a steam train with potbelly stoves in the coaches and an observation car straight out of "Hello, Dolly!". It operates on weekends during March, April, November and December. Weekdays on May 1 through October 31. Call 717-687-7522 for time schedules.

The New Hope and Ivyland steam railroad is mentioned in the article on that town.

EXCURSION BOATS

The sight-seeing cruise has been with us a long time - the fancier excursion cruise has become more popular within the last few years.

Sightseeing usually involves some narration and access to hot dogs, soda and beer. Excursion boats often have cocktail bars, restaurant or buffet service, and music or entertainment. The entertainment may range from a single guitarist to a five piece band. Here are some of the larger cruises that are currently afloat. The excursion type vessel also caters to groups for birthdays, engagement parties, proms and business bashes.

Circle Line Tour: A standard sightseeing attraction for many years, the ferry leaves from 42nd St, NYC and travels around the island of Manhattan via the Hudson River, New York Harbor, East River and Harlem River.There's the standard 3-hour or a half-circle two-hour tour. (A one-hour tour departs from *South Street Seaport* for a ride around the harbor.) An announcer (or canned tape) points out the Statue of Liberty and all the monuments, skyscrapers, bridges and churches with appropriate anecdotes and facts. Too bad most of the tourists on board don't understand English! Still the big thrill is to wave at all the other excursion boats out there and of course you do get to see New Jersey as well as New York when you're on the Hudson. Coffee and hot dogs available. Sailings vary by season and prices vary with the length of the tour. *Telephone*: 212-563-3200 / www.circleline.com.

NY Waterways: It began as a commuter ferry between Weehawken and New York City. It filled a real need, leading to further service from Hoboken and Jersey City. A bus meets the ferry on the New York side and takes passengers to destinations within a confined loop. Now this popular line has expanded into limited cruises. You can take the boat from Weehawken to Kykuit, Sunnyside and other Tarrytown destinations on weekends during warm weather. There's a popular ferry to Yankee Stadium and the Mets Shea Stadium. Also special cruises from Weehawken on July 4th, New Year's Eve and for well known Broadway shows. *Telephone*: 800-533-3779.

The Spirits: The Spirit of New Jersey leaves from Liberty State Park and sails into the Hudson River and New York Harbor. This large, enclosed boat seats 300 people and offers a choice of lunch, brunch, cocktails, dinner and dancing or group festivities. The typical lunch or dinner will be buffet and afterwards the waiters turn into entertainers or a live band plays for dancing. Although they do take walk-on passengers, it's best to reserve beforehand. Groups of course must reserve. *Telephone.* 201-333-3603..

A similar excursion boat, **The Spirit of Philadelphia,** departs from The Great Plaza at Penn's Landing (right across from the Camden aquarium) to circle the Philadelphia Harbor and provides Broadway entertainment for lunch. *Telephone.* 215-923-1419. And those who want to leave from Manhattan can always board the sister ship, **The Spirit of New York** which departs from West 23rd St and 12th Ave. Call 212-727-2789 for that one.

The Lady: Want to experience the ambience of a Mississippi paddle-wheeler? You can, on this 85-foot custom built excursion boat which used to dock at Atlantic Highlands and cruise the Navesink river. Now it has moved north to Liberty State Park in Jersey City (Exit 14B on the Tpke.) where it berths at the Liberty Landing Marina to join the crowd in New York Bay. Cruises for lunch, dinner (and of course group charters). Their office is still in Monmouth County and their telephone is still 732-291-4354.

The Jersey Shore: Here you will find several versions of sightseeing and excursion boats. **"The River Queen,"** a simplified version of a Mississippi River paddle boat, cruises for lunch, afternoon sightseeing, etc., This boat, which sails from Bogan's Basin in Brielle, and its sister ship the **"River Belle"** which leaves from Point Pleasant Beach are both popular with groups, especially senior citizens groups. The boats cruise the inland waters of the Manasquan River and Barnegat Bay so the water is calm and sightseeing is mostly of the docks and patios of shore homeowners plus an occasional bridge. Some cruises have narration, but there is no entertainment except for the special Dixieland band cruises that run on Wednesdays during the summer. Telephone. 732-528-6620.

Further down at Wildwood Crest (Park Blvd. on the bay side) there is a **Captain Sinn's Sightseeing Center** (609-522-3934) which runs sightseeing cruises as well as whale-watching trips and dinner cruises. And the **Cape May Fishing & Sightseeing Center** (609-898-0055) in Cape May operates whale and dolphin watching cruises plus a shorter wine and cheese harbor cruise. Of course the whale-watching trips go out into the ocean but whether or not they actually spot any whales depends on the time of year. There are a number of other short sightseeing cruises that leave from Otten's Harbor in Wildwood and the Cape May Yacht Basin in Cape May, most with narration (although the evening trips usually favor band entertainment).

The A.J. Meerwald is New Jersey's first and only tall ship! Actually, it's an oyster schooner that has been restored and is berthed (along with a small museum) in BiValve, a port in Burlington County. Luckily, it also visits other ports (such as Highlands, Philadelphia and Atlantic City) during warm weather and takes on paying passengers who can help hoist the rigging and trim the sails. Winter, it's booked for school groups. *Telephone*: 856-785-2060.

The Cape May-Lewes Ferry now offers a new $27,000,000 four-deck ship to make the 70-minute trip across Delaware Bay to Lewes. Boat runs are about every forty minutes during peak season. Of course these ferries take cars also since their main business is transportation. However the new ships resemble cruise liners in that they have elevators, modern decor, fancy restaurants and can cater groups. The older ferries also make regular run (and sometimes have special events) so call first if you want the "fast" ferry. The terminal is at the tip of Cape May County. *Telephone:* 800-717-7245.

CULINARY INSTITUTE OF AMERICA

Want to run a day trip and fill up the bus? Try The Culinary Institute of America and seats will fill up fast. Groups often wait months for reservations. If you go on your own, you may find it easier to reserve a table at this school where budding chefs cook, clean and serve in the restaurants on the first floor.

What makes CIA so popular? Since many of the graduates go on to found chic, ultra-expensive restaurants, there is the feeling of getting in on the ground floor of a good thing. But if the cooking is done by seniors, the waiters must be freshman, because the service can vary from efficient to inept.The food, however, is always good, if not necessarily in the sublime category.

Set high on a hill overlooking the Hudson Valley, the red brick Institute includes classrooms, student dorms, several restaurants and a well-stocked bookstore. *The Escoffier Room,* which specializes in the formal, multi-course European meal includes a large window which allows patrons to watch the chefs at meal preparation. A typical formal meal might include a light hors d'oeuvre, a soup, a main course followed by salad, and then a handsome dessert. The *American Bounty Room* offers faster service and includes such staples as roast beef and American pies.

Other eating areas include the informal *St. Andrews Cafe,* and the Italian *Caterina de Medici* for formal fare. A tour of the CIA is available. You pass all the classrooms where students may be beheading fish or pushing pastry through a tube. There is a rolling graduation here, so classes go on continuously. If you are combining a trip to the Institute with a visit to the neighboring historic houses at Hyde Park be sure you allow plenty of time, since lunch is a leisurely affair here.

HOURS: Call first
LOCATION: Hyde Park, NY (3 miles north of Poughkeepsie).
TELEPHONE: 914-471-6608

RENAULT WINERY

Let's face it, a winery tour is just about the most popular kind of industrial tour there is. The art of winemaking is so ancient, and the slightly fermented air in the cellars so heady that there is always a party air about these tours. And since wine-tasting is involved, everyone seems to have a good time.

Historic Renault Winery calls itself the best little tour-house in New Jersey. You learn about the early wine presses and dosage machines, and some tour leaders play to the crowd, threatening to send the women in to stomp the grapes or the men in to clean the barrels. The tour includes a sip of wine and some history of the place. The winery is situated way out in the Pine Barrens about 16 miles northwest of Atlantic City where the sandy soil lends itself well to grape production.

There are various stops in rooms full of antique wine-making equipment, Venetian glassware and small wine-tasting rooms. Then it's into the cellars where giant vats store the wine. These oak and redwood vats are fifty and sixty years old and would have to be replaced today by stainless steel, as the old cooper's craft is lost .The guide explains how the wine is poured off and other facts. If I learned one salient fact here it was to never buy cooking wine. It seems that food companies buy the wineries' rejects, then add salt (that's a law), bottle it and sell it.

Aside from its tours, Renault Winery also serves lunches at a charming bistro outside the main building called The Wine Garden. There is also a weekend gourmet restaurant, open to the public by reservation. In the fall, grape stomping festivals take over. Groups can also reserve for these.

> **HOURS:** Daily. Tours are Mon. - Sat.: 10:30-4; Sun.: 12-4
> **ADMISSION:** $2.00 for tours. Under 18 free.
> **LOCATION:** Bremen Ave., Egg Harbor City, Atlantic County. Take Garden State Parkway exit 44 (if coming from north only!) and right onto Moss Mill Rd., then 6 miles to Bremen Ave.
> From Atlantic City. Route 30 to Bremen Ave.
> **TELEPHONE:** 609-965-2111

OTHER AREA WINERIES

Wineries are a fast growing segment of New Jersey's agricultural scene and they seem to be popping up all over. New ones have sprung up in Warren, Hunterdon and Somerset counties. While many do not have traditional tours, they all welcome visitors on weekends and special occasions. Most of these wineries combine forces for a large spring and fall wine tasting festival, where food, entertainment, and an admission charge await. Hayrides and grape stomping also.

Even without festivals, tracking down wineries on fall weekends has become a popular activity. And tracking it is, because many of these places are on winding narrow roads where street signs don't exist. Luckily the Wine Council puts out a map, complete with directions. Call 609-292-8853 for this.

As for tours, the newer wineries (which often look like suburban ranch houses), are run scientifically with fiberglass and steel equipment There isn't much to see and the information tends to be technical. The big thing is the wine-tasting, At a long bar, an attendant will pour wine into little cups and explain its type and texture. Often they start with light, dry wines and proceed to woody and fruit-flavored ones. Naturally, you are expected to buy a few bottles after all this work.

As for the barefoot grape stomping parties - these are usually reserved for groups and include food, wine and the right to enter an open barrel and squish grapes through your toes. Great anger therapy. Among the wineries in Warren County are the **Four Sisters** (908-475-3671), **Alba** (908-995-7800) and **Tamuzza** (908-459-5878). More southerly ones include **King's Road Vineyard** in Hunterdon County (800-479-6479) and **Cream Ridge,** near Great Adventure (609-259-9797). In Pennsylvania, The **Sand Castle Winery** offers popular tours. This vinyard along the Delaware River was developed by brothers from Czechoslovakia and offers European style wines and a full tour. Telephone: 800-PA2-WINE.

THE MEADOWLANDS

Meadowlands Sports-Arena Complex was built in the middle of a wide open area, convenient to the Lincoln Tunnel so it could attract folks from both sides of the river. More then twenty-five years later, the biggest problem is traffic tie-ups, especially when all three buildings are holding events. There are covered crosswalks for pedestrians to get from one parking lot to another. The complex consists of;

1. THE RACETRACK: Both harness and flat racing have their season at this modem, sparkling facility with its glassed-in, climate controlled Grandstand. There are restaurants here for those who want to combine a night out with dining out. The fancy one is **Pegasus,** up on the top level of the track. It gives you a bird's eye view of the race, buffet stations, and high prices. Or you can opt for the tiered restaurant which gives a better view of the track but rather ordinary food.

For those watching the race from the grandstand a large 15 x 36 foot video matrix screen allows you to watch the action on the far side of the field and also flashes the results almost immediately.

2. GIANTS STADIUM: So named because the football team of that name makes its home there, but soccer teams, The Jets and college champion football teams play on the same turf—at least so far. Special headliner concerts show up here as well. The stadium has a seating capacity of 78,000 color coded seats and a video matrix scoreboard that delights the kids. The outside parking lot is the scene of flea markets, antique shows, petting zoos and a three-week carnival in the summer.

3. CONTINENTAL AIRLINES ARENA: It boasts a striking modem design that arches eleven stories high. The arrangement of seats (approximately 20,000) allows good viewlines. However, a shortage of personnel sometimes closes off the lower concourse so you may have quite a hike if you go for snacks. The Arena hosts basketball games, ice shows, Ringling Brothers Circus, rock shows and many other entertainments.

FOR THE MEADOWLANDS COMPLEX

PARKING:	Fee varies. Come early to avoid jamups.
LOCATION:	East Rutherford, Bergen County.
DIRECTIONS:	From NJ. Turnpike northbound - take Exit 16W for direct access. From NJ Turnpike southbound - take Exit 18W. From Garden State Parkway northbound - Exit 153A to Route 3 East From G.S.P. south-Exit 163 to Route 17S to Paterson Plank Road East
TELEPHONE:	201-843-2446

OTHER RACE TRACKS & RODEOS

MONMOUTH PARK: Oceanport, Monmouth County (Use GSP Exit 105). The oldest and to many, the most attractive of Jersey's racetracks, close to the seashore. There are plenty of picnic tables along the outside track, so families often come and enjoy a lunch. Indoor and outdoor seating at grandstand. Cafeteria, food stands plus a restaurant in the clubhouse. Thoroughbred racing from late May through September. *Telephone: 732-222-5100*

FREEHOLD RACEWAY: Park Avenue, Freehold, Monmouth County (Take Route 9 to junction of Route 33). *Telephone.* 732-462-3800. A beautiful track with flags flying, right in the heart of horse breeding country. Harness racing runs from January through May; then August to December. Fairs and flea markets operate in between.

ATLANTIC CITY RACE COURSE: Junction of Route 40 and Route 322, Atlantic County (Atlantic City Expressway Exit 12). *Telephone.* 609-641-2190. Thoroughbred racing June 1 - Sept. 30.

GARDEN STATE PARK Rte 70 and Haddonfield Rd. Cherry Hill, Camden County. *Telephone.* 856-488-8400. Harness racing Wed.-Sat., Sept.-Dec.: Thoroughbred racing Tues.-Sun., Feb.-June. Site of a popular flea market (q.v.)also.

COWTOWN RODEO: Yes, it does exist and its a regular rodeo with bucking broncos and all that stuff. It runs every Saturday night from the end of May to the end of September at 7:30 p.m. rain or shine. The audience sits on outdoor bleacher seats. Also site of flea market. *Admission:* Adults: $10.00; Children: $5.00; 12 and under free. *Location:* US Route 40 eight miles east of Delaware Memorial Bridge (Woodstown), Salem County. *Telephone:* 856-769-3200.

U.S. EQUESTRIAN TEAM HEADQUARTERS: Not that they're in residence that often, but there are several events open to the public at the team headquarters in Gladstone. One, *The Festival of Champions,* includes show jumping, dressage and things like four-in-hand competitions (for teams of horses). There is a charge for special events. The stables and show rings are located on Pottersville Road, Gladstone, Somerset County. *Telephone:* 908-234-1251.

OTHER NEW JERSEY ARENAS & AUDITORIUMS

PNC BANK ARTS CENTER: Formerly known as The Garden State Arts Center-which was certainly a more pleasing name. A beautiful white concrete amphitheatre designed by Edward Durell Stone is the setting for nightly concerts and loads of special events throughout the summer.The "shell" is covered and offers seating for several thousand while additional thousands can be accommodated on the lawn. The lawn people, however, can no long bring their chairs but must buy them from the concessionaires. There are also strict rules about bringing in outside food and drink. This has increased the Center's profits but brought quite a bit of grumbling from customers.

The shell is open on all sides so that there a delicious breeze from the nearby seashore wafts through the auditorium (although I hear new barriers have cut this down somewhat.) Shows at the Center range from pop singers to rock acts with a few ethnic festivals thrown in. Everyone from The Beach Boys to operatic divas have appeared here. The season runs from late June to early September.

Adjacent to the Center is the **New Jersey Vietnam Veteran's Memorial** Pavilion. (800-648-VETS) Located in Holmdel, Monmouth County. Take Exit 116 off The Garden State Parkway, follow signs. *Telephone:* 732-335-0400, 732-442-9200.

OCEAN GROVE AUDITORIUM: A cavernous 7,000 seat auditorium built in the late Victorian age is one of the attractions of this quiet camp-meeting town right next to Asbury Park on the shore.

The Great Auditorium with its majestic organ, has recently been refurbished and restored. It is now home to many family-style entertainments plus a lecture series. Typical attractions are singers (including pop singers) choral groups and festivals. Again, this is for the summer season only. Located at 54 Pitman Ave., Ocean Grove, Monmouth County. *Telephone.* 732-775-0035.

BLOCKBUSTER-SONY MUSIC ENTERTAINMENT CENTRE. Commonly known as the **E-Center.** On the Camden waterfront across from Philadelphia, this state-of-the-art facility with a seating capacity of over 25,000 is a recent venue for rock groups and other entertainers. Some indoor capacity for smaller theatricals. Secured parking nearby. One Harbor Blvd., Camden. *Telephone:* 800-833-0080.

NJPAC. Opened in October, 1997, **The New Jersey Performing Arts Center** is the jewel that is supposed to revive Newark, culturally and financially. A beautiful building with a 2750 seat auditorium worthy of the greatest opera houses and a small 500 seat intimate theater, plus an indoor restaurant. But they should have allowed more lobby space and put in escalators—the traffic flow (for people that is) is sticky. Plenty of secured parking surrounds the Center. The place for orchestras, ballet, jazz, tap, chorales, and musicals. One Center St, Newark. From Rte. 280 take Rte. 21 (McCarter Highway), follow signs. *Telephone.* 888-GO-NJPAC.

NEW JERSEY BASEBALL STADIUMS

Remember the old-fashioned baseball park where you went with the kids, ate hot dogs and cheered the locals on? They seemed the stuff of movie folklore rather than real life for many years. Then a major league baseball strike a few years ago made the average baseball fan so angry at the seeming greed on the part of both players and management, that the fans struck. Disgusted with overpriced tickets, food, parking fees and whatnot, the fans wanted a local team to root for. So new baseball stadiums began to rise all over New Jersey. Most have teams that are affiliated with the majors. The stadiums offer bleacher seating with average capacity of between 3500 and 4500. Here is a summary of the teams and parks presently on hand.

Atlantic City Surf:
The Sand Castle, on Route 40 East, Atlantic City. 609-344-7873 / www.acsurf.com

Newark Bears:
Riverfront Stadium, Bridge St., Newark. 973-483-6900 / www.newarkbears.com

New Jersey Cardinals:
Skylands Park, Route 565, Augusta, Sussex County. 973-579-7500 / www.njcards.com

New Jersey Jackals:
Yogi Berra Stadium. One Hall Drive, Little Falls (on Montclair State University campus). 973-746-7434 / www.jackals.com

Somerset Patriots:
Somerset Ballpark, East Main St., Bridgewater. 908-252-0700 / www.somersetpatriots.com

Trenton Thunder:
Mercer County Waterfront Park, Trenton. 609-394-8326 / www.trentonthunder.com.

INDEX

C

G

H

K

L

M

REGIONAL INDEX-NEW JERSEY

Leaming's Run Garden
Ocean City
Ocean City Historical Museum
Stone Harbor
Stone Harbor Bird Sanctuary
Wetlands Institute
Wildwood
Wildwood Crest

CUMBERLAND COUNTY
Belleplain State Forest
Bridgeton Tour
Cohansic Zoo, Bridgeton
Pine Barrens
Wheaton Village

ESSEX COUNTY
Branch Brook Park
Cora Hartshorn Arboretum
Eagle Rock Reservation
Grover Cleveland Birthplace
Edison Labs/Glenmont
Jersey Explorer Children's
    Museum
Montclair
    Israel Crane House
    Montclair Art Museum
    Presby Iris Garden
Newark
    Ballantine House
    Branch Brook Park
    New Jersey Historical
    Society
    Newark Museum
    NJPAC
South Mountain Reservation
Turtle Back Zoo
Yogi Berra Museum

GLOUCESTER COUNTY
Gloucester County Tour
Hunter-Lawrence House,
    Woodbury
Mullica Hill Antiques
Red Bank Battlefield Park
Scotland Run Park

HUDSON COUNTY
Afro-American Museum
Excursion Boats, Hoboken
Hoboken
Jersey City Museum
Liberty State Park
Ellis Island
Liberty Science Center
Statue of Liberty
Secaucus Outlets

HUNTERDON COUNTY
Black River & Western Railroad
Flemington Outlets
Hunterdon Museum of Art
Hunterdon County Park
Hunterdon Historical Museum
Lambertville
Marshall House
Northlandz
Pick-Your-Own Farms
Round Valley State Park
Spruce Run State Park
Twp. of Lebanon Museum
Voorhees State Park

MERCER COUNTY
Belle Mountain Ski Area
Grounds For Sculpture
Hopewell Museum
Howell Living History Farm
Kuser Farm Mansion
Mercer County Park
NJ State Police Museum

Princeton
    Bainbridge House
    Drumthwacket
    Morven
    Princeton Art Museum
    Princeton Battlefield
    University Tour
Stony Brook Park
Trenton
    New Jersey State House
    New Jersey State Museum
    Old Barracks
    William Trent House
Washington Crossing State Park

MIDDLESEX COUNTY
Cheesequake State Park
Discovery House
East Jersey Olde Towne
Edison Memorial Tower
Johnson Park
Kearney Cottage
Middlesex County Museum
New Brunswick
    Buccleuch Mansion
    Hungarian Center
    NJ Museum of Agriculture
    Rutgers Geology Museum
    Zimmerli Art Museum
Proprietary House
Roosevelt Park

MONMOUTH COUNTY
Allaire State Park
Allen House
Asbury Park
Avon
Belmar
Brielle
Deal
Deep Cut Gardens
Englishtown Auction Sales

Freehold
    Covenhoven House
    Monmouth Battlefield State
        Park
    Monmouth County
        Historical Society
    Freehold Raceway
Keansburg Amusements
Longstreet Farm, Holmdel
Monmouth Museum
Monmouth Park Racetrack
Ocean Grove
Owl Haven
PNC Arts Center
Poricy Park Nature Center
Sandy Hook
Spring Lake
Thompson Park
Turkey Swamp Park
Twin Lights Lighthouse

MORRIS COUNTY
Chester
Cooper Mill
Craftsman Farms
Dover Flea Market
Fosterfields
Frelinghuysen Arboretum
Great Swamp Outdoor Center
Hacklebarny State Park
Historic Speedwell
Hopatcong State Park
Meyersville Grange Flea Market
Morris County College
    Planetarium
Morris Museum
Morristown
    Acorn Hall
    Jockey Hollow
    Macculloch Hall
Museum of Early Trades and
    Crafts

251

Raptor Trust
Schooley Mountain Park
Willowood/Bamboo Brook
Whippany RR Museum

OCEAN COUNTY
Barnegat Lighthouse State Park
Beach Haven
Double Trouble State Park
Island Beach State Park
Lebanon State Forest
Long Beach Island
New Egypt Flea Market
Ocean County College
    Planetarium
Ocean County Historical
    Museum
Ocean County Park
Point Pleasant
Popcorn Park
Seaside Heights
Seaside Park
Six Flags Great Adventure
'Tip" Seaman Park
Toms River Seaport Museum
Tuckerton Seaport
Wells Mills Park

PASSAIC COUNTY
Abram S. Hewitt State Forest
American Labor Museum
Dey Mansion, Wayne
Fairy Tale Forest
Garret Mtn. Reservation
Greenwood Lake
Norvin Green State Forest
Paterson
    Great Falls
    Lambert Castle
    Paterson Museum
    Paterson Tour
Ringwood Manor

Skylands
Van Riper-Hopper House
Weis Ecology Center

SALEM COUNTY
Cowtown Rodeo
Fort Mott State Park
Hancock House
Parvin State Park
Salem Tour

SOMERSET COUN1Y
Buck Gardens
Colonial Park Rose Gardens
Delaware and Raritan Canal
State Park
Duke Island Park
Golf House, Far Hills
Great Swamp
New Jersey Renaissance Festival
Raritan Valley College
    Planetarium
Scherman-Hoffman Sanctuary
Somerset Environmental
Education Center
Somerville
    Duke Gardens
    Old Dutch Parsonage
    U.S. Bicycling Hall of Fame
    Wallace House
U.S. Equestrian Team
Washington Rock State Park

SUSSEX COUNTY
Delaware Water Gap
Franklin Mineral Museum
Gingerbread Castle
Hidden Valley Ski Area
High Point State Park
Millbrook Village
Mountain Creek
Old Monroe Schoolhouse

Olde Lafayette Village
Space Farms Zoo
Sterling Hill Mine
Stokes State Forest
Swartswood State Park
Vernon Valley Ski Area
Waterloo Village
Wawayanda, State Park
Wild West City
Worthington State Forest

UNION COUNTY
Belcher Ogden Mansion
Bowcraft Amusements
Boxwood Hall, Elizabeth
Dr. Robinson Plantation
Drake House, Plainfield
Miller-Cory House
Reeves-Reed Arboretum
Trailside Nature Center
Trailside Planetarium
Warinoco Park
Watchung Reservation

WARREN COUNTY
Alba Vineyards
Allamuchy State Park
Delaware Water Gap
Four Sisters Winery
Jenny Jump State Forest
Lakota Wolf Preserve
Land of Make Believe
Merrill Creek Reservoir
Pequest Trout Hatchery
Shippen Manor
Stephens State Park
Tamuzza Vineyards
Well Sweep Herb Farm

NEW YORK STATE

HUDSON VALLEY AREA
Boscobel
Culinary Institute of America
Hunter Mountain Ski Area
Hyde Park
Kykuit
Lyndhurst
Philipsburg Manor
New York Renaissance Faire
Ski Windham
Sterling Forest Ski Area
Sunnyside
Van Cortlandt Manor
Vanderbilt Mansion
West Point
Woodbury Common

NEW YORK CITY

MANHATTAN
American Museum of Natural
  History
Chinatown
Circle Line Tour
Cloisters, The
Empire State Building
Forbes Galleries
Frick Collection
Lincoln Center Tour
Madison Square Garden
Metropolitan Museum of Art
Museum of Modem Art
NBC TV Tours
N.Y. Stock Exchange
South Street Seaport
U.N. Headquarters
World Trade Center

BROOKLYN
Aquarium
Brooklyn Botanic Gardens

BRONX
Bronx Zoo
NY Botanical Gardens
Wave Hill

STATEN ISLAND
Staten Island Zoo

PENNSYLVANIA

BRANDYWINE VALLEY
Brandywine Battlefield State
    Park
Brandywine River Museum
Longwood Gardens

BUCKS COUNTY
Andalusia
Lahaska
Mercer Mile, Doylestown
New Hope
Pennsbury Manor
Pearl S. Buck House
Rice's Flea Market
Sesame Place
Washington Crossing Park

PHILADELPHIA AREA
Barnes Foundation
Fairmount Park Houses
Franklin Institute
Franklin Mills Mall
Independence Mall
Philadelphia Museum of Art

Philadelphia Zoo
Please Touch Museum
United States Mint

POCONOS AREA
Big Boulder Ski Area
Bushkill Falls
Camelback Ski Area
Delaware Water Gap
Jack Frost Ski Area
Shawnee Mountain Ski Area
Shawnee Place

OTHER PA AREAS
Crayola Factory
Dorney Park -
    Wildwater Kingdom
Hershey Rose Gardens
Hersheypark
Reading Outlets
Strasburg Railroad
Valley Forge

DELAWARE
Cape May-Lewes Ferry
Hagley Museum
Nemours
Winterthur

Can't find a copy of NEW JERSEY DAY TRIPS in your local bookstore? Want to send a copy to a friend in another state? Just photocopy the coupon below and send, with check or money order, to:

THE WOODMONT PRESS
P.O. BOX 108
GREEN VILLAGE , NJ. 07935

Please send me _____ number of copies of
NEW JERSEY DAY TRIPS @ $14.00 a copy.
Postage and handling are $2.50 extra.

I am enclosing $_____

Postage $2.50

TOTAL $_____

Send book to:

NAME_____

ADDRESS_____

CITY/STATE/ZIP_____

*For 2 or more copies add .50 to postage for each additional copy.